MW00800970

Symbiosis and Ambivalence

12

SYMBIOSIS AND AMBIVALENCE
Poles and Jews in a Small Galician Town

Rosa Lehmann

Berghahn Books
New York • Oxford

First published in 2001 by
Berghahn Books

© 2001 Rosa Lehmann

All rights reserved.
No part of this publication may be reproduced in any form or by
any means without the written permission of Berghahn Books.

Library of Congress Cataloging-in-Publication Data

Lehmann, Rosa.
   Symbiosis and ambivalence : Poles and Jews in a small Galician town / by Rosa Lehmann.
     p. cm.
   Includes bibliographical references (p.)
   ISBN 1-57181-794-8 (alk. free)
    1. Jews--Poland--Jaśliska--History. 2. Holocaust, Jewish
(1939-1945)--Poland--Jaśliska. 3. Jaśliska (Poland)--Ethnic relations. I. Title.

DS135.P62 J29965 2001
305.892´404386--dc21   00-050776

British Library Cataloguing in Publication Data

A catalogue record for this book is available from the British Library.

Printed in the United States on acid-free paper.

Cover photos by David Niemeijer.

CONTENTS

TABLES, FIGURES AND MAPS

To David and Bente

PREFACE

This study is dedicated to the people of Jaśliska; to the Jews who perished and to the few who survived, and to the Poles who cherish the history of their town.

*L*earned scholars and important writers have dedicated many works and debates to the subject of Polish-Jewish relations. Perhaps the most popular and widespread view of Polish-Jewish relations is that Poles are virulent anti-Semites and that the Polish Jews have been their unfortunate victims. Among others this view is confirmed by Claude Lanzmann, who in his 1985 film 'Shoah' presents the Poles as the naive, indifferent, and even culpable by-standers of the Nazi genocide of the European Jewry (Lanzmann 1985). Since then, many authors—Poles and Jews—have contested or defended the view of the Pole as the eternal anti-Semite. The present study provides no ready answer to the question whether Polish anti-Semitism is special or not (see for example Grynberg 1983; Mendelsohn 1986; Irwin-Zarecka 1989b). Instead my study attempts to explain the complex nature of Polish-Jewish relationships, which have been the outcome of composite historical processes.

With this work I hope to offer an original contribution to the understanding of Polish-Jewish relationships. My study is original because it deals with ordinary people and not with the public discourse and because it focuses on the interaction between Poles and Jews without passing judgement on the people concerned. It should be noted that this work has its origin as an academic thesis. This being the case, my observations do not necessarily coincide with the perception of my Polish and Jewish informants.

ACKNOWLEDGEMENTS

*F*irst of all, I would like to thank my colleagues and friends of the University of Amsterdam, the Free University of Amsterdam, the Jagiellonian University of Cracow, and the University of Warsaw for their invaluable support of my research in practical and intellectual terms: Anton Blok, Jeremy Boissevain, Dorota Czerwińska, Rena Fuks-Mansfeld, André Gerrits, Rob van Ginkel, Longina Jakubowska, Zdzisław Mach, Daniel Meijers, Elżbieta Meijknecht-Proń, Ot van den Muijzenberg, Jacek and Ewa Nowak, Annamaria Orla-Bukowska, Anna Ostrowska, Andrzej Paluch, Zofia Sokolewicz, Jojada Verrips, and Piotr Zabrzycki. I would like to specifically thank Hans Vermeulen, who has been influential in shaping the present text through his many comments and suggestions on earlier drafts. Special thanks are also due A. Gebhard who translated a lengthy Hebrew document for me, and Arianne Zwiers who translated the Yiddish story by Opatoshu that opens each chapter. Finally, this text has greatly benefited from the editing work of Peter Mason and Norma Fain Pratt, who corrected the text for language and style.

Of course gratitude is also due to the people of Jaśliska, especially my hosts Emilia and the late Władysław Długosz. The support of Helena and Zdzisław Orlik and their son Medard was priceless. Without their introduction to the village and constant guidance during my stay in Jaśliska, I would not have been able to collect as much material as I have done now. My work would have been much harder without the historical knowledge provided by Zdzisław (including the access he granted me to his private archives and the archives of the primary school in Jaśliska) and the local knowledge provided by Helena. Special thanks are also due the priest of Jaśliska, father Barań, who generously permitted me to study the parish archives, the postman, and the numerous other villagers who made our stay there such a pleasure.

This is also a good occasion to express my appreciation of the way I was granted access to the many offices, libraries, museums, and archives in Poland. Special thanks are due to the mayor of the community council in

Dukla, the director of the historical museum in Dukla, the personnel in the court of law in Krosno, the director of the lyceum in Rymanów, the staff of the episcopal museum in Krosno, the personnel of the historical museum and the open-air museum in Sanok, and the people of the Jewish Historical Institute in Warsaw. The access I was granted to the Polish State Archive was also very helpful. I would like to thank the archivists of the departments in Skołyszyn, Sanok, Rzeszów and Przemyśl for guiding me round the archives. Outside Poland I would like to thank the YIVO Institute for Jewish Research (New York) and the Yad Vashem Archives (Jerusalem) for providing me with valuable documents and assistance.

I am also much indebted to my interpreters, Wojciech Mrozek, Bożena Marszałek, and Edyta Krakowiecka. There is no need to mention that without their help I would have spent more time studying Polish grammar books than talking to informants.

I am especially grateful to the few Jewish survivors of Jaśliska who have been willing to share with me some of their memories of a world they have lost. Their contributions have been very important as they revealed a glimpse of the Jewish perspective on prewar Polish-Jewish relations. I realise that the Jewish informants belong to a generation that has suffered many times its share. For them the recollection of memories can be very painful.

A final word is due to my family: in particular my grandparents who gave me emotional backing, my father Bernd Lehmann who supported me in many ways, and my parents-in-law Rudo and Leidie Niemeijer, who have contributed to the completion of this work in more ways than I can mention here; they not only supported me materially and emotionally, but also took the effort to read earlier drafts of this work, and furnished me with many substantial comments and suggestions. Of course, I am much indebted to my husband David Niemeijer who suffered the inconveniences of living with an anthropologist, and a perfectionist at that. He was the one who inspired and stimulated me to plunge into this complex subject. I am very grateful for his feedback during the process of research and writing, and for his help in editing the manuscript and designing the maps.

There are many more people who helped me in one way or another and whom I have not been able to mention here; my thanks are also due to them.

This study was financially supported by: Amsterdam School for Social Science Research, Amsterdamse Universiteitsvereniging, Dr Hendrik Muller's Vaderlandsch Fonds, Fundatie van de Vrijvrouwe van Renswoude, Netherlands Organisation for Scientific Research (NWO), Nuffic, Scientific Research Society Sigma Xi, Stichting Bekker-La-Bastide-Fonds, and the University of Amsterdam fieldwork fund.

Map 1 Jaśliska and surroundings

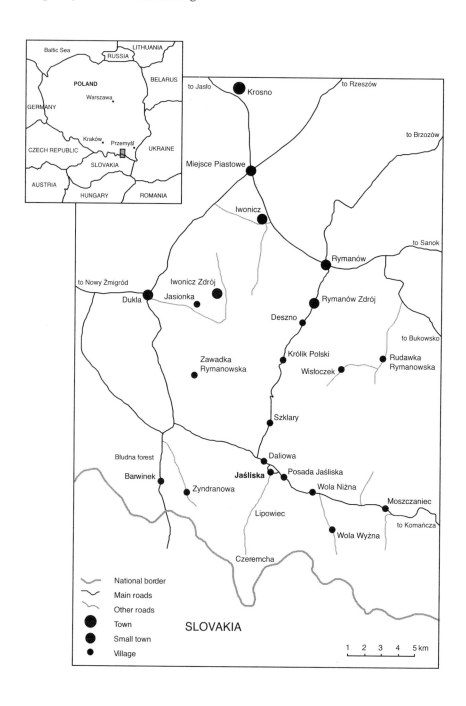

Map 2 Resettled and destroyed villages surrounding Jaśliska

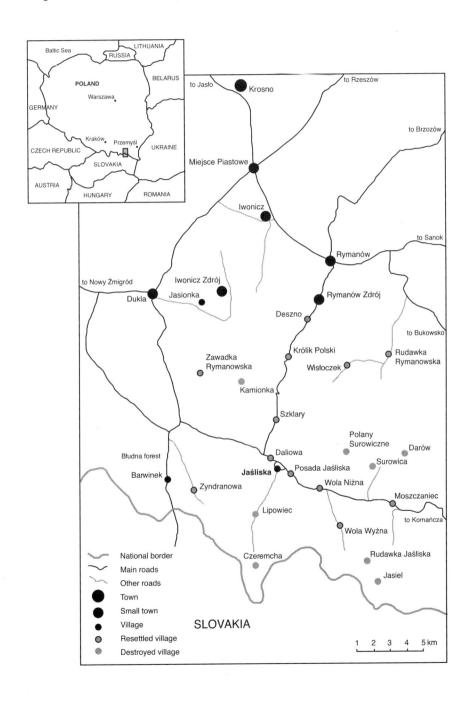

INTRODUCTION

Marcin Kwiatek, already past his eighties and white as a pigeon, had been lying in his bed the whole winter. The bones of his hands and feet were hurting. When springtime closed in he felt much better. And suddenly, it was on a Friday at the end of April, a feeling of joy descended upon him; a new happy feeling that he would no longer need the support of his neighbours. Marcin stepped out of bed, dressed himself, and for the first time since the cold and difficult winter, left his little house near the entrance of the Jewish cemetery of Melawe [...] The cemetery, which he had taken care of for decades, was neglected. The tombs were destroyed and pulled out. Above the ruined graves branches of walnut trees were moving, old beech trees rose in their places and they rose and moved as they had done for ages (Opatoshu 1951: 312).[1]

During the interbellum period (1918-1939) over three million Jews lived in the cities and small towns of Poland. The Polish Jews had their own institutions, were engaged in many occupational fields, and were divided by differences in social class, political faction, and religious conviction. There were big city Jews and village Jews, poor petty traders and wealthy industrialists. There were Orthodox Jews, assimilated Jews, and atheists. There were socialists, Zionists, and right-wing activists. Then came the Shoah. In five years the Nazis murdered over three million Polish Jews, leaving the Jewish community almost completely annihilated. Of the few Jews who survived many did not want to start anew in Poland and they migrated to the United States, Argentina, Israel, and other destinations. All in all, by the early 1960s some thirty thousand Jews remained in the country, about one-tenth of the postwar total (Irwin-Zarecka 1989a: 59). In 1968, a violent anti-Zionist campaign spurred on by the Polish security police caused two-thirds of the remaining Jews to leave Poland. During the 1980s another group of Jews, mainly the younger generation, chose to escape political oppression and economic decline by leaving the country. Since then, migration from Poland to the more attractive countries in the West has never really ceased.

Notes for this section begin on page xxii.

At present a few thousand Jewish men and women live scattered over a few major centres (in particular Warsaw, Cracow, and Lublin); their average age is seventy years. In fact, the Jewish community is seriously threatened by a lack of young and active members (Niezabitowska and Tomaszewski 1993: 7, 16). This was the pattern until the mid 1990s. Since then, a remarkable recovery seems to have taken place. In Warsaw, for instance, a Jewish nursery was recently created. This reflects a growing consciousness and recognition of Jewish roots; in other words, a coming out process. Whatever their precise numbers, as a consequence of the Shoah, the Jews have stopped being one of Poland's largest ethnic minorities. It is striking, therefore, that Jews still play a conspicuous part in present-day Poland. In many ways, Poles are still wedded to their Jewish fellow nationals. In her article on Poland's Jewish ghosts, Wisse (1987: 25) justly stresses the Poles' unusual relationship with the Jews when she quotes Black's Medical Dictionary: 'Following the amputation of a limb, it is usual for the patient to experience sensation as if the limb were still present. This condition is to be referred to as a phantom limb. In the vast majority of cases, the sensation passes off in time.' For many Poles, however, the irritating sensation left by their Jewish 'phantom limb' still lingers on.

Poland, 1990—The landscape is abundantly filled with landmarks of Poland's Jewish history. Every town, even the tiniest, has a Jewish cemetery. Most cemeteries are neglected, destroyed, or overgrown with plants and trees; very few are still in use. Synagogues are used for many purposes (as libraries, garages, warehouses), others have fallen apart or have been rebuilt as museums. A single synagogue is still used for religious services and is occasionally visited by native Jews, though it is frequented in greater numbers by Jewish tourists who have come to visit the 'Old Country'; the country of their parents and grandparents. Streets and villages still carry names that bear witness to the former Jewish inhabitants. All over Poland one can find Polish men and women who resourcefully cherish, take care of, and exhibit former Jewish houses, cemeteries and properties, and in this way earn some extra money. The memorial sites commemorating the Nazi war crimes further remind one of Polish Jewry and their fate.

Poland, 1990—The presidential election campaign was reduced to the simple question of who was or was not a Jew. Lech Wałęsa strengthened his own position by calling himself a true Pole, suggesting that Mazowiecki, his main political opponent, was a Jew. The Polish electorate did not want to be governed by Jews, for 'all the bad things come from the Jew-politicians'.[2] So the Polish constituents decorated Mazowiecki's posters with the Star of David or with the word 'Jew', and then voted for a true Pole: Lech Wałęsa.

One year after the elections I still heard some people referring to Mazo-wiecki as 'Jude Mazowiecki'. Long before the elections took place, some former advisors and present opponents of the president had been 'unmasked' as Jews.

Warsaw, 1993—Television fragments of 'Anatevka', the melodramatic musical about Russian Jewry, evoked to nostalgic reflections by my Polish fellow viewers. Still more interesting were the fragments of two stage plays I watched on television. The first drama about a poor Polish peasant family (mother kills rich foreign visitor who turns out to be her son) depicted the traditional Polish Jew, namely, the Jewish tavern-keeper. Within his small territory, the Jewish character sold beer and vodka, meddled in Polish affairs, gave crucial information and advised his Polish clients. A Polish friend of mine helpfully explained that 'before the war' Jews ran saloons and taverns in villages and towns. In those days all information, also from the outside world, ran through the tavern and was treasured by the tavern-keeper. The Jews, therefore, had much influence. The same friend commented on a television fragment about the perils of a Polish aristocratic family. Here again Jews were present, this time in the person of an assimilated Jew. The Jewish character was a talkative elderly man who, in contrast to the other people present, had enthralled the young men and women. His accent was a special 'Jewish' one and his manners were also 'Jewish', as my friend explained. I, however, did not notice anything special.

Kraków, 1992—The image of the Polish Jew turns out to be a very lucrative one. Tourist shops sell wooden sculptures and paintings that picture the prewar shtetl Jews: old Jewish men with crooked noses and backs, wearing long beards and black clothes, reading the Talmud or playing the violin. Books with 'Jewish Jokes' find a ready sale in the kiosks on the street. The kosher vodka, produced under rabbinical supervision and decorated with a Chanukah menorah or an ugly grinning Orthodox Jew, is exported to all countries in the world, especially those with large Jewish communities. The kosher vodka is also sold in the Polish shops and is consumed in large quantities, because 'what is kosher is best,' a Polish salesman once explained to me.

Poland, 1989—Poland experiences an upsurge in academic and popular interest in the Polish Jewry. Between 1987 and 1989 an unprecedented amount of literature on Jewish subjects entered the book market in Poland. The literature covers all fields from the Bible and other Jewish holy scriptures through the Shoah, to history, fiction, poetry, Jewish humour and even Polish-Jewish cuisine. The treatments are on different levels from scholarly approaches to personal accounts, memoirs, or pure entertainment (Gross

1991: 295).The influx of literature on Polish Jewry in Poland is not confined to Polish (Jewish and non-Jewish) authors only. Translations from contemporary world literature on Jewish (and non-Jewish) subjects have also appeared, of which many Jewish authors have Polish roots (e.g., Bauman, Singer, Kosinski).

Poland, 1991—New publications on Polish Jewry still fill magazines and book stores. Recent connections between Israeli and Polish publishers even increased the number of publications on Poland's Jews which exclusively serve the Israeli and Polish market. As Gross (1991: 308) observed, 'the Polish market is for the time being "absorbent" and waiting for "merchandise"'. At the same time, other cultural fields (theatre, arts, music, literature, and film) have recently discovered their own Jewish heroes, who are now considered to be part of Poland's cultural heritage (e.g., Kantor, Schultz, Polanski). Moreover, numerous festivals of Jewish culture and concerts with Jewish music attract large audiences. The remarkable Polish interest in the Jews, as well as the recent habit of claiming that famed Jewish personalities are Polish, might well be described as a 'requiem for the Jewish people' (Gross 1991: 295).

Rymanów, 1992—I came across a clear example of such 'claiming', when I met the director of the secondary school in Rymanów and one of the teachers. Our first meeting was something of a trial. Why didn't I study the history of Rymanów? Did I know that there had been a large Jewish community living there, and that it had produced two famous rabbis? Here I must note that I had never mentioned my interest in Jewish history. The teacher proudly added that the Jew Isidor Isaac Rabi, a famous physicist, was born in Rymanów.

A few months later we met again and as if to prove his previous statement, the teacher gave me copies of two newspaper articles and one letter. The articles were written in memory of Prof. Dr Isidor Isaac Rabi, who had died on 11 January 1988. The letter, written by a representative of the American embassy, expressed Prof. Dr Rabi's thanks to the Rymanów municipality. It turned out that the famous physicist had visited his home town in July 1971. Indeed, the man was someone to be proud of. Prof. Dr Rabi had been a pioneer in exploring the atom, had won the 1944 Nobel Prize for Physics, and had been a 'strong intellectual influence' on succeeding generations of physicists.[3]

The frank admiration of the local teacher is notable for two reasons. Though born in Rymanów in 1898, Isidor Isaac Rabi was still a baby when his parents took him to New York's Lower East Side. Ninety years later he died in Manhattan as an American citizen. What is more, considering the fact that the physicist Rabi was of Jewish descent, he was less a Pole and more a Jew, at least in the strict view of the former Communist authorities. This, however, did not keep the teacher from claiming the celebrated Jewish physicist as part of the Polish cultural heritage, and more specifically of Rymanów. He even considered the story of the local Jewish hero to be a perfect reason to study the 'highly interesting history' of his town.

The conspicuous role of the Jew in Polish culture lies at the heart of the present study. The study originally began as an academic thesis (Lehmann 1995) and was prompted by the upsurge of popular and academic interest in the Polish Jewry in the early 1990s. The Polish discourse on the subject indicates that, in addition to being an interesting subject by itself, the Polish-Jewish past is a very Polish issue as well.

I decided to carry out my research in Jaśliska, a small peasant community in southeastern Poland, which I selected for a number of reasons. First, the small size of the community allowed a degree of overview. Second, its inhabitants were native Poles. Third, before the outbreak of the Second World War one-quarter of the residents were Jews. Research in Jaśliska was conducted in two rounds: in the summer of 1992 and in the winter of 1993. After the completion of fieldwork, I began a quest for former Jewish residents of Jaśliska. Part of the material presented in this study is drawn from interviews with five Jaśliska-born survivors of the Shoah. The interviews were conducted between 1993 and 1996 in Belgium, Canada, and the United States. The accounts of the Jewish informants were used to complement the picture that was put forward by the Polish informants.

The initial focus of investigation was the impact of the Shoah on Polish-Jewish relations. Questions that related to this topic were: how did the Poles cope with the extermination of the local Jews; in what way did the Shoah affect life in a small Polish community; and finally, how did the Shoah alter Polish-Jewish relations? However, during fieldwork and while writing the present text, the main focus of attention shifted from an experience-oriented approach to an approach focusing mainly on concrete interaction. As a result, the memory of the Shoah no longer occupies a prominent place in the present study. Instead, the crucial foci of investigation shifted to Polish-Jewish interactions before the Second World War as well as to the Poles' perception of the Jews and of prewar Polish-Jewish relationships. My intention has been to analyse the link between local history and the local attitudes towards the Jews. In this analysis the views of the older as well of the younger generations are included. The idea is that the divergent views held by subsequent generations display the dynamics of the present-day Polish attitude towards the Jews.

Recent studies have come to address the issue of coexistence between Jews and Poles and conclude that, while it is true that Jews and Poles periodically found themselves in confrontation, most of the time they lived in cooperative symbiosis (Rosman 1990; Kamińska 1991; Wróbel 1991; Orla-Bukowska 1994; Lehmann 1997; Hoffman 1998). Through a case-study approach, in which I used first-hand archival and anthropological sources that are connected in time and space, my own findings in Jaśliska supports this notion for the interwar period. In this rural context—low industrialisation level and low level of class mobility—mutual dependencies between Polish peasants and Jewish entrepreneurs fostered a relationship that was characterised by reciprocity and cooperation rather than conflict. This study explores the conditions that gave rise to this type of peaceful coexistence. It is argued that the strict ethnic boundaries between the Polish and Jewish communities, as well as the patron-client relations that had developed between the members of the two communities, were of crucial importance in the maintenance of a political and social equilibrium.

Chapter one discusses the theoretical and methodological implications of my study of Polish-Jewish relations and introduces the underlying research question. Chapter two deals with the early history of Jaśliska, the early history of the Jews in Poland, and the initial Polish-Jewish relations in the area of study. Chapters three to five deal with the main spheres of interaction—the spatial, economic, and social spheres—between the Poles and the Jews during the nineteenth and early twentieth centuries. Chapter six presents the case study of 'the converted Jewish woman', whose story covers various aspects of Polish-Jewish relations in prewar as well as in postwar Poland. Chapter seven deals with the destruction of the Jewish, Polish and neighbouring Lemko communities[4] during the Second World War (1939-44) and the civil war that followed (1944-47). The case material that is presented in the earlier chapters form the basis for a reassessment of the quality of the relationship that linked the Poles with the Jews in prewar Poland in Chapters eight and nine. We find that the Polish-Jewish relations in the interwar years were characterised by interdependence and symbiosis. Accordingly, the Poles' attitude towards the Jews in the research village is marked by ambivalence rather than by anti-Semitism alone.

For reasons of privacy the names of the (Polish and Jewish) informants have been replaced by pseudonyms.

Notes

1. Translated from Yiddish to Dutch by Arianne Zwiers. From Dutch to English my translation.
2. NRC Handelsblad, 24 August 1990, page 6.
3. International Herald Tribune, 13 January 1988; New York Times, 13 January 1988.
4. As a result of a complex of historical and political factors, written sources and my informants used many different terms to denote this minority group, calling them Ukrainians (*Ukraińcy*), Lemkos (*Lemkowie*), or Rusyns (*Rusnacy* or *Rusini*). See the notes to Chapter two for an explanation of the usage of the terms Lemko and Rusyn in the present text.

THE JEW LEGEND

'Wladek,' Janek turns to the oldest boy, 'have you ever seen a Jew?' 'No, I have never seen one. I must have been one year old, maybe one year and a half, when the Germans expelled the Jews from Melawe.' 'Nor have I seen one' (Opatoshu 1951: 316).

Introduction

*T*he quotations opening each chapter originate from *The Jew Legend*, a story written in the United States in 1951 by the Polish-Jewish author Joseph Opatoshu (1887-1954).[1] In *The Jew Legend* Opatoshu reflects on the relationship between Poles and Jews in the past, present, and future. Besides being a very beautiful story, *The Jew Legend* is a story with a vision which forty years after its first printing has not lost its illustrative power. In the first section of this chapter I will consider the contents of Opatoshu's story in more detail, as the story gave rise to the research question that underlies the present study: how can there be anti-Semitism, or for that matter philo-Semitism, in a country where there are no longer any Jews? Following this short summary, I will briefly enter into the current debate on anti-Semitism in Poland. This debate, carried on from the early 1980s,[2] reveals an important dilemma which directly relates to the above-mentioned research question. Finally, I will discuss the different views on the origins and persistence of anti-Semitism. This discussion will form the basis for the framework which is used in the further analysis of Polish-Jewish relations. The chapter closes with a discussion of the research site and the fieldwork conducted in southeastern Poland.

Notes for this section begin on page 18.

The Tale of the Polish Jews

The Jew Legend

> Marcin Kwiatek, an old white-haired man in his eighties, wakes up from a long
> sick-bed. For the first time since the cold and difficult winter, the old man feels
> strong enough to leave his little house at the entrance of the Jewish cemetery of
> Melawe, a formerly Jewish town. Sitting on a bench in front of his house, he
> watches the ruined walls of the cemetery. Snatches of his long life pass through
> his mind: the small *shul*[3] on the square, the old Jewish cemetery which was kept
> by his father, and where he, Marcin, was born, grew up, and married Jadwiga.
> After his father died the care of the Jewish cemetery passed to Marcin Kwiatek.
> The old man recalls the names of each former Jewish inhabitant and the way he
> had served them as their *shabbes goy*.[4] Memories of the good old days fill the old
> man with sadness and joy. Suddenly, voices from the cemetery disturb the old
> man's day-dreaming. They are the voices of children playing in the bushes. Four
> boys around the age of ten approach 'grandfather' Marcin, take their seat, and
> invite him to tell them his most exciting stories. The children, having by chance
> heard of the former Jewish inhabitants, try to find out from the old man who
> those people were, what had happened to them, why they perished. Marcin
> Kwiatek patiently answers the manifold questions. Thus begins the legend of
> those who had ceased to be, and the legend seems to bring them to life again.

The above excerpt presents a summary of *The Jew Legend*. As a tale *The Jew
Legend* is about postwar Poland. The old Jewish cemetery symbolises the
death of millions of Polish Jews and marks the end of centuries of coexistence between Poles and Jews. The old white-haired Marcin Kwiatek[5] rep-
resents the past, in that he is the sole witness to a world that no longer exists.
When he dies, all ties with that past will be lost forever. While he is still alive,
the old man and cemetery-keeper whose duty it is to guard the souls of the
deceased transmits the complex 'truth' about the Jews to successive generations. The young children represent the future postwar generations, who
may be ignorant but nevertheless sense the spirit of a people that are no
longer there. Even stripped of its symbolism, the story by Opatoshu still
holds true. In Poland of the 1990s Jewish cemeteries are overgrown and
deserted, while the transmission of 'facts' has become the exclusive domain
of white-haired men and women. Anticipating my own experiences in the
field, I found that *The Jew Legend* highlights certain important aspects with
respect to postwar Polish-Jewish relations.

To start with, *The Jew Legend* stresses the impact of the *Shoah* on postwar Polish-Jewish relations. Opatoshu makes it very clear that to talk about
the Jews of Poland is to talk about millions of dead. In the story the main
Polish character Marcin Kwiatek mourns over his one-time Jewish neigh-

bours, the Jews of Melawe. Encouraged by his young listeners, he tells about the wartime period, and when he condemns the genocide he implicitly touches the issue of guilt. The painful truth of the Shoah leads him to idealise the past and to present an ideal picture of prewar Polish-Jewish relations. In the eyes of the old man it was the German 'bastards', not the Poles, who cruelly disturbed the harmony between the Polish and Jewish inhabitants of Melawe.

The Jew Legend further draws attention to the different perspectives of the *successive generations*. In the story 'grandfather' Marcin and the four children hold different views about the Jews. The intellectual gap between the old man and the children exemplifies the gap between the generations who witnessed the prewar times and those who did not. While the first base their opinion on 'real life' experiences, the latter base their opinion solely on hearsay, that is, notions and views transmitted to them by the older generations. In the story the 'real life' experiences of grandfather Marcin and the 'symbolic' experiences of the children often clash. Opatoshu implicitly suggests that the merely symbolic presence of the Jew in postwar Poland may give way to a mythical representation of the Jew, or a Jew legend.

Another theme that is closely related to that of generational differences is the theme of Polish *ambivalence*. The ambivalent attitude towards the Jews becomes particular striking in the short discussion between the children and the old man. In the discussion a curious mixture of ideas and notions are reviewed: the Jew as the murderer of Jesus Christ versus the pious Jew; the Jew as a charitable human being versus the Jew as an evil character; the alien Jew versus the native Jew; the rich Jew versus the poor Jew. While the children present an outspokenly biased and negative image of the Jews, the old man is unmistakably positive about his one-time Jewish neighbours. At the same time, despite all biases, the children display an exceptional curiosity regarding the Jews. Opatoshu thus clearly suggests that the Poles' attitudes towards the Jews are inherently ambiguous.

Finally, *The Jew Legend* addresses the aspect of *interdependence* between Poles and Jews in prewar Poland. Marcin Kwiatek served the Jews as a *shabbes goy* and in this way earned a decent living. The relationship between Marcin Kwiatek and the Jewish community was primarily an economic one, but had also a social side. At the home of the rabbi, Marcin was one of the family and he participated in most Jewish religious festivals. The dependence of the old man on his former Jewish neighbours is revealed by the miserable situation in which the old man finds himself after the Shoah. Lacking the support of the Jews from Melawe he now lives on charity and he misses the rich social life of the past. Opatoshu seems to suggest that the

Shoah not only harmed the Polish Jews but also harmed the Polish Gentiles, as the Shoah took away a people whose contributions to the Polish culture and economy were vital.

In a poetic manner *The Jew Legend* deals with the theme which also underlies the present study: the amputated Polish-Jewish relationship. Constituting an estimated ten percent of the country's total population, Jews formed the second largest national minority in prewar Poland and they occupied important economic niches. The Shoah put an end to the Jewish community in Poland, as well as to centuries of Polish-Jewish interaction. This crucial transition lies at the very heart of the research question: how did the transformation of physical contact into mere symbolic contact change the Poles' views of the Jews? In his story Opatoshu gives some clues to possible changes in perception and attitude. One of these includes the notion that Poles of all generations will have difficulties in coming to terms with the Polish-Jewish past, precisely because of the experience of the Shoah. Neither the Poles nor the Jews had been prepared for a definite farewell. Therefore, Jews will live on in the memory and imagination of the Polish people, just as they have done in the centuries before, despite their physical absence in the real existing world.

On 'Traditional Polish Anti-Semitism'

The recent interest in various aspects of the Polish-Jewish past in Poland can be explained in terms of a broader intellectual need to explore the 'blank spots' of Poland's national history. As Irwin-Zarecka (1989a: 175) puts it: 'What began as [a] re-discovery of Poland's Jewish heritage has been a gradual recognition that not all of the country's history is decent and honourable.' In order to investigate the unknown and painful episodes of history, the main focus in the debate on Poland's Jewish past has been on anti-Semitism and the Shoah. The traumatic experience of the Shoah, which Poland witnessed closely, and also the events of 1946 and 1968, the years of pogroms, anti-Semitic campaigns, and mass emigration of the Jews from Poland, became main issues of public reflection in Poland after a silence of almost forty years. One aspect of the debate needs special attention. Despite its original positive incentive, the debate on Polish anti-Semitism and the Shoah is weighed down by the problem of guilt. An important topic in the discussion, for example, is the attitude of the Poles to their Jewish fellow citizens before and during the Second World War. As a consequence, many publications implicitly or explicitly investigate the link between prewar Polish anti-Semitism and the Final Solution of European Jewry (Heller 1977; Friedman 1980; Grynberg 1983; Goldberg 1986; Gutman 1986; Bartoszewski 1987b; Krakowski 1988; Bryk 1990; Błonski 1990; Levine 1991).

The fact that so much attention is paid to the history of Polish anti-Semitism cannot only be explained by the Poles' own need for critical reflection. In post-Holocaust memory Poland holds an exceptional place: it was where most of the world's Jewish population lived before the war, and where the extermination of European Jewry took place (Hoffman 1998: 2). The history of Polish anti-Semitism, therefore, is not only subject to debate inside Poland, it is also the special concern of outsiders.[6] Most of the Nazi concentration camps were built in Poland, and it is often said, or implicitly suggested, that the Nazis counted on the collaboration of the Poles in their project of extermination. The screening of the documentary *Shoah* in 1985 by the French director Claude Lanzmann strongly directed public opinion in this direction (Lanzmann 1985). In a way, the film was a successful attempt to validate the long established view that Polish anti-Semitism is special, or as Hoffman (1998: 5) puts it, the view that 'ordinary Poles were naturally inclined, by virtue of their congenital anti-Semitism, to participate in the genocide, and that Poles even today must be viewed with extreme suspicion or condemned as guilty for the fate of the Jews in their country'. Although this view may provide some people with a satisfactory explanation of how such a human tragedy could have happened (as well as an answer to the question of who is to blame), it also intensifies the argument between the advocates of a Polish and a Jewish point of view.

To a certain extent, the exploration of Poland's Jewish history has become the battleground of two opposing views, that is, a Jewish and a Polish point of view (Gutman 1986; Mendelsohn 1986; Scharf 1986; Turowicz 1988; Zimand 1989). While Polish participants have gone on the defence and, accordingly, attempt to counter the current claim that all Poles are anti-Semites and that Poland's Second World War record is worse than that of many other occupied countries, Jewish participants who tend to read the entire past as a bitter contest between oppressors and victims, seek to draw from the Poles a confession of guilt and, as a rule, are always disappointed by them.[7] The current splitting of parties between a Jewish camp (though not all its participants are Jews) and a Polish camp (though not all its adherents are Poles), must also be viewed in the light of the historical gap between Polish and Jewish social scientists. Where Polish scholars have always tended to pay minimal attention to Jewish affairs and Jewish subjects,[8] Jewish scholars have dealt exclusively with Jewish subjects which they studied in isolation from Polish society (Hertz 1988; Tomaszewski 1993; Orla-Bukowska 1994). No doubt this exclusivist attitude has led, and still leads, to numerous misunderstandings. The contrasting views, however, do not lead to anger and hurt alone. In the past few years, a number of Polish and Jewish authors have expressed the wish and have attempted to bring to life a Polish-Jewish dialogue (for example Polonsky 1990; Bartoszewski 1998; Hoffman 1998).

Anti-Semitism in Poland: a Structural or Cultural Problem?

Structure versus Culture

A broader sociological discussion of anti-Semitism might help us gain insight into the question of why there is anti-Semitism in Poland without Jews. For the matter of convenience, I will distinguish two contrasting views that hold implicit assumptions on the origins and persistence of anti-Semitism. In the first view, the socio-economic position of the Jew is decisive in creating that stereotype. In the second view, the cultural climate of the host society is decisive in creating the anti-Semitic stereotype of the Jew.

The first view is typically voiced in the literature on the so-called *middleman minorities*,[9] although some aspects of this view are also implicit in sociological studies on Polish Jewry (Golczewski 1986; Kieniewicz 1986; Levine 1991). The aspects of the middleman minority situation that attract special attention in the middleman minority theory are the economic niches of the minority, the 'alienness' of the minority in the host society, the cultural attributes of the minority, and finally, the socio-economic explanations of host hostility (Zenner 1991). Middleman minority theory stresses the real socio-economic position of the middleman minority, and as such explains anti-Semitism in terms of the vulnerable role Jews occupy in the economy. Explained in terms of the quality of the minority group (their number, objective role, and 'alienness') anti-Semitism is rendered 'sociologically inevitable', while the Jews themselves are seen as the source of anti-Semitism.

The second view is typically voiced by authors who are in search of the dynamics of anti-Semitic behaviour and thought (Hertz 1988; Irwin-Zarecka 1989a; Oldson 1991). These authors lay stress on the analysis of the political and cultural climate of a society that generates anti-Jewish ideas and attitudes. The thesis maintains that anti-Jewish ideas have a creative power in and of themselves, as they are nurtured and perpetuated by the political and cultural elites over time, and carry a specific meaning and relevance to the contemporary society. Although these authors believe there is no such thing as 'good anti-Semitism', they do distinguish between degrees of anti-Semitism and recognise the ambiguity in anti-Jewish behaviour and thought. On Hannah Arendt's observation that, '[i]t is hardly an exaggeration to say that Romania was the most anti-Semitic country in prewar Europe,' Oldson (1991: 163-164) for example, critically comments:

> [...] we must note that she is correct to a degree. The anti-Semitism here, however, does not correspond to that of the Nazis [...] Romanian anti-Semitism did not render the Jew simply an object to be destroyed. In the old kingdom, at least the Jew remained human—although abused in a horrific and criminal manner that epitomized man's inhumanity to man, he was not merely written off as a disposable, inert commodity. Viewing the Jews in this fashion permitted both the barbarities with all the deficiency of methodology employed by the Nazis and likewise the final survival of a majority of the Jewish population of the old kingdom [of Romania].

The views presented above point to an important dilemma. On the one hand, it is safe to assume that anti-Semitic imagery is positively correlated with the Jews' socio-economic position in the host society, or for that matter, with direct 'real life' experience. This link may be illustrated with the image of the Jew as usurer, sorcerer, and Christ-killer, which found general acceptance in medieval Europe at the time when Jews became specialised as money-lenders. It was during this period that a permanent association was made between the infidel Jews and the recurrence of Christ-killing (Zenner 1991). On the other hand, the Jews' socio-economic role in Poland's history cannot possibly explain why the Jews still play an important role in contemporary Polish society. By now, the Jews have ceased to play that part in Polish society, but the (anti-Semitic) stereotype of the Jew still exists. On this dilemma Hertz (1988: 1) comments:

> [...] antagonism to a certain people, defined in the case at hand as anti-Semitism, is not dependent on their numbers, their objective role, or their 'alienness.' It is not the few Jews in Poland who are the source of anti-Semitism but certain deep and wide-ranging diseases that eat away at the society in which those Jews live. Jews become only a convenient means to facilitate the polarization of certain feelings and reactions. Even if there were not a single Jew in Poland today or if no Jew were playing the slightest part in Polish life, it is likely that some forms of anti-Semitism would still exist. The living would be replaced by their own ghosts. In Poland the traditions of anti-Semitism have left such deep traces that the Jew as symbol could suffice entirely.

If this dilemma reveals one thing, it is the importance of cultural notions. Taking into account the instrumental and creative power of cultural notions, the fact that certain 'symbolic' experiences can persist even when 'real' experiences prove the contrary is rather the rule than the exception. An example is provided by Glassman (1975), who studied the images of the Jew in medieval England. From the time of the expulsion of the Jews from England in 1290 until the period of the re-establishment of a small Jewish community in the seventeenth century, the English people rarely saw or met Jews. Despite their virtual absence, the Jews were considered an accursed group of usurers, sorcerers, and adversaries of God, who with the support of the devil were found guilty of every conceivable crime that entered the popular imagination. If there was no way to verify the incidents of Jewish treachery, why did these images persist? Glassman (1975: 152) concludes that the popular image of the Jew had developed out of the need for Christianity to show itself superior to Judaism and to justify its claims that it was the new Israel.

In other words, the complexity of feelings and perceptions cannot be reduced to direct results of experience since these facts themselves might be a social construction. Apparently, cultural notions can continue to convey anti-Semitic attitudes without the need for a structural component. Does that, however, imply that structure is irrelevant? I would say no. Even proponents of the 'culture' view cannot deny the impact of 'real life' experience.[10] But where the structure of society can play an important role in the development and formation of anti-Semitic attitudes, these attitudes (such as stereotypes), once developed, can continue to persist long after the specific roles that induced their development have ceased to exist. Many of our present-day stereotypes have their origin in the Middle Ages and have not applied to a real life situation since their conception. In fact, one may even consider, as Van Arkel (1984) does, that the lack of contact between Jews and non-Jews—which is an implicit consequence of the lack of a 'structure' in present-day Poland—supports the persistence of anti-Semitic views, attitudes, and behaviour.

If we are to understand the present-day attitudes of the Poles towards the Jews, we will have to look back to the structure of prewar society. As Opatoshu already showed, it was during this period that the basis for the present-day attitudes was laid. Of special interest should be the link between the structure of the prewar society and the associated cultural notions. The foregoing discussion drew attention to the fact that values and ideas relating to the Jews cannot simply be explained from the 'facts', but involve a certain degree of social construction. At the same time these social constructs cannot be seen separately from the structure of society, in that they often perform important functions in maintaining these structures. To understand the complex relationship between views and attitudes on the one hand and physical experience on the other, it is necessary to understand the structure of society, determine the way 'facts' lead to socially constructed notions and, finally, to investigate how these notions perform an important stabilising function in regard to that structure.

Because of the complex interplay between culture and structure, it is important to acknowledge the changes in the position of the Jews in Polish society over time. The role of the Jews when they first settled in the Polish lands in the twelfth century was a very different one from that of the early twentieth century. Each successive period, however, had an impact on the following periods in terms of both the structure of society and the cultural notions regarding the Jews.

Jews in Poland: Their Economic Role

Interactions between Poles and Jews before the Shoah cannot be explained by a single description or notion. The socio-economic position of the Polish Jews and their related 'role' in the host society shifted with time, due to socio-economic and political processes that took place in the society at large and within the Jewish community itself. In addition to the historical fluctuations, there have been regional variations as well. Firstly, the socio-economic position of the Jews and their relationship with the host society depended on the policy of the authorities on whose lands they resided: the Roman Catholic Church, the nobility, or the king. Secondly, members of the highly stratified Jewish community occupied different positions at different times and in different places. The rich Jews and the poor Jews, the town Jews and the village Jews, occupied various positions and as such maintained divergent relations with the host society. Finally, in the ethnically diverse regions, Jews did not always constitute an exclusive local minority, while in some towns and villages they even formed a local majority. This element, being part of an ethnically diverse or homogeneous landscape, also influenced Polish-Jewish relations. Or, as Hundert (1986: 57) puts it: 'Therefore, when surveying [Polish-Jewish] relations in the context of the Jewish economic role, chronological and geographical distinctions must be taken into consideration as well as the more obvious differences in the quality of relations between Jews and various social groups.'

But let us return to the different stages in the history of the Polish Jews. The overview given below covers the period from the establishment of the Jewish community in Poland during the twelfth century to the disintegration of that community after the Second World War. In general terms, the first phase included the Jews' expulsion from their homeland and their subsequent settlement in southern and western Europe as a *trade diaspora*.[11] In the twelfth century wealthy Jewish individuals settled in Poland. These rich individuals worked for the Polish kings as minters, bankers, or commercial agents, and probably attracted a complement of petty servants, tradesmen, merchants, and religious functionaries who formed the early communities (Rosman 1990: 36). In their new host country Jews then served as culture-brokers between the local customers and foreign Jewish traders who sought outlets for their products and services.

A second phase in the history of the Polish Jews started with the large influx of Jewish refugees from Germany and Spain in the fourteenth and fifteenth centuries. A substantial Jewish minority filled the commercial entrepreneurial niche, first as subjects of the Polish king and serfs of the Polish treasury, and later, from the sixteenth century onwards, also as subjects of the Polish nobility and magnates.[12] Hence, the Jews' gradual integration in Polish commerce, trade, distribution, and administration coincided with an effective royal and magnate policy, stimulating the Jews to take up managerial and commercial activities. The king as well as the magnates granted the Jews privileges, allowing them to maintain a large measure of political and cultural autonomy, while at the same time guaranteeing their protection (Rosman 1990). Local Jewish communal autonomy, which was more ramified and more developed in Poland than anywhere else in Europe, was a fact for centuries.[13] The Jewish community developed its own language (Yiddish), preserved its own religion (Judaism), and created a new spiritual movement (Hasidism) which further marked it off from the surrounding society (Rosman 1990). In forming a separate estate within the feudal society, and linking the estate of the peasant serfs with the estate of the Polish nobility, the Polish Jews then served as ideal economic *middlemen* or *brokers*.

Due to the processes in the modern period—decline of traditional authority, development of key political institutions, adherence to nationalist ideologies, social mobility, and an increase of the division of labour—the Jews' role as middlemen or brokers became an anachronism, while their status as a separate estate and alien body in the host society was no longer authorised.[14] Though most Jews continued to be active in traditional occupations, such as trade, crafts, or tavern-keeping, they no longer served as intermediaries between two hierarchical social estates. Especially in the bigger towns, Jews found employment in new economic sectors such as learned professions, industry, and modern (capitalist) commerce. Small-business activities would soon form the main source of income for many Jewish families, as well as for those who left for the United States in search of a better life. Adaptation to the new social situation changed the outlook of the Jewish community. Political, economic, and religious differentiation split the community into numerous factions that had a secular, assimilationist, nationalist, or traditional religious outlook. Being part of a highly differentiated and mobile society, the Polish Jews took up a new life as independent *ethnic entrepreneurs.*[15]

The hey-day of modern Jewish life in Poland took place after 1918, as Poland regained its sovereignty. After 1918 Jews became citizens of the Second Polish Republic, and accordingly participated in Polish public life. However, although the majority of Jews adopted the Polish nationality, Jews never became accepted as full-fledged Polish citizens. With the severe economic crisis in the 1920s and 1930s, and the rise to power of a right-wing totalitarian regime in 1935, the Polish Jews frequently fell victim to economic and political anti-Semitism. During this period many more Jews migrated to countries where economic oppression was less severe. For those who remained in Poland the invasion by Nazi Germany in 1939 was the beginning of the end. Only a few hundred thousand Polish Jews survived the Final Solution carried out by Nazi Germany in the period between 1939 and 1944. After the war the few remaining Polish Jews integrated in the socialist structure of People's Poland, as both the Jews and the Jewish community were strongly encouraged to assimilate and become invisible.[16] Today the spirit of the 'Old Country' lives on in Jewish centres where Jewish migrants established their new communities and founded ethnic enterprises and Jewish immigrant associations called *landsmanshaftn*.[17]

Jews in Poland: the Cultural Implication

Despite the Jews' varied socio-economic role in Polish society, the value system that defined their status and identity remained fairly stable over time. This value system was linked with the feudal structure that—on Polish territory—lasted for almost half a millennium. Feudalism came into being during the Middle Ages, was maintained and developed throughout the history of the noble republic, and survived its fall in 1795. From the second half of the nineteenth century the system no longer had a legal basis, but the main features survived due to prevailing social values, which possessed 'a power no less than that of the strictest legal provisions' (Hertz 1988: 60). In practice, therefore, the estate character of the life of the Polish Jews existed until the outbreak of the Second World War. Hertz, who writes about the Jews' role in Polish culture, uses the concept of caste to describe the position of the Jews in Polish feudal society. It is debatable whether caste is a more suitable term than estate; unlike castes, estates were created politically by manmade laws rather than by religious rules of ritual purity.[18] For the sake of argument, I follow the terminology of Hertz (1988) in his interesting reading of the value system in feudal Poland.

According to Hertz (1988: 59-61), the Polish caste system (that consisted of four castes, namely, the nobility, the burghers, the peasants, and the Jews) had the following characteristics. Firstly, a caste was a *closed* group. Leaving the caste was difficult, if not impossible, and was connected with attempts to erase any traces of caste background. Participation in the caste required absolute acceptance of a number of rules that defined the caste's identity. These were religious, legal, linguistic, moral, and professional rules. In that sense, a caste was also a *cultural* organisation, as specific cultural features marked the caste and distinguished it from the cultures of other groups in that system. In addition, a caste was an *economic* organisation, because a number of economic activities resided within the model of the caste and determined the way its members would act. Finally, a caste occupied a definite place in the society as a whole, as it was assigned a specific status within the social *hierarchy*. As such, caste members were subject to definitions which strictly determined their behaviour and attitudes both in and outside the caste: 'The definition of a Jew embraced a world of beliefs and moral, political, and legal principles; it embraced a world of economic activities and allotted to the Jews definite functions and tasks in that world. This created a comprehensive stereotype, one that had been systematized and conditioned by emotions' (Hertz 1988 : 68).

The relationship between a non-Jew and a Jew was structured by the prevailing stereotype. Irrespective of whether a Jew was considered favourably or not, he was expected to follow the requirements of the stereotype and to act the way a Jew should act. Generally speaking, this stereotype took the following form:

> [...] the Jew was a person not only of another faith, language, and tradition, but also of another morality. He was scheming and evasive. He thought only about his own profit and sought to cheat Christians. He had all the features folklore everywhere in a precapitalist economy endowed upon every merchant. In Poland, where merchants, especially small merchants, were nearly exclusively Jews, those features were ascribed to the entire caste (Hertz 1988 : 68).[19]

In practice the expectations were rarely disappointed. This, according to Hertz (1988: 69), is a universal characteristic of caste systems; caste members accept the rules imposed by people outside the caste and follow them, whether 'at issue are the local populations in the colonial countries, the American or South African blacks, the peasants in old Poland, or, finally, the Jews.' In Poland, the caste system was accepted as self-evident by all the people concerned, and was considered both normal and proper almost up to the twentieth century. Once the Jews had found a place within that system, they not only accepted the rules imposed on them, but even made these rules stronger in order to preserve their position in regard to other social groups. The nobility, the burghers, and the peasants did the same within their own caste organisations.

In addition to the stereotype of the Jewish merchant and usurer, the 'sociology' adopted by the Polish nobility sustained the rigid set of social values and rules on which the caste system was based. This sociology included definitions applied to the 'inferior ranks' of the society, in which the peasant was a boor (*cham*), the burgher a petty bourgeois (*łyk*), and the Jew a scab (*parch*). These terms designated rigid social groups that were placed in a definite socio-political, economic, and cultural framework, and each group was subject to distinct, and superior value judgements (Hertz 1988 : 72). These judgements, however, were not only applied in relations between nobles and non-nobles. They also expressed relations between the lower ranks. For the burgher too the peasant was a *cham* and the Jew a *parch*, while the peasant saw the Jew as a *parch* and the Jew saw the peasant as a *cham*.

This is not to say that the peasant, burgher, and landlord held the same views about the Jews. The image of the Jew was one thing in the world of the landowning nobility and another in the world of the burghers or the peasants. Nor is this to say that the views were always the same. In each period or situation different valuations crossed with each other, leading to ambivalent attitudes and definitions. Hertz points out that such definitions did not necessarily attest to the existence of deeper inter-group conflict or hatred. A peasant, nobleman, or burgher who called a Jew a *parch* was defining the place of the Jewish caste, passing a value judgement on that caste, and fixing its position in the entire structure of the society. Although that judgement may not have been flattering, it was not a sign of hostility. To quote Hertz (1988: 73): 'In the conditions of a caste system such judgements could be perfectly well contained within a framework of peaceful and tension-free relations.'

In the analysis of Hertz, caste identity structured inter-group relations and determined the nature of inter-group contact between the Poles and the Jews. Hertz's concept of caste identity largely overlaps with the concept of ethnic identity as defined by Barth (1969): as a category that provides individuals with identities for the purpose of social interaction. In fact, ethnic difference continued to exert an influence on Polish-Jewish interaction when values and judgements associated with the caste system were on the wane. This was especially true for the countryside, where cultural differences were highly standardised and protected by an extensive value system. Moreover, there is evidence that the Polish and Jewish communities made serious efforts to keep up a certain cultural distance during the interwar years too. Following Barth (1969) we could explain this as an attempt by the ethnic communities to preserve the complementary difference which characterised their society in the face of close interethnic contact. Seen from this perspective, stereotypical views and behaviour do not necessarily result from (or point to) interethnic conflict, but might just as well entail a classic symbiotic situation (Barth 1969).[20]

An Ethnographic Case-Study Approach

The Case of Jaśliska

The foregoing discussion has pointed out the various aspects which should be taken into account when studying Polish-Jewish relations: the impact of the Shoah, the generational perspective, the socio-economic relations, and the cultural implications. All these aspects have a historical dimension, that is, they change with time or refer to processes in time. This research also deals with processes in time: the structural transformation of Polish-Jewish relations and its impact on perceptions and views. Although a great deal of attention will be paid to the history of this relationship, the present study aims to present more than a mere reconstruction of the past. It starts from the view that in order to understand certain aspects of social reality one needs to investigate the way in which they came into being.

My approach to the subject is that of a case study. A large number of case studies have been written on particular Jewish communities by scholars of Jewish history, but few such authors were concerned with Polish-Jewish interaction. Moreover, the studies that are concerned with Polish-Jewish relations per se mostly deal with specific themes (for example, Jewish assimilation trends, anti-Semitism, postwar relations) on a macro level, and, as a consequence, often deal with events or tendencies that are unrelated in time or space. The work by Rosman (1990) is different in that it explores magnate-Jewish relations within the confines of the *latifundium* owned by one wealthy magnate family. Following Rosman, I would argue that it can be useful to employ first-hand archival and anthropological sources which are connected geographically and chronologically to each other. This, in turn, allows new insights that cannot be gained when using secondary or macro-level sources.

This study presents the case of Jaśliska, a former town and present-day village in southeastern Poland. The archival and anthropological sources that I employ relate to Polish-Jewish relations in this specific locality over a period of almost one hundred years, starting with the Jews' settlement in the small town in the second half of the nineteenth century and ending with the destruction of the Jewish community in 1942. Attention is also paid to the period before the Jewish settlement, as well as to the period after the destruction of the Jewish community, but in those cases too the sources that are used directly relate to the research area. By presenting a detailed ethnographic study of a specific case, my intention has been to contribute to a more accurate understanding of the relationship between Poles and Jews at the micro-level.

My approach to the analysis of Polish-Jewish relations is in agreement with Barth (1969) as it rests on the premise that actors use ethnic identities to categorise themselves and others for purposes of interaction. In this study much attention will be paid to the ethnic boundary between the Polish and Jewish communities in prewar Jaśliska. The various forms of interaction will be organised thematically and, accordingly, will be viewed from the different domains of interaction: the spatial, the economic, and the social domains. The types of contact between Poles and Jews, the significance of these contacts for each party, as well as the scope and limit of interaction between Poles and Jews will be investigated for each of these domains. The danger of a thematic approach is that it is likely to result in a static picture of past social relations. I have tried, though, to discuss the themes in such a way that the historical dimension will not be lost. Chapter seven is different in that it focuses on the destruction of the Jewish and Polish communities during and in the years directly following the Second World War.

Another important, but less extensive, part of this study will be an analysis of cultural notions regarding the Jews. These cultural notions are expressed in the views, opinions, and stories about the local Jews as they were told to me by my Polish informants. The changes in these views will be studied by reviewing the different perspectives of successive generations. The accounts show that views and valuations of the Jews by the Polish informants are often expressed by assessing the Polish-Jewish relationship in prewar Jaśliska. This implies that the 'factual' interpretation of the prewar relationship by the informants largely overlaps with their 'subjective' interpretation of that past, and for that matter, with their view of the local Jews. Hence the informants' views of the Jews, as well as the different generational perspectives, will be dealt with in constant conjunction with the informants' recollection of facts about Polish-Jewish relations in prewar Jaśliska.

The Ethnographic Present

Research in Jaśliska was conducted in the summer of 1992 and the winter of 1993. The fact that I worked and lived in the place where I conducted research spurred my integration in the village. Still, I found that the villagers were extremely suspicious and uncommunicative at first. It took much effort and much time before I gained the confidence of the informants. Besides the introverted character of the peasant community, the language problem formed another obstacle in trust building. Although I had some education in Polish prior to my stay in Poland, I did not have such a command of the language that I could do without the help of an interpreter. The latter assisted me during interviews with informants and during visits to governmental bodies such as the State Archive and the Court of Law. With (and at times without) the assistance of an interpreter, a second visit to the village certainly helped to do away with most of the doubts on the part of the villagers. It was during that last but short visit that I learned most about the village.

Jaśliska is a typical example of a town like thousands of others which existed in prewar Poland: a town with a large minority of Jewish entrepreneurs in the centre and a small majority of Polish peasants on the outskirts. At the outbreak of the Second World War Jaśliska had an estimated 1,100 inhabitants, of which one quarter were Jews. Like many other towns in prewar Poland, Jaśliska suffered greatly from the Great Depression in the 1920s and 1930s, and it lost its town rights in 1934—in spite of the town's impressive historical record as a prosperous trade centre of Hungarian wine. Today, Jaśliska has just under 500 inhabitants and is primarily a peasant village. According to the 1988 national census (GUS 1988) about 36 percent of the active population were full-time farmers. At present there are few prospects in the village for non-farm income. In 1990 the state liquidated the local State Farms (PGR's), which were the main employers in the area. This resulted in an alarmingly high unemployment level among the middle-aged men and women. The people that have secure jobs are those in the service sector, like the priest, the postman, the teachers of the village primary school, the doctor and the shop assistants. Jaśliska is also the site of a small convent, where six nuns live and work.

I chose Jaśliska as the research site for a number of reasons. First, the small size of the community meant that I had easy access to it. Second, before the Second World War one quarter of the inhabitants of Jaśliska had been Jews. Compared to the proportion of Jews in the whole of Poland (10 percent of the prewar population), the proportion of Jews that lived in Jaśliska is fairly representative; they constituted a modest but significant minority.[21] At present, as in most other cities, towns, and villages of Poland, there are no Jews in Jaśliska. Thirdly, the large majority of Poles who inhabit Jaśliska today are indigenous to the village. This fact is important if one takes into account the history of wars and deportations in the region.

Crucial in the assessment of the collected data is the way in which I introduced the research topic to the informants. I introduced myself as a student of sociology who was interested in the local history of the town and in family histories. Neither the informants nor the interpreters who assisted me during fieldwork knew that I was primarily interested in Jaśliska's Jewish past. The reason why I did not make the research topic explicit was that I expected it to be a sensitive one. The stories told about Jews and related topics (including the topic of the villagers' seizure of former Jewish property) were told without prompting. The advantage of this strategy is obvious; the memories, stories, and opinions on the Jews were largely brought up by the informants themselves, and as such they partly reveal their actual relevance to the lives of the informants. On the other hand, because of my reluctance to directly approach the subject, some crucial information only reached me in a late phase of fieldwork. All in all, I was positively surprised by the enthusiasm with which the informants engaged in story-telling about the Jewish past of their community.

The fieldwork activities have not been limited to empirical research in Jaśliska. I spent a considerable part of the time on archival research on matters pertaining to the village. The bulk of archives were visited during the summer, when I investigated the real estate registers (*księgi wieczyste*) in the court of law in Krosno for the period 1874-1940 and the municipal council in Dukla for the period 1945-1965. In addition, considerable time was spent in the State Archives, whose departments are spread over many towns. During the winter, stress was put on contact with the villagers who in the absence of agricultural work had more leisure time and, as a result, were less reluctant to talk. Most interviews were conducted in Jaśliska, some in the neighbouring villages, and one in Nysa (southwest Poland). In addition to my own field material, I used the interviews of Polish students carried out in Jaśliska in 1978, 1979, and 1985 which were in the archives of the open-air museum in Sanok.

In the period between 1993 and 1996 I conducted a series of interviews with Jewish survivors of the Shoah who were former residents of Jaśliska. Because the informants live scattered over Europe and North America, I met them at different times over this three-year period. The Jewish informants who will turn up in this study are Samuel O. (1911-1995), his wife Pearl O. (1911, now living in Toronto, Canada) and his two brothers Jacob (1914, New Jersey, U.S.A.) and David O. (1920, Toronto, Canada). Besides the members of the family O. I further met Morty L. (1921, New Jersey, U.S.A.), and Josko S. (1918, Antwerp, Belgium). With the exception of Pearl O. all informants were born in Jaśliska. At this point the testimonies of Israel B. (1901) and Mordechai D. (1909), both survivors of the Shoah, should also be mentioned. The testimony of Israel B., a former resident of Jaśliska, was recorded by Josef Litwak on behalf of Yad Vashem in Jerusalem (Litwak 1969). The testimony of Mordechai D., former resident of Kraków who passed Jaśliska as a prisoner of war, was recorded by Róża Bauminger in Kraków (n.d.).

Notes

1. Hertz (1988: 30-31) wrote the following biographical note on Opatoshu: 'Joseph Opatoshu was a Jewish writer who wrote in Yiddish on Jewish themes. He was a Jew both as a man and as a writer. Spiritually bound with Jewry, its past and traditions, he also believed in its future. He was a Jewish nationalist, and the slogans of the assimilationists were foreign to him. But at the same time Opatoshu was deeply bound to Poland. He owed a great deal to Polish culture, a debt of which he was fully aware. He was interested in Polish affairs until the end of his life, and far from Poland, in New York City, he collected Polish books and kept up relations with Polish writers.'
2. The timing of this debate can partly be explained by the increasingly tolerant attitude of the Communist regime regarding Jewish affairs during the early 1980s. The little space which was created gave birth to a public discussion which, once established, could not be reversed (Irwin-Zarecka 1989a). By the mid-1980s the debate on Poland's Jews was carried on by the three mainstays of Polish society: the opposition (members of the underground movement Solidarność and members of the so-called 68 generation), the Roman Catholic Church (particularly progressive Catholic intellectuals), and the Communist regime (in the person of prominent journalists and writers). The Special Issue on Poles and Jews which was published in 1998 by the monthly magazine *Więź* (The Bond) gives a very interesting overview of the opinions and reflections held by the three mainstays of Polish society over the last thirty years (1960-1998), as it comprises a selection of texts (essays, pamphlets, memoirs, interviews) which have influenced the debate on Christian-Jewish and Polish-Jewish relations in Poland (Bartoszewski 1998).
3. Yiddish for synagogue.
4. A Christian who on Jewish holidays such as the Sabbath does work which is prohibited to Jews. It was customary for Jewish communities to employ a Christian to work for them as *shabbes goy*.
5. Kwiatek, the last name of the old man, in Polish means 'flower' which stresses the cheerful character of the old man.
6. By 'outsiders' I mean persons (Jews and non-Jews alike), who did not live through the war in Poland, either because they are from a later generation, or because they were elsewhere at the time. Besides non-Poles and non-Jews, who for one reason or another have devel-

oped an interest in Poland's Jewish past, these also include historians, journalists, and writers of (Polish-)Jewish descent, as well as members of the Polish émigré community. The latter two groups turned the tolerant Polish climate to good account and have greatly contributed to the debate on Poland's Jews.

7. An example of such countering of arguments is provided by Grüber (Jewish historian) contra Szczypiorski (Polish writer) and Milo Anstadt (a Polish-born Jewish writer) in NRC Handelsblad, 3, 15, 26 November, 8 and 28 December 1994.

8. This is not to say that Jews were never discussed in Poland. On the contrary, a great deal was written about them, but there were rarely honest attempts to study and understand Jewish culture. To write about Jews was to write about the 'Jewish problem' (Irwin-Zarecka 1989b). Historically, the presence of the Jews became formulated as a major social problem in eighteenth- and nineteenth-century Poland, when the notion of the modern nation state was introduced (Cała 1986; Lichten 1986). The so-called 'Jewish question' continued to be a major political issue in postwar Poland (Hirszowicz 1986). Today, scholars of Poland's Jewish history still discuss the 'Jewish problem', which they now rightly refer to as a major 'Polish problem' (Kieniewicz 1986; Bartoszewski 1987a; Krajewski 1998).

9. See especially Zenner (1991) and Bonacich (1973). The term *middleman minority* originates from Becker, an American sociologist, who attempted to prove that those traits which may be associated with the Jews also appear in other ethnic groups noted for their commercial abilities, such as the Scots, Chinese, Parsis, and Armenians. Becker's comparisons placed equal stress on several middleman groups, thus focusing attention on comparison. Other appellations denoting similar groups include *pariah capitalists*, *middle class minorities*, *permanent minorities*, *trading minorities*, *marginal trading people*, and *trading diasporas* (Curtin 1984; Vermeulen 1991; Zenner 1991).

10. Hertz (1988: 197), for example, concludes that '[...] judgements on and images of people who belong to other ethnic groups [...] are the fruits of historical experience, the results of our contacts with others from outside our group.'

11. The term 'trade diaspora' is used by Curtin (1984) to denote the interrelated net of commercial communities, or trade settlements in alien towns. According to Curtin, the most common institutional form of cross-cultural trade after the emergence of city life was the trade settlement. Commercial specialists would leave the home community to go and live in alien towns, most likely a town important in the life of the host community. Upon arrival the strange merchants could settle down and learn the language, the customs, and commercial ways of their hosts. They could then serve as cross-cultural brokers, helping and encouraging trade between the host society and people of their own origin who moved along the trade routes (Curtin 1984: 2).

12. The term 'magnates' refers to powerful and wealthy noblemen or noblewomen, members of the elite of the nobility (aristocracy) who took the lead in furthering its political and economic interests. This group consisted of ten to twenty families in each generation and were distinguished by ongoing high economic standing, several generations of service in the Polish Senate, marriage connections with other aristocratic families, a high level of education, and recognition accorded by contemporaries (Rosman 1990: 7).

13. Each main Jewish community (*kehilla*), with its satellite communities, constituted a distinct corporation run by an oligarchic group of some twenty men called the *kahal*. These *kehalim* were organised into regional councils (*Vaad Galil*), which in turn were loosely confederated on the national level as the Council of Four Lands (*Vaad Arba Aratzot*) and the Council of the State Lithuania (*Vaad Medinat Lita*) (Rosman 1990: 37). This form of highly developed Jewish communal autonomy lasted from the middle of the sixteenth century until its abolition by the Polish Diet in 1764. In the nineteenth and twentieth centuries less centralised forms of Jewish communal autonomy existed.

14. According to Rosman (1990) the process of displacing the official Jewish community from its medieval role as intermediary between the Jews and the surrounding society started already with the abolition of the Council of Four Lands (the institution that organised Jewish autonomy at the semi-national level in Poland) in 1764. When in 1795 Poland lost its sovereignty to the Russian, German and Austrian empires, a new era set in that also affected the position of Poland's Jews.

15. For this term see Vermeulen (1984: 22-23).

16. As Irwin-Zarecka (1989a: 50-55) convincingly shows, the shift towards 'invisibility' was not simply a reaction to the anti-Semitic climate in the years immediately following the Second World War. Most Polish Jews who resolved to stay and to take part in the rebuilding of Poland were already highly Polonized. In addition, the official 'internationalist' doctrine in postwar Communist Poland prohibited differentiation between Jews and non-Jews. To illustrate this point, none of the postwar censuses distinguishes between different ethnic or religious identities as was common before the war (see for example GUS 1988). Moreover, the lessons drawn from the Holocaust prevented the Jews from maintaining their Jewish identity: 'If the tragedy was not to repeat itself, the Jews were never to be singled out again' (Irwin-Zarecka 1989a: 55).

17. For a discussion of *landsmanshaftn* in New York (Russian and Polish Jewish immigrant associations) see also Weisser (1989).

18. By using the term 'caste' rather than 'estate' to denote the sharp differences and rigid barriers between a small number of strata in feudal Poland, Hertz implicitly takes a stand in the debate on whether the caste system is specific to Hindu culture, or whether its principle features are more widely found in other societies. In the first position, caste cannot be defined independently of the 'caste system', which is specific to classical Hindu society. In the second argument, the term caste is extended to embrace the stratification of ethnic groups, for example in the southern states of the U.S.A. (Abercrombie, Hill et al. 1984: 29). In an introduction to Hertz's *Jews in Polish Culture,* Dobroszycki observes that Hertz's use of the concept cannot be separated from Hertz's experience in the United States, where he had sought refuge during the war and where he would later settle permanently. Hertz was to a considerable extent inspired by research conducted in the United States on all possible aspects of human relations, in particular that of American blacks. This influence is detectable in the frequent comparisons he makes between the situation of the Jews in Poland and the position of the blacks in the U.S. According to Dobroszycki (Hertz 1988), the sociological concept 'caste' gave rise to Hertz's approach, categories, and ideas (directly relating to the processes he observed in the United States), and enabled him to find an illustrative and historically accurate means for presenting an image of the Jews as they had been seen in Poland for centuries and also as they had come to see themselves.

19. It must be borne in mind that a dislike of trade occupations prevailed in Poland. The country's economic backwardness and the traditions of the nobility had created an atmosphere of contempt for trade as a profession. It was an economic activity given very low status, and people who pursued it were not respected. Accordingly, trade fell to the caste occupying a very low place in the social hierarchy, that is, to the Polish Jews (Hertz 1988: 69).

20. Barth (1969: 18) defines ethnic symbiosis as the positive bond that connects two or more ethnic groups in an encompassing social system which is based on the complementarity of the groups with respect to some of their characteristic cultural features. This is the situation where two or more ethnic groups provide important goods and services for each other, i.e. occupy reciprocal and therefore different niches but in close interdependence.

21. Here it must be noted that before the war the proportion of Jews in some towns and villages in this part of Poland exceeded 50 percent.

Chapter 2

THE SETTING

The children, about ten years old, who lived in the vicinity of the Jewish ceme-tery, sat down close to Marcin. Because Marcin spent his whole life on the cemetery, and because he always knows of something to tell about the dead, about the past, the children feel attracted to him (Opatoshu 1951: 314).

Introduction

*I*n this first empirical chapter the settings in which Polish-Jewish relations in Jaśliska developed will be explored. It begins with the early settlement of the Jews in the Polish lands (Hebrew: *Polin*) in the early thirteenth century, through the period of Jewish exclusion from Polish merchant towns, until their gradual settlement in Jaśliska in the second half of the nineteenth cen-tury. We will find that feudal structures laid the basis for Polish-Jewish inter-actions in the province of Galicia[1] until well into the twentieth century. This is remarkable, as feudal obligations in Galicia were lifted in the first half of the nineteenth century (1848). The slow recovery from feudal conditions can be explained by the low level of economic development in the region that left the feudal patterns of exploitation virtually intact.

Feudal Relations: The Gentry, the Jews, and the Peasant Serfs

Early Jewish Settlement in Poland

During the twelfth, thirteenth, and fourteenth centuries, Jews from Germany, Bohemia, and Moravia were attracted to the growing towns and cities of

---

Notes for this section begin on page 37.

Poland and filled the commercial and entrepreneurial niche in this country of nobility and serfs (Rosman 1990: 36-37). Compared to Western Europe, the Jews in Poland enjoyed a favourable legal and economic status. The basic rights of the Polish Jews were laid down in the 1264 charter on the Jewish liberties in Poland, ratified in 1334, 1453 and 1539 by the respective Polish kings. The charter legally defined the Polish Jews as serfs of the state treasury (*servi camerae*) and subjects of the Polish king, and at the same time secured the Jews' economic and religious inviolability. Poland's religious toleration made it an attractive land of settlement for Jews aiming to avoid religious persecution in Western Europe.

> Notwithstanding certain minor feudal obligations in privately owned towns (obligations that were shared by other townspeople) the Jews were free men, entitled to travel, change residence, swear and sue in court, bear arms, and own homes and businesses. In principle, they were allowed to deal in any commodity and could sell retail as well as wholesale. Jewish religious practice was completely licit and church-inspired restrictions on Jewish dress or behaviour were rarely taken seriously (Rosman 1990: 37).

In practice the privileges on paper did not always hold up. Over centuries the Polish lands were ruled and owned by the Polish Crown, the Latin Church, and the richer ranks of the Polish nobility (*szlachta*). The legal and economic position of the Jews depended to a considerable extent on the policy of the respective owner on whose land they resided: the king, the bishop, or the (magnate) landlord.[2] When a Jew found himself under the jurisdiction of a powerful, despotic nobleman, when a royally chartered town's patriciate convinced the king or bishop to grant their town a privilege *de non tolerandis Iudaeis*, or when a clergyman incited a blood libel or a host desecration trial, the nominal legal status of the Jews did not count for very much (Rosman 1990: 38). Moreover, as time passed the Jews' main antagonists, the petty nobility and the royal patriciate, became more successful in eliciting official restrictions on Jewish settlement and economic rights in royally chartered towns, because the position of the Polish king was weakening.

Particularly during the sixteenth century but also during the seventeenth and eighteenth centuries, dozens of crown cities and towns, including major centres like Lublin, Warsaw, and Wilno, attempted to exclude Jews from residing in their jurisdictions. Other discriminatory legislation aimed at reducing or eliminating Jewish competition, forbade them to engage in retail trade, limited Jewish wholesale merchants to certain specific goods, or forbade them to lease shops or stores on the marketplace of the town (Hundert 1986: 57). Frequently, guild charters not only excluded

Jews from the guild's trade but also limited or prohibited Jewish acquisition of raw materials used by the guild, or forbade them to sell imported products of the same type as those produced by the guild (Hundert 1986: 58). Relations between Jews and Christian merchants and craftsmen became especially strained during the seventeenth century. This was not only due to the growing number of Jewish craftsmen and the increasingly difficult economic situation, but also because of the widening influence of Jewish merchants who increasingly controlled the raw materials which the craftsmen needed, and marketed goods which competed with the craftsmen's products (Hundert 1986: 59).

With the 1569 Union of Lublin, Poland gained vast open territories in the Ukraine. These large and sparsely populated lands were given to the magnates, who set about organising them as Polish feudal estates. The magnates and Polish noblemen, who rejected direct involvement in commerce as a distasteful and unnoble pursuit, needed people to serve as administrators, to develop commerce, and simply to fill the new towns they established. Jews, increasingly subject to pressure from the nobility and townsmen to limit their settlement and economic rights in the crown territories in western Poland, were attracted eastward to the lands of the magnates, who offered them free—even subsidised—settlement, religious freedom, and abundant economic opportunity (Rosman 1990: 40). 'The ideal Jewish settler,' Rosman (1990: 39) concludes, 'was someone with a good reputation, ready cash and commercial skills'. While originally the Jews came to Poland in connection with their services to Polish kings, by 1765 more than half of the 750,000 Jews in the Polish Commonwealth lived on privately owned *latifundia* under the direct jurisdiction of nobility—especially magnate owners (Rosman 1990: 39).

The foundation of Polish-Jewish economic relations was laid during the period of the Second Serfdom (1550-1850). Polish feudal structures were spurred on by the acquisition of new lands in the East and increasing exports of Polish grain to European markets during the sixteenth century. Levine (1980) points out a distinctive feature of Polish feudalism: the sharp bifurcation between the commercial and the natural (non-commercial) sector of the economy. The natural sector was made up of the small productive units of the feudal estates in which the peasants worked the lord's land a certain number of days a week in exchange for the right to cultivate a small strip of land. From the grain produce the peasant would have to provide himself and his family with food, pay additional cash rent to the lord, pay tithes to the Church, and market any possible surplus for money to meet the fixed obligations as well as to buy whatever commodities he could not produce. However, the peasant's freedom to sell surplus on local markets was restricted through the rule of the landowning gentry as well as through his own poverty.

The absorption of Jews into the economy of the gentry's feudal estates served social and political aims as well as economic incentives. Levine (1980: 240) stresses the significant role of the Jews in 'linking the natural and commercial sectors of the feudal economy and in providing the mechanisms by which the economic contradictions inherent in feudalism could be transcended and the fictions of [feudal] autarky could be sustained.' The economic activities of the Jews constituted a potential threat to the feudal economy. As merchants in towns and peddlers in the countryside, Jews facilitated the peasants' efforts to maintain a market relationship, causing cash to flow from the feudal estates, and enabling the peasants to strengthen their economic and social position in relation to the landowning gentry. In order to preserve both the feudal autarky and the patriarchal social relations on the estates, the gentry restricted Jewish commercial activities and eliminated Jewish crafts. Instead, Jews were absorbed into the closed feudal monetary circuit and the set of economic relations known as the *arenda*.

The Jewish Arrendator

Rosman stresses the importance of the arenda in Jewish economic life during the sixteenth and seventeenth centuries. He defines an arenda as a lease of property or rights, transferred from the lessor to the lessee, in exchange for a pre-set rent (1990: 107). Such control meant that the lessee could pocket any income produced by the leased property or rights. For a Polish landlord who possessed many properties and rights, leasing arrangements held several attractions. First, they provided him with cash. Second, they were an efficient method of exploiting his numerous holdings with a minimum of effort. Without arrendators, administration, revenue collection, and bill paying would have been much more cumbersome. Furthermore, leasing reduced the risks for the landlord, as the lessee was expected to absorb any loss (Rosman 1990: 107-108).

In practice the term arenda referred to a lease of monopoly rights and was mostly held by Jewish arrendators, whereas leases of real estate (such as villages and manors), signified by the term *dzierżawa*, were usually held by Polish noblemen. Arenda provided a livelihood for a significant part of the Jewish families and was considered to be a traditional Jewish occupation by non-Jews and Jews alike. Documentary sources show that the word 'arrendator' (*arendarz*) was often used interchangeably with 'Jew' (*Żyd*) which, paraphrasing Rosman (1990: 112), 'bespeaks the numerical predominance of

Jews in this sphere'. The fact that noblemen were reluctant to engage in an occupation that they considered undignified kept the field of arenda almost exclusively Jewish.

A common form of arenda leasing involved the leasing of most of the rights and monopolies on a given area. This super-lease, normally including the liquor production facilities, taverns, bars, mills, tolls and taxes (and sometimes also the ponds and tobacco) of a town or group of villages, was referred to as 'general arenda', 'town arenda', 'village arenda', or simply 'tavern arenda' or 'brewery arenda'. The general arrendator who held this lease usually leased out components to sub-arrendators. Candidates for holding a general arenda were wealthy Jewish individuals or groups of individuals and sometimes the council of a Jewish community (*kahal*) itself. The sub-arrendators were people of modest means who viewed their lease as a *miha* (Hebrew), a means of making a living, and not as capital investment. Leases were usually held for one to three years, depending on the local customs and the arenda contract (Rosman 1990: 116).

The best known and most often exploited right available for the arenda was the right to propination (*propinacja*), meaning the exclusive right of the landlord to manufacture and sell alcoholic beverages within his domain (Rosman 1990; Levine 1991). With the decline of dependable labour supplies and stable market outlets for grain in the seventeenth and eighteenth centuries, the propination provided an important solution to the shipping and marketing problems, as it created a profitable end product for Polish grain.[3] Congruent with their prior involvement in the arenda, Jews were recruited to organise the increasingly important monopoly of the production and sale of alcohol. In the middle of the eighteenth century 20 to 30 percent of the Jewish population was involved in some aspect of alcohol production. According to the census of 1764-65, a majority of Jews in villages as well as 15 percent of the Jews living in towns, were involved in alcohol-related enterprises (Levine 1980: 223-224). However, although profitable as business, propination also provided a suitable device to accentuate the advantages and reduce the disadvantages of the economic relationship between the serfs and the Jews. Levine (1980: 240) explains:

> Encouraging the serfs to spend their surplus on drink would keep the money within the natural sector of the feudal economy; siphoning off their surplus would preserve feudal autarky. At the same time, it would absorb Jews into an enterprise which would limit their development of local markets that were not controlled by the gentry. The peasants would be induced to raise a surplus, but this surplus would still be beneficial to the feudal lord even if it had to pass through the hands of the Jewish innkeeper.

In other words, the propination as a siphoning-off mechanism was a remedy for the inefficiencies and failures of the coercive surplus extraction, and a 'feeble effort of the gentry to maintain their profits despite uncertain returns on grain, while preventing the Jews and serfs from gaining the modicum of freedom that participation in exchange markets allows' (Levine 1980: 240-241). In their capacity of tavern-keepers, Jews not only masked the gentry's efforts to personally dominate the serfs and to exploit them economically, but they also functioned as safety valves for social tensions. Jewish 'exploiters' therefore were the first to fall victim to rebellious peasants, vengeful clergy, and political agitators (Jews and non-Jews alike). As suppliers of alcohol, Jews came to be blamed for the peasants' poor standard of living, their low productivity, their rebelliousness and destructiveness (*dezolacja*). This view is clearly voiced by Demian (cited in Macartney 1970: 195-196) in his 'Darstellung der Oestereichischen Monarchie' (1804), a guide to the Austrian monarchy as it was in the author's day:

> The Galician peasant in particular is a peculiar mixture of servility and refractoriness, of stupidity and cunning; in particular, the frequent enjoyment of brandy has become a terrible necessity—no less than meat—for him. When the peasant drives to market, he calls in on the way there at several Jewish taverns, leaves the payment till the return journey, then on that repeats all his visits and drinks away half, sometimes all, the money he has made at the market. He swills down twenty to thirty glasses at a sitting. His wife is not a hairsbreadth behind him. On Sundays and holidays they walk to the church in their best clothes, but barefoot, carrying their boots under their arms. At the entrance of the village in which the parish church stands they put on their boots; after Divine Service they take them off again in the same place and then go into the taverns with their husbands or kinsfolk. There they drink brandy till sundown, without eating so much as a morsel of bread; then they start off, singing, for their villages, which are often a couple of leagues away, and often spend the whole night lying in heaps on the road. Usually it is the Jews who provide this, the Galician peasants' fount of happiness, brandy, which serves him as a means to drive away all cares, tonic, as medicine, to cheer him up and even to appease the pangs of hunger. At their frequent meetings the Jew enters into intimate conversation with him, listens to his complaints and often gives him sound advice. In these frequent conversations he learns what each peasant possesses, what he has to sell, what he is short of and what he can do without. Now the Jew is already master of the poor helot's property. Very soon the peasant drinks himself into indebtedness to the Jew, and this does not worry the creditor. He does not recite his sins to the peasant until he knows that the latter is no longer able to purge them with money. Then a composition is made, and the Jew takes everything the peasant offers in lieu of payment in cash, and renews his credit.

Jaśliska: Portrait of a Polish Episcopal Town

The Foundation

The history of Jaśliska begins with the incorporation of the Sanok lands into the Polish Kingdom in 1341. In those days the last monarch of the Piast dynasty, King Casimir the Great, colonised the sparsely populated lands by a settlement policy based on the pattern of the so-called 'Magdeburg Law'. This settlement charter stipulated feudal dues and services similar to those enforced in towns and villages throughout the country (Hann 1985; Reinfuss 1990). Part of this colonist policy was the establishment of Jaśliska in 1366, then called by its German name *Hohstath*, when King Casimir the Great appointed a Hungarian merchant as the first owner of the town, granting him fourteen *lanów*[4] of arable land and pastures, allowances from rent and fines, and the privilege to build houses and a castle. In the same privilege the Polish king gave one *lan* of land to each individual settler, who in addition was exempted from paying dues to the Crown (so-called *wolnizna*) during the first twenty years after settlement (Fastnacht 1962; Kozakiewicz 1966; Gajewski 1996). After the first few decades following its foundation, the name of the town was changed to the Polish *Jaśliska*,[5] presumably because this was the name that was already in use to denote the settlement where the town was erected (Gajewski 1996).

While originally Jaśliska was established in connection with a royal charter, little less than a hundred years later the Roman Catholic Church took over the control of the town. In 1384 Maria, the Empress of Hungary, gave part of her lands to the episcopate of Przemyśl, hereby making a first concession to the Church's expansive ambitions in the area. When in 1434 the bishop of Przemyśl bid for the lands of Sanok, the Polish king delegated the authority of Jaśliska to the bishop (Kozakiewicz 1966). From that time onwards, Jaśliska belonged to the episcopate of Przemyśl and together with some neighbouring villages formed a separate episcopal dominion or *klucz*.[6] When in the sixteenth and seventeenth centuries Jaśliska emerged as one of the most important royal trading centres between Poland and Hungary, it did so under the close supervision of the Roman Catholic Church. The successive Polish kings as well as bishops granted the town numerous privileges to stimulate economic growth. Indeed, the state and church representatives supported each other in their ambition to exploit the lucrative trade in the areas of control (Kozakiewicz 1966). The trade character of the town left its imprint on the town's population. While it appeared that by the seventeenth century the majority was Polish, at least six inhabitants were Hungarian and one was Scottish. In addition, a considerable portion of the town dwellers came from other parts of the Polish kingdom (Gajewski 1996).

Among the products traded in Jaśliska such as cattle, honey, vodka, fish, plums, and cereals, the most valuable was Hungarian wine (Orlik 1979). The numerous transactions that were registered in the town books, as well as the large cellars that were built beneath the houses (so-called 'Hungarian houses')[7] covering an area equivalent to the whole market square, are a witness to the large-scale wine trade in the town, which exceeded other major trade centres. In order to secure high profits from the lucrative wine trade, the commercial activities in Jaśliska were strictly regulated and protected by numerous constitutional acts and royal privileges. In 1578, for instance, it was decreed that 'there is no other road for wine to go than through Jaśliska, Dukla, Rymanów, Sądecz, Biecz, Nowy Targ, Krosno, Sambor and Stryj' and in 1579 Jaśliska was granted the privilege to store and levy tax on wine (Bostel 1890: 810). To enlarge revenues from the wine trade, only Hungarian tradesmen were allowed to import wine from Hungary. In 1615 King Sigismund III ordered that 'no single citizen of the Polish state may fetch wine in Hungary, not by himself, nor with the help of a deputy, under the penalty of the confiscation of wine plus 500 *grzywien*[8] fine'. To suit the action to the word, guards were called to stop 'any form of disobedience, so that the tax on liquor, income and traffic, a right that is primarily reserved to the Polish Republic, will not be lost' (quoted in Bostel 1890: 810-811).

The numerous privileges could not prevent the gradual decline of the wine trade during the seventeenth century. Despite the measures taken to counter any form of 'disobedience', some 'stubborn' individuals would still 'go to Hungary and fetch wine' or 'pay and send inferiors' to do the job for them. And there were those who 'help backsliders enter the town for their own good, as well as those who cowardly attack the town guards' (quoted in Bostel 1890: 811). At the same time, because of over-taxation and firm royal control, many Hungarian merchants avoided the customs and storage facilities in Jaśliska to such an extent that even the local townsmen began to worry. In 1639 the issue was raised during a public meeting, after which nine carters, who were suspected of taking secret routes, were put on trial and were administered an oath to the effect that they would never again fail to cross Jaśliska (Bostel 1890: 811).

Handicrafts evolved parallel with the increasing involvement in commerce. In the course of the sixteenth century four large guilds (*wielkie cechy*) were established, embracing several industrial specialisations, including blacksmiths, potters, saddlers, bar-keepers, tailors, shoemakers, furriers, and weavers (Orlik 1979). The privileges included many regulations and prohibitions that were supervised by the bishop of Przemyśl. It was forbidden to import or trade foreign-made products into the region subject to the privilege. In addition, the amount of products that could be sold or purchased by craftsmen was restricted. A shoemaker, for instance, was not allowed to sell more than ten shoes or purchase more than twenty-five large skins during fairs (*jarmarki*) or markets (*targi*). Disobedience was punished with the confiscation of the marketed products, with fines, or even with the loss of one's guild membership (Kozakiewicz 1966; Orlik 1979). To stress his control over the guild institution, the bishop demanded active participation in religious ceremonies by all members of the guild, while evasion and failure to participate was punished with a small fine. In like manner, members of the guilds had to pay a yearly allowance to the bishop (Orlik 1979).[9]

A Multi-Ethnic Environment

The bishop's rule over the town determined the exclusively Roman Catholic character of Jaśliska well into the nineteenth century. To preserve religious uniformity, the bishop severely restricted the settlement rights of all non-Roman Catholics (Prochaska 1889; Bostel 1890). In this the bishop was strongly supported by the petty nobility, merchants, and artisan guilds of the town, who held all potential rivals in contempt. Jews, who had escaped religious persecution in central and western Europe and started to populate the Sanok lands from the second half of the fifteenth century, were considered the main antagonists by the Roman Catholic townsmen. The predominantly Greek Catholic *Rusyn* environment formed another potential threat to Roman Catholic rule in the area.

Most early settlers in the Sanok lands came from the East, particularly in the later phase of colonisation when the richer lowlands were already densely populated. The religiously Orthodox Eastern Slavs were descendants of the Kievan Rus' federation and are commonly referred to as the *Rusyn* or *Ruthenian* people (Magocsi 1978).[10] Another ethnic group that settled in the highlands of the Sanok lands were the Vlach pastoral nomads, who originated in the Balkans and who, during the fourteenth and fifteenth centuries, migrated in several waves from Transylvania to the northern parts of the Carpathians. The Vlach shepherds eventually abandoned their nomadic life and were assimilated by other groups in this region, but they left permanent marks on the economy and culture of the *Rusyn* communities (Reinfuss 1990). In contrast to the lowland areas where the Magdeburg settlement charter was applied, colonisation of the upland areas was patterned on the Vlach charter (*ius Valachium*). In this charter dues were expressed not in terms of crops or money but in terms of animals, their skins and their cheeses (Hann 1985: 19). Indeed, Rusyn economy was based on a combination of arable farming and animal husbandry until well into the twentieth century (Reinfuss 1990).

By the end of the sixteenth century there was a clear-cut distinction between the Polish villages in the lowland areas and the Rusyn villages in the upland areas with respect to economy, language and religion (Hann 1985). When in 1596 the Roman Catholic Church and some of the Orthodox clergy signed a union in Brest-Litovsk, many Orthodox subjects of the Polish Commonwealth became adherents of the Greek Catholic or Uniate Church.[11] Hann (1985; 1988) stresses the small impact these religious changes had at the level of the parishes. The Greek Catholic Rusyns continued to practice the Byzantine rite and to use the 'old style' Julian calendar.[12] Nor did the rapprochement between the Orthodox and Roman Catholic bishops lead to a dissolution of the religious and ethnic boundaries between the Polish and the Rusyn villages. One example is the case of Jaśliska, where Greek Catholic Rusyns were forbidden to settle by decree of the Roman Catholic bishop. This restriction is clear from the fact that during the seventeenth century the town authorities of Jaśliska more than once appealed to the privilege which was granted to the town by the 'forbears of the present bishop' and which says that 'rusyns' (*rusznaczy*), elsewhere denoted as 'people of the Greek Catholic faith' (*ludzi greckiej religii*) '... are forbidden to have houses in the town or to take up residence in the town' (quoted in Bostel 1890: 806).[13] By 1630 the town's regulations were such that no single Greek Catholic confessor lived in the town, with the exception of two privileged persons (Bostel 1890: 806).

Jewish Exclusion from Jaśliska

Little is known about Jewish settlement in the Sanok lands (*Ziemia Sanocka*) until the nineteenth century. Sources indicate that the first Jews settled in the area during the second decade of the fifteenth century, but their numbers were not very impressive. The first registered Jews were two brothers from Ransburg, Nachem and Lazar, who took up residence in Krosno in 1426 (Horn 1970: 4). A more intensive influx of Jewish immigrants, partly refugees from Western Europe, took place from 1560 to 1570. During this period the total number of Jews is estimated at some 240 persons, though Horn (1970: 7) considers this is probably a low estimate. The Jews tended to concentrate in the larger centres of the region, particularly in Lesko and Rymanów (see map 1). Between 1630 and 1640 the Jewish population almost quadrupled, making up some 800 persons. Still, Jews constituted only 1.6 percent of the total population in the Sanok lands and 6.2 percent of the population living in towns. The percentage of Jews inhabiting the Sanok lands was much lower than the percentage of Jews in Eastern Galicia and probably was the lowest in the whole of Poland. For this reason the Polish Diet (*Sejm*) agreed in 1648 to lower the amount of Jewish head-tax in this region 'to save the very few of them' (Horn 1970: 9-10).

As is clear from the figures presented by Horn (1970) there were no Jews among the first foreign settlers in Jaśliska. From the second half of the sixteenth century the number of Jews in the region increased, but they settled mainly in the traditional Jewish centres such as Rymanów and Lesko. This pattern changed during the seventeenth century, when the growing number of people caused the Jews to move to other towns in the area. The communal records of Jaśliska offer evidence of frequent Jewish attempts to settle in small towns in this period. However, the Polish townsmen, merchants, and craftsmen successfully hindered the Jews from settling in Jaśliska by means of the privilege *de non tolerandis Iudaeis*. This exclusionary measure indicates that the Polish townsmen feared the competition of Jewish merchants, even at a time when in the whole Sanok region the Jewish population numbered less than a thousand.

The first written record on the exclusion of Jews from Jaśliska is in the town book dated 1593. It tells of a secret meeting of 'ordinary townsmen' who after serious deliberation agreed that 'whoever rents a room in his house to the Jew Lazur, who takes in toll, then such a man is subject to a fine of ten *grzywny*, which he owes the populace and the gentlemen councillors' (quoted in Bostel 1890: 805). In 1608 the bishop decreed that 'for the safety of the townsmen' Jews were forbidden to buy a farmstead, shop or lot in Jaśliska, or to lease houses or to engage in trade, except during fairs or markets (Prochaska 1889: 269; Bostel 1890: 805).[14] While this privilege *de non tolerandis Iudaeis* met the interest of both the Roman Catholic bishop and the townsmen, the communal records also show that their interests clashed at times. When in 1611 the Jews brought a charge against the authorities of Jaśliska who kept them from taking up residence and buying wine *even* during fairs and markets, the bishop gave his vote to the Jews (Bostel 1890; Horn 1970).[15] Likewise, in 1630 the bishop and the leaseholder (*dzierżawca*) of the manor to which Jaśliska belonged partly lifted the ban on Jewish settlement and decreed that 'no single townsman is allowed to admit a Jew into his house to pass the night or store his merchandise, *except for* the current Jewish arrendator' (italics mine, quoted in Bostel 1890: 806). Indeed, sources show that the first Jewish settlers were tax-farmers (*pisarze poborowi*) on behalf of the leaseholder at the customs of Jaśliska (Horn 1970).

Thus, even during the period of *de non tolerandis Iudaeis*, the attitude of the wealthier ruling stratum toward Jewish involvement in the town's economy was fairly ambivalent. For the bishop and the leaseholder (respectively *de jure* and *de facto* owner of the town) the economic activities of the Jews held several attractions. First, the role of the Jews as intermediaries between the town and the countryside stimulated trade as well as crafts in the town and in the region. Second, the Jewish involvement in the *arenda* (particularly tax farming) provided the town's rulers with cash. Finally, taking into account the important contribution of the Jews to the local economy, and the general economic decline in the region since the seventeenth century, the exclusionary policies proved counter-productive. However, the residence of Jewish arrendators and their families in Jaśliska by no means implied the beginnings of a sedentary Jewish community in Jaśliska, as an arenda lease was valid on an average for only three years (Rosman 1990). When after the first partition of Poland in 1773 Jaśliska was placed under the jurisdiction of the Austro-Hungarian empire and the 'enlightened' Austrian policies weakened the power of the Polish gentry and the bishops, the true influx of Jews in Jaśliska began. At that time, Jews had already settled in most of the villages surrounding Jaśliska, as we learn from a census carried out in the Greek Catholic deanery of Jaśliska in 1767 (Budzyński 1991).

Modern Times, or the Decline of a Small Town

Austrian Colonisation of Southeastern Poland

The downfall of the Polish kingdom coincided with the decline of royal control over the vast Polish territories as well as with the overall decline of the Kingdom's economy. The seventeenth and eighteenth centuries were marked by warfare and a sharp decrease of prosperity, trends which also affected Jaśliska. A series of wars caused havoc to the town, while the passing Polish armies who came to protect the area against foreign intruders, carried off all surpluses (Orlik 1979).[16] As a result, trade and handicrafts declined and many townsmen left the region. In 1681 the town book comments that 'after repeated complaints of the impoverished town population [...] about the unbearable guard-duties, hearth-taxes, income-taxes, and the *ex quavis Rzeczpospoliteae causa*[17] imposed levy, the townsmen started to leave the town already twenty years ago' (quoted in Bostel 1890: 815). To ensure the Church a certain amount of income, the bishop decreed that the deserted grounds should be sold to a well-to-do person who had the means to start a profitable business. However, to avoid a total exodus, he allowed the town council to hand over the land free of charge 'in the event that no candidate would show up' (quoted in Bostel 1890: 815).[18]

After the first partition of Poland in 1773, Galicia was placed under the jurisdiction of the Habsburg monarchy.[19] Austria consistently promoted a 'colonial policy' in the former Polish province. The province was set aside as a market for products—chiefly the so-called 'inferior' products for the 'use of Galicia'—produced in the industrial areas of the monarchy, and the province was used as a source of extra tax revenues. In respect to taxation, the Austrian government followed the example of the large Polish landowners. The landowners developed only those branches of industry that served to increase the profits from their vast estates, that is, the production and sale of alcohol. In fact, about one-third of the mechanised industry in Galicia at the end of the nineteenth century consisted of beer breweries, distilleries and mills (Mahler 1990). Austrian rule was further characterised by an enlightened control over its Polish subjects. The Austrian constitution of December 1867 granted Galicia significant political autonomy, while the franchise of the Galician peasantry in 1848 freed the peasants from feudal obligations and reduced the power of the bishop, who no longer had the highest authority. In addition, the farmers were given the lands on which they had previously been working. In practice, however, this meant the peasants were required to repurchase the lands by paying concealed taxes (Orlik 1979).

Poverty in Galicia, notorious since the end of the eighteenth century, became especially pronounced during the last decades of the nineteenth century. Whereas neighbouring countries and other provinces in Austria participated in the general process of capitalist development, with the resulting increase in industry and standard of living, Galicia was barely touched by these economic developments. The progress of industrialisation in Galicia was only about one-fifth of that of Austria as a whole. In 1900 more than 80 percent of the Galician population was still engaged in agriculture (Mahler 1990: 126). The industrial backwardness of the country was mainly the result of social relations in the agrarian economy. The concentration of land in the hands of wealthy landowners was greater here than in any of the other former provinces of Poland.[20] The purchasing power of the largest part of the population was extremely low because of the feudal conditions in the villages and towns. Sources indicate that in Galicia at the end of the nineteenth century the consumption of such staples as grain, meat and potatoes was one-half of that in western Europe. According to the Austrian income tax figures, the per capita income of the population in Galicia was one-tenth of the rest of Austria. As a result, an estimated 55,000 people died of starvation annually in Galicia (Mahler 1990: 127).

Modern means of transport, large-scale industries and commercial enterprises in new urban cores pushed aside former centres of industrial and commercial life. Jaśliska, being remote from the new urban centres, lost its former central position alongside the north-south trade route. As commercial activities were no longer profitable, economic life became centred on farming and on the processing of raw materials such as stones and wood.[21] Handicrafts were employed to provide local farmers with necessary products like shoes (shoemakers), clothes (tailors), and agricultural tools (coopers). Since people were, as one informant put it, 'free to move and borders were open,' regional trade guaranteed some additional income. Fairs were held twelve times a year (on Christian holidays) and attracted locals as well as merchants from the Austrian-Hungarian countries. The marketed products, apart from manufactures, were crops, horses, sheep and cattle. Additional income from trade was badly needed since agricultural produce was hardly sufficient to sustain the whole populace.

The local inheritance system, an outdated rotation system (*trójpolówka*), as well as the poor mountain soils resulted in yields below subsistence level (Orlik 1979: 22). A detailed cadastral survey conducted in 1851 shows that many plots were already highly fragmented (Hann 1985: 25). Though surplus was no longer extracted from them, the peasants now paid land tax for plots too small 'to pasture a goat on' (Orlik 1979: 50). It was in those days that farmers adopted the practice of pre-harvest (*przednówki*) to compensate for food shortages. Hailstorms, pestilence and a sequence of epidemics further affected agricultural production and caused heavy losses among the town's population. In 1831 a cholera epidemic swept the town, causing the death of eighty-four inhabitants. A typhoid epidemic in 1847 decimated even larger numbers of the population. During this epidemic at least 121 people died, while the surviving inhabitants withdrew to the forests. In 1862 an angina epidemic caused the death of fifty-six children. A typhoid epidemic swept the town in 1915, probably brought by passing Russian armies, causing the death of still more people (Orlik 1979: 32).

The decreasing opportunities to sell crops and handicrafts locally, as well as the alarmingly low level of industry in Galicia, forced many families to leave the town and emigrate 'for bread'. Emigration, in particular to the Americas, became so widespread that at the turn of the century each peasant household in Jaśliska had at least one member who lived and worked overseas (Orlik 1979).[22] Another way to earn some extra income was through seasonal migration. Most seasonal migrants went to work as agricultural labourers in Slovakia and Hungary during the high season. In return for their services the peasant workers were paid in kind, the most valuable product being wheat.[23] On seasonal migration Andrzej F. (72) commented: 'Before the First World War when this region was ruled by Austria local people made a little on the side through the cultivation of beetroots and through harvesting like we used to say 'na Węgrach' [in Hungary].' Smuggling was another tried method by means of which the people sought to compensate for the decline in local market outlets. Indeed, the smuggling activities proved to be lucrative and soon overtook official trade.[24]

Despite the extreme poverty, informants claimed that peasants were relatively well off during the Austrian times. As an informant (65) put it, 'people praised Austria, for they remembered King Staś, the last king of Poland. Our Polish landlords *(panowie)* used to exploit the peasants, whereas they were living comfortably on their landed estates.' The peasants' subordinate position and the landlords' arbitrary rule during the reign of the Polish kings are expressed in the legend of Saint Isidor, the patron of the farmers, as was told to me by the same informant:

> *When old women wove, they had a picture with them on which Saint Isidor was painted. Once Saint Isidor had to plough the land. It was on Easter, on Monday. And the landlord asked: 'Who is ploughing?' Isidor looked through the window and said: 'The bulls are ploughing'. And the landlord said: 'You, go to the fields!' But Saint Isidor said: 'I will go to celebrate our holy day.' Thereupon Saint Isidor took a candle and started to sing religious songs. The wind was blowing, but the candle burned. It was Saint Isidor who carried the candle. Then a storm came and the landlord noticed that the candle kept on burning. At this sight the landlord became frightened and made his rule less severe. He gave pieces of land to the obedient peasants, at least that is what they told me. If one was a good worker he got some five are of land. For good behaviour one would get a piece of garden. Good behaviour meant keeping your head close to the ground, being obedient. The peasants who were very obedient, like slaves, were even treated better. (Jan S., 65)*

In the late nineteenth century the administration of some of the remaining manors was managed by the non-native Sidor family. The Sidor family hired peasant workers, especially women, to harvest or work the fields. *Pan* Sidor, lessee of the local manor during the interwar years, is remembered as a tall, diligent and modest person, leading the same poor and hard-working life as the peasants.

Austrian Enlightened Policies and the Jews

Austrian rule altered the conditions of life for its Jewish subjects as well. The policies of the Austrian government towards Galician Jewry were marked by repressive as well as enlightened tendencies. However ambiguous the policies of the successive Austrian rulers, they all paid similar attention to the so-called 'Jewish problem', as their main objective was generally to adjust the large number of Galician Jews within the structure of the Habsburg empire.

The Austrian 'Code of Regulations Concerning the Jews' (1776) allowed Jewish communal autonomy to stand, but only in return for large amounts of 'protection' and 'toleration' taxes. In the years between 1785 and 1789 a reform policy was carried out which aimed at the improvement of the conditions of the Jews and their ultimate assimilation. The patent of 1785 dissolved the supreme council (which was established in 1776) and in the same year rabbinical civil law was decreed invalid. The so-called 'Patent of Toleration' (1789) aimed at the abolition of all legal differences between Jews and non-Jews and abolished Jewish autonomy, the *Kahals*, and the jurisdiction of the rabbinate. In this period the expulsion of the Jews from the villages began: various trade branches, peddling, and arenda (among others the right to propination) were prohibited to them. At the same time the restriction on Jewish craftsmen was abolished and Jews were actively encouraged to take up agricultural work by lowered taxes. In 1789 Jews were included in the obligation to do military service and had to adopt German names. Government-sponsored schools were established and attendance was made compulsory. At the same time, the practice of special taxation of Jews was extended with the tax on ritually slaughtered meat, marriage tax, residence tax, and candle tax (Landman 1941; Roth 1971).

The legal restrictions and obligations introduced by the Austrian government met with passive and active resistance. Jews, for instance, prevented their children from attending the government-sponsored schools and in 1806 all the Jewish schools in Galicia were closed. The plan for settling 1,410 Jewish families on government-owned land, initiated in 1786, also failed, and by 1822 only 836 Jewish farmers were registered in all of Galicia (Roth 1971).[25] All in all, the conditions of the Galician Jewry deteriorated (rather than improved) by the introduction of special taxation and the numerous occupational restrictions. Close to one-third of the Jewish population was deprived of its means of livelihood, while the majority of the impoverished Jews remained active in traditional occupations where there was an enormous competition. According to the official estimates, at least one-third of the Jewish population consisted of *luftmentshn* (persons without a definite occupation), who lived on odd jobs or who had no trade and often no means of subsistence at all. Even those directly engaged in trade (approximately one-third) were primarily petty tradesmen and shopkeepers. About one-fifth were engaged in crafts and small industry (primarily in the clothing industry). Despite all the legal restrictions, approximately one-fifth of the Jewish population lived in villages as innkeepers, tradesmen, and money-brokers (Mahler 1985: 6).

Parallel with the economic hardship of Galician Jewry their political emancipation began. The revolution of 1848 heralded a new era of political freedom, mobility, and land reform. The 1848 Galician parliament, which included three Jews, rescinded the special taxes on Jews, and in the constitution of March 1849 Jews were granted equality of rights. At the end of 1851, however, the government revoked the constitution and restricted the civil rights of the Jews, only to lift most of the restrictions between 1859 and 1860. The Austrian constitution of 1867 finally abolished all restrictive laws against the Jews (Landman 1941). The enlightened Austrian policies also annulled the restrictions on Jewish settlement in the former episcopal towns. Although a considerable part of the grounds of the Jaśliska community were still in the hands of the Przemyśl diocese, from 1848 onwards Jews had free entrance to the town (Sulimierski, Chłembowski et al. 1882). However, the first two Jewish families settled in Jaśliska as early as 1808 (Yad Vashem 1984). It is generally agreed that the larger influx of Jews started in the second half of the nineteenth century (Orlik 1979; Grzesik and Traczyk 1992; Gajewski 1996). By the early 1920s Jaśliska counted 224 Jewish residents, who made up one quarter of the town's total population (GUS 1924: table 23).

Notes

1. Historical name for the region that is now part of southeastern Poland and mid-western Ukraine.
2. Magnate is a term to denote the elite of the nobility, consisting of the most powerful and wealthy noblemen. Although magnates represented only a small percentage of the total nobility (probably ten to twenty families in each generation), their significance for the nobility and for Poland was considerable (Rosman 1990: 7-8).
3. As a result the manufacture and sale of grain-based intoxicants dramatically increased. In 1564 income from the manufacture and sale of alcohol accounted for 3 percent of the overall income of royal properties. About two centuries later (1789) the proportion of revenues reached 40.1 percent (Levine 1980).
4. Historical unit of measurement.
5. The name Jaśliska is probably derived from Jasiółka, a small stream that passes the town.
6. Defined by Rosman (1990: 218) as the basic unit of a *latifundium* consisting of a town or towns, villages and several manors.

7. Many of these cellars are still preserved and are now used to store (processed) agricultural produce during the winter.

8. A monetary unit, usually used to express the amounts of monetary fines (Rosman 1990: 217).

9. Apart from handicrafts the townsmen also engaged in construction work (such as masons, painters and architects). Jaśliska also specialised in the production of mill stones—still the main symbol in the city arms. It is also from these days that the ingenious water supply system dates, which ceased to function as late as the 1960s. Bogusław K. (82 years old), whose family history in Jaśliska can be traced back over three hundred years, took part in repairing and laying the old water pipe system and is still nicknamed after his skills (*równik*).

10. As a result of complex historical and political factors, written sources and my informants used different terms to denote this specific minority group, calling them Ukrainians (*Ukraińcy*), Lemkos (*Lemkowie*), or Rusyns (*Rusnacy* or *Rusini*). In this chapter the term Rusyn is used (both as an adjective and as a noun) to denote the people whose origins can be traced back to the early Rus' and Vlach migrations. The term Rusyn (Polish: *Rusnak* or *Rusin*) was chosen because this is the name which I encountered in the source material (for example in Prochaska 1889; Bostel 1890; GUS 1924). As I explain below, using the currently fashionable term Lemko in this chapter would be an anachronism.

    Historically, the term Rusyn had a primarily religious connotation and was used to denote the people who belonged to the Greek Catholic or Orthodox Rus' Churches. With the national awakening after 1848, the term Rusyn was used by Rus' nationalist leaders to indicate both the religious and national affiliation of the people inhabiting Subcarpathian Rus' (Magocsi 1978). In the early twentieth century, Polish ethnographers carried out detailed academic research on Rusyn subgroups and their territorial boundaries and introduced another set of names reflecting the geographic and ethnographic characteristics of the Rusyn subgroups: Lemkos (*Lemkowie*), Bojkos (*Bojkowie*), and Hutsuls (*Hutsulowie*). In terms of their geographic location and ethnographic characteristics, the Rusyn communities which surrounded Jaśliska belonged to the territory which in interbellum Poland was commonly referred to as Lemkovina (*Łemkowszczyzna*). The change of the political climate after the Second World War induced the Polish authorities to label the Lemkos (due to border shifts following the war the Bojkos and Hutsuls resided mainly outside Poland) as 'Ukrainian terrorists' and 'Nazi allies', and their official status was that of a Ukrainian minority (Hann 1985; Hann 1988). Currently, in post-communist Poland, the term Lemko is commonly used again (Mach 1993; Czajkowski 1994; Czajkowski 1995).

    Taking into account the complex history of the group under consideration, I should like to stress that I use the term Rusyn as a historical term identifying religious affiliation rather than ideological commitment to a particular ethno-national identity, as it would be an anachronism to use the term in a way that became fashionable in later centuries. In later chapters, however, I use the term Lemko because both the terms Rusyn and Ukrainian make implicit assumptions about the ethno-national identity of the people involved, and are as such a political statement. On the other hand, the term Lemko as it is currently used by the Lemko inhabitants of Poland and in the Polish public debates is primarily a term identifying geographic origin and cultural heritage.

11. The Greek Catholic Church was subordinated to the authority of the Roman Pope and accepted the Roman Catholic dogmas, while it preserved the Orthodox liturgy and the right to marry for lay clergymen. Hann (1988) formulates three Greek Catholic doctrinal points that conflict with the Orthodox faith: (1) the use of unleavened bread in the Eucharist; (2) belief in the existence of Purgatory; and (3) the Procession of the Holy Spirit from the Father and the Son. The official conversion of the Rusyn community

started nearly a century later, as a result of the protracted conflict between the Greek Catholic and Orthodox rulers (Hann 1985; Hann 1988; Reinfuss 1990).

12. The new year in the Julian calendar begins thirteen days later than in the Roman Catholic Gregorian calendar (Reinfuss 1990: 144).

13. When, for example, in 1605 twenty-seven persons bade for the privilege to become citizens of the town, two men were dismissed, one for being an illegitimate child (*illegitime natus*), the second for being a Rusyn (*rutenus*). Admittance of these persons would have been an act 'contra privilegia civilia' (Bostel 1890: 806-807).

14. So much is clear from the following excerpt quoted in Bostel (1890: 805): 'For certain and important reasons it is forbidden and illicit for any Jew to buy or venture on a house, shop, or place to live in or to lease or purchase no matter what commodities [...] No matter what pretext, one should not tolerate or lease to Jews a single shop or store room, nor harbour them in one's own house, the one who does will be subject to a fine which is for the citizens to decide.'

15. In 1611 the bishop of Przemyśl decreed that Jews were free 'in conformity with the old customs' to visit the fairs and markets in Jaśliska and to take up residence in town 'until they have bought their things and have found a carter to take the things away with them' (quoted in Bostel 1890: 805). In addition, he reprimanded the town authorities, whom he forbade to close the town gate to Jewish merchants during fairs and markets (Horn 1970: 14).

16. In 1657 armies of the Hungarian prince Jerzy Rakoczy surrounded the town. In 1704 the Tartars repeatedly attempted to attack the town. The services paid to the constantly passing Polish army units (for the whole episcopal dominion to which Jaśliska belonged) ranged from a total of 900 Polish złoty in 1633 to a total of 40,935 Polish złoty in 1714 (Orlik 1979: 14-15).

17. Taxes paid in support of the Polish Republic.

18. The declining reputation of Jaśliska may be illustrated with the example of what happened to the land of Istwan Hungwarus, merchant and resident of Jaśliska, who left the town with his family in 1684. When a certain Jan Wątroba, peasant and resident of Jaśliska, wanted to convert the grounds to his own use, the town council decided that Jan Wątroba had to make his wishes public three times during the local markets and four times at the neighbouring fairs, so that 'a buyer or interested party' could apply for the land of Istwan. Since no one applied, the council assigned the land to Jan Wątroba and registered him as the new and legitimate owner (Bostel 1890: 815).

19. The three-way partitioning of Poland is often explained as a unified attempt by the despotic Austrian, Russian, and Prussian rulers to crush the enlightened political reforms in Poland. The first such attempt was made in 1772, when Austria, Russia and Prussia signed the treaties of the first partition. These treaties assigned Galicia to the Austrians, western Prussia to the Germans, and the Polish northern Provinces to the Russians (Davies 1986). After the Polish diet (*Sejm*) had voted for the liberal constitution of 3 May 1791, a legal act which formulated the principal of democracy and the rights of the people and the nation, the second and third partition soon followed. In 1793 the north-eastern part of Poland (Byelorussia, Volhynia) passed to the Russians. In 1795 central Poland was divided into an Austrian, Russian and Prussian part (Davies 1986; Walicki 1990). The region of southeastern Poland and north-western Ukraine is commonly referred to as Western and Eastern Galicia (called after the historical region *Ruś Halicka*). During the rule by the kingdom of Poland-Lithuania (1386-1572) and the Polish-Lithuanian Commonwealth (1569-1795) Galicia was known as Little Poland (*Mało Polska*) (Roth 1971: 265).

20. About 40 percent of all the land in Galicia was held by landowners possessing more than fifty hectares, and 37 percent of this land was in the hands of owners who possessed more

than a hundred hectares. On the other hand, in 1902, 71 percent of all the peasants in Galicia had holdings of less than five hectares and 44 percent had holdings of less than two hectares (Mahler 1990: 126).

21. In the course of the nineteenth century the quarry industry developed and a large number of peasants from Jaśliska found work in the local mines. During the interwar years emphasis on this branch shifted to the neighbouring village of Posada Jaśliska and during the Great Depression the quarry eventually went out of production.

22. Between 1880 and 1900 some 135 inhabitants from Jaśliska left for the United States, while a few went to France, Brazil, Argentina, and Uruguay. The majority of those who left stayed in the country of emigration because of the better living conditions (Orlik 1979: 35).

23. Other seasonal migrants who went further away were paid in cash due to the difficult transport conditions (essay by Henryk Olszański, Sanok 1985).

24. Especially the coopers who sought new areas of distribution specialised in smuggling. But also the local Jews are said to have been devoted smugglers during the interwar period (Litwak 1969).

25. This failure was largely due to the ambiguous Austrian policies regarding the Jews. Legislation in 1784 prohibited Jews from renting rural properties from Christians, except for several hundred Jewish colonists whose number decreased from year to year due to the harassment by Austrian officials (Landman 1941; Mahler 1985). The prohibition against Jews' acquiring agricultural land remained valid until 1867, when all restrictive laws against the Jews were lifted.

Chapter 3

SPHERES OF INTERACTION

Spatial Integration

'Is it true, grandpa, that all Jews and even the little boys wore long coats like rich men do? And that the walls of the market square, the Plotsk street and the War-saw street, the shops and the workshops were theirs?' (Opatoshu 1951: 316).

Introduction

By the time Jews set foot in Jaśliska the town had lost much of its initial grandeur. The numerous wars which marked the end of the Polish kingdom (1650-1773) and the subsequent Austrian colonial policy (1773-1918) had turned Jaśliska into a feudal agrarian community of secondary importance: the Hungarian merchants had long departed from the town, the Polish inhabitants were turned into enslaved peasants, while the nobility of the small town had lost their privileges and had joined the landless and the poor. In this setting, the economic interests of the Jewish settlers and the Polish residents no longer clashed. Indeed, Jews chose to settle in the small town because of the profitable economic prospects (new outlets) it offered them in a predominantly agrarian area. Also the Poles were likely to profit by the face-to-face interaction with the Jews, as the latter gave them the opportunity to obtain cash and purchase non-farm products locally.

Once a Jewish family had decided to settle in Jaśliska, the first thing to arrange was a place to live. As most houses were already inhabited, Jewish settlers would have to purchase the properties from the actual owners. A primary condition for the success of such transactions was the availability of

---

Notes for this section begin on page 57.

money and the supply of land. Since Jews had money and many Poles were in need of cash, supply and demand easily met. Two factors contributed to an additional supply of land. First, by the end of the nineteenth century many peasants had left the town in search of better living conditions. Though most of these emigrants usually returned after a short stay abroad, there were those who never came back and left their lands and houses deserted.[1] Second, the wave of epidemics between 1831 and 1862 presumably contributed to an additional increase of empty houses. Although the conditions for settlement were suitable, the Jews, who during the second half of the nineteenth century, at the height of the agricultural crisis, started to inhabit the town's centre in ever growing numbers, were not exactly welcome. They not only seized the grounds and houses of the indigenous Poles, but they also secured a position that turned them into fairly prosperous residents.

Patterns of Settlement

Sources on Jewish Settlement

Informants confirmed that the process of Jewish settlement started in the early nineteenth century. Aged informants claimed that their parents and grandparents had witnessed the arrival of the first Jewish settlers. As Daniel S. (82) explained: 'My father told me that he could remember the time when there was only one Jewish family living in Jaśliska.' Middle-aged informants maintained that their grandparents and great-grandparents had been witnesses of the first Jewish settlers ('Grandparents of our grandparents used to tell that only one Jew came to Jaśliska'). Most young informants, however, had no clue and dated the period of settlement earlier. Wieńczysław W. (28) stated that Jews settled only in places where 'they considered it profitable'. According to him, Jews used to live in Polish towns, but later moved to the province whenever they saw that 'trade was needed'. Joanna L. (22) argued that since trade is connected with Jews, they probably settled in Jaśliska from the fourteenth century onwards. Other informants said that the main influx of Jews started at the turn of the twentieth century and was completed after the First World War. Josko S. (75), a former resident of the town, claimed to be a descendant of the first Jewish settlers:

> *The first Jews were my grandparents. They were the first Jews who came to Jaśliska [...] My father was S. My grandfather was Hanjaków. My great-grandfather was Szmul. My great-great-grandfather was the father of Szmul, Kalman. And Kalman's father was Chab Nusim S. And Nusim S. lived in Rymanów. He had three children, three sons, and they went to live in Jaśliska. His three children were Mechl S., Kalman*

S. and there was Leibish S. Leibish S. did not live in the small town, but went to live in Wola.[2] [...] This was a hundred, maybe a hundred and fifty years ago.

Josko S. dates the first Jewish settlers five generation back, which points to the rather recent character of Jewish settlement in the Jaśliska. The account of Josko suggests that the first Jews came from Rymanów, a town approximately 20 km from Jaśliska (see map 1), which indicates that population movements took place on a rather local scale.

Jews first appear in the Austrian administrative registers for the election to the Galician Diet (*Sejm*) in 1867 (WAPK 1867a; WAPK 1867b). In these registers fifteen Jews are listed out of a total of 163 potential voting members. Among them were two ancestors of Josko S. (75), Kalman and Mechl S., both generous taxpayers to the Austrian treasury.[3] These figures indicate that Jews, who were enfranchised in 1860, had started to settle in Jaśliska already before 1867. Taking into account the strict regulations on suffrage (minimum age, minimum income, male sex, and Polish nationality) Jewish families in 1867 totalled at least fifteen, making up an estimated 9 percent of the town's total population.[4] During the fifteen years that followed, the number of Jews increased steadily, forming an estimated 17 percent of the town's total population in 1882.[5] As Table 3.1 shows, the number of Jews in Jaśliska for the period 1889 to 1938 fluctuated between 20 and 30 percent. At the turn of the twentieth century, the settlement process came to a halt and, in the almost forty years that followed, the proportion of Jews remained stable at around one quarter of the town's total population.

Table 3.1 Population of Jaśliska according to Religious Faith

Year	Roman Catholic	Mosaic	Others	Total	Percentage of Jews
1889	≈695	201	≈10	906	22
1900	634	293	9	936	31
1921	642	224	10	876	26
1938	813	≈286	≈10	≈1109	26

Notes: some figures have been estimated, which is indicated with a ≈-symbol.

Sources: Główny Urząd Statystyczny (1924), Pismo Diecezjalne (1938), Yad Vashem (1984).

If one compares these figures to the general pattern of settlement in the Sanok district in the early twentieth century, the proportion of Jews in Jaśliska was normal for this type of small town (*miasteczko*). According to the census of 1921, as many as two-fifths of the total Jewish population of the district lived in rural communities (*gminy*). Within these rural communities,

23 percent of the total population living in small towns consisted of Jews, compared to 3 percent of the total village population.[6] Figures for the adjacent Krosno district display the same pattern. Here also a quarter of the total population living in small towns consisted of Jews, which far exceeded the ratio of Jews living in villages (GUS 1924). Still, a relatively large proportion of the region's Jewry settled in villages. This can be explained by the low level of urbanisation and the consequently large number of villages in the region. By 1921, 90 out of 122 villages in the Sanok district were inhabited by Jews, housing 26 percent of the region's total Jewish population.[7] Quite often these Jewish village communities consisted of only one or two families. By 1921, Jews had also settled in the neighbouring villages of Jaśliska, among them Posada Jaśliska (fifty-five Jews), Daliowa (twenty-four), Czeremcha (ten), and Lipowiec (three) (GUS 1924).

Additional documentation on Jewish settlement in Jaśliska is provided by the cadastral or real estate registers (*księgi wieczyste*), which document the history of land ownership in Jaśliska. Figure 3.1 summarises the data from these registers (for details see Appendix). The pattern it shows is one of an extreme increase of the proportion of Jewish building lots for the period 1874 to 1905, as well as a gradual decrease of this proportion after 1905.

Figure 3.1 Proportion of Building Lots Owned by Jews

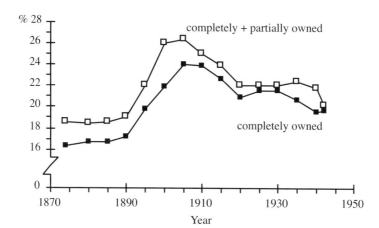

The momentous growth of the Jewish community in Jaśliska took place in the second half of the nineteenth century, congruent with the increase of Jewish capital in the town's real estate. During this main period of settlement Jews also invested in holdings of communal interest. The real estate registers mention that Jews had built their House of Prayer already before 1874. Other sources claim that by 1883 Jews had established a Jewish school, bank and cemetery (Orlik 1979: 27).[8] The decrease in the proportion of Jewish real estate in the period 1905 to 1942 indicates that Jewish settlement in Jaśliska was completed at the end of the nineteenth century. It also indicates that several Jewish families had left the town, presumably in search of better living conditions.

A Jewish Centre

Several informants were able to carefully mark out the lots Jews once inhabited.[9] Most informants, however, simply stressed the overwhelming concentration of Jews in the centre of Jaśliska. Statements like 'the whole town was Jewish' and 'on the market square only Jews were living' were commonly heard. The division between a Jewish centre and a Polish periphery is clearly expressed by the common notion that the Jews lived in town, whereas 'the people' (read: the Poles) lived on the outskirts.[10] As one informant clearly put it: 'Jews did not want to live in the fields.' The real estate registers and the cadastral map (1896) largely confirm the informants' observations. Figure 3.2 pictures the Jewish settlement pattern in Jaśliska. Clusters A-J indicate the Jews' preference for different parts of the town in terms of earliest settlement. It must be noted that differences between the clusters A-D are minimal, since most houses were owned by Jews already from the start of the real estate registers (1874). The shared median of first settlement for clusters A-D is 1874, while the median for clusters E-I ranges from 1886 to 1911. In terms of the lots that were first abandoned with the decline of the Jewish population after 1905, the pattern shifts a little. Clusters A, B, D, F and G are clearly preferred sites. Once owned by Jews, most lots in these clusters stayed Jewish until 1942. The year of departure for the other (less popular) clusters ranges from 1906 to 1935.

These figures indicate that Jews settled first and foremost near the market square (with the exception of cluster E that was only occupied later and relatively soon abandoned). Another favourite was the Dalejowska street, which is the road leading to Kraków and, more importantly, to the neighbouring towns of Dukla (20 km from Jaśliska) and Rymanów (18 km).[11] Jews were less likely to settle in the Lwowska street, presumably because of its inconvenient location: off the road from the main traffic and at a relatively large distance from the centre.[12] The road to Hungary (Węgierska street) fell mainly outside the scope of interest as trade with Hungary had gradually declined (see Chapter two). The figures also indicate that Jews were less likely to settle on the outskirts of the town. Jews first settled in the centre and only later moved to the periphery, which is in accordance with the informants' observation that Jews moved out only when the market square grew 'overpopulated'. When Jews settled on a site in the periphery, they left this site relatively soon (with the exception of cluster G), in some cases after just one year. The repeated transactions suggest that Jews did not always live on the lots they owned. The transactions in the real estate register also witness bargains and settlements of debts (see Chapter four).

Figure 3.2　Clusters of Jewish Houses in Jaśliska.

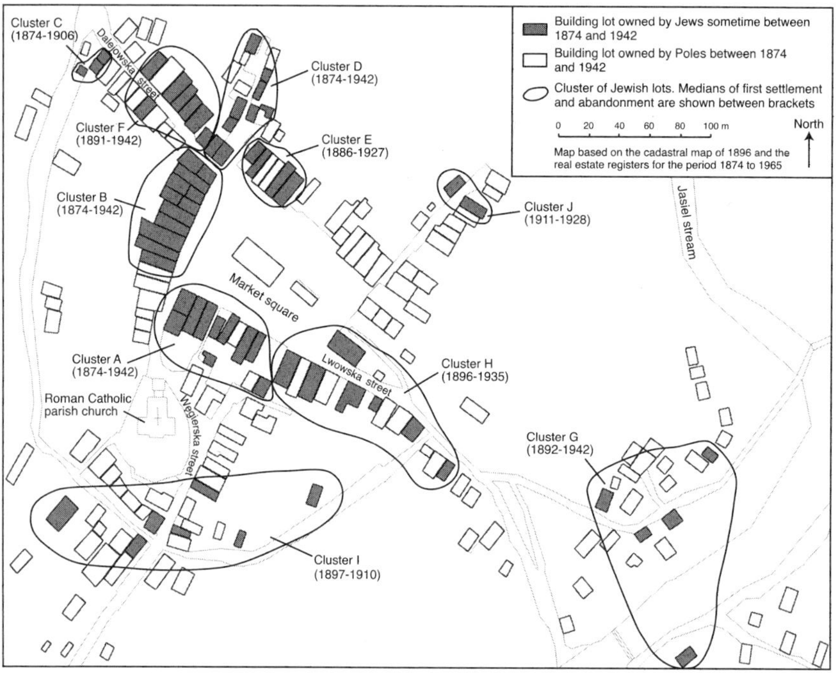

Over the years the pattern of Jewish settlement in Jaśliska appears rather stable. Maps 3, 4, and 5 in the Appendix mirror the Jews' inclination to concentrate in the north-western part of the market square and the Dalejowska street, irrespective of year or period. Notable is also that the north-eastern part of the market square remained exclusively Polish. Although the Jews resided within a clearly defined area, maps 3 to 5 show that the Jews did not live in a closed Jewish quarter. Since there were only few sites to settle on, Jews lived relatively scattered over the town. Jewish houses could be found at a considerable distance from the centre and from each other, while in proximity to Polish dwellings.

The Jews, the Town, and Trade

Informants clearly connect Jewish settlement in the town's centre with the Jews' involvement in trade. As an informant put it: 'Jews settled in town because they wanted to do business (*gesheft*)'.[13] Upon the arrival of the Jews trade was in safe hands, for not only were Jews 'the best traders', but they quite 'lived on trading', a notion which informants usually confirmed with the popular aphorism 'Where ever a Jew is, is a shop.'[14] Informants claimed that of the various taverns selling vodka and wine only one belonged to a Pole and that the rest were Jewish. Jews further advanced their *gesheft* by introducing shops in which they sold all kinds of products. It so happened that in the town 'all shops were Jewish and the best houses too.' On the Jews' commitment to trade the local historian Orlik (1979: 26-27) writes: 'From the mid-nineteenth century, local trade to the largest extent was conquered by the Jewish element flocking to Jaśliska. Jews took in hand the trade in wine, textiles, bar-keeping and milling. All around the market square Jewish shops appeared selling hardware, clothes and food.'

Obviously, Jewish commercial activities changed the appearance of the town, which in the last few centuries had developed into a feudal munici-pality mainly inhabited by peasants and craftsmen. Jews had special 'Jewish houses' for their commercial activities, and they were the first to build stone houses which had an urban look. The physical transformation of Polish houses into Jewish shops perfectly symbolises the engagement of the Poles and the Jews in distinct economic sectors. Whereas the Poles were farmers and earned a living from their farmland and livestock, Jews were traders and earned a living from products which they did not produce themselves. The transformation of the town's centre into a Jewish quarter for commerce is best illustrated by the following observation:

> *When a Pole lived in the centre he could sell his house [to a Jew]. The house was not fit for trading but for farming only. There was a big entrance hall, one living room, and one kitchen, if I remember well. The Poles, for example, had one room in which they lived and worked as coopers and one kitchen in which the women used to cook. A Jew, in contrast, used to separate the front part of the house and build a shop there. Behind the shop they had a kitchen. They were sitting and cooking in the kitchen and when somebody entered there was a bell on a steel spring, it made a special sound. The bell hung on the door and rang when somebody entered. Thereupon the Jewish woman came and asked: 'Can I help you? What would you like to have?' Then she served the customer. (Jan S., 65)*

Jewish Merchants and Polish Peasants

The Austrian and Polish administrative registers supply valuable informa-tion on the economic activities pursued by both Poles and Jews, as well as their contributions to the Austrian treasury through income and land tax during the nineteenth century. Among the sixteen Jews registered in 1870, four farmers were listed, as well as four merchants, three tavern-keepers, two propinators,[15] one mercer, one butcher, and one moneylender (WAPK 1870a; WAPK 1870b). These figures indicate that one-third of the Jews in Jaśliska earned a living from the manufacture and sale of grain alcohol, one-third earned a living from other types of trade, and one-quarter earned a living from farming. The butcher and moneylender constitute the remainder. Jewish involvement in the production of alcohol and trade (two-thirds of the total) lends support to the general view that Jewish taverns, saloons, and shops were part of everyday life in the nineteenth and twentieth centuries in Jaśliska. Still, a quarter of the Jewish males registered farming as their main occupation. This contrasts with the informants' assertion that Jews were not active at all in the agricultural sector.

Polish professional distribution was less diffuse. Of the 114 Poles listed on the registers of 1870, 106 were farmers, six were craftsmen (of whom only one worked as a full-time craftsman), while the royal postman and the priest constituted the remainder (WAPK 1870a; WAPK 1870b). This implies that 93 percent of the Poles were active in farming, 5 percent were engaged in handicrafts (mostly in combination with farming), while less than 2 percent were employed in services (i.e., the postman and the priest). Apparently none of the Polish taxpayers was registered as a full-time merchant (trading alcohol, food, metalware or other products), which partly explains the Jews' prevalence in this sector. On the other hand, the large number of Polish farmers easily exceeded the number of Jews in the agricultural sector. Figure 3.3 reflects the notable contrast in the distribution of Poles and Jews for the different economic sectors: trade, service, handicrafts and agriculture.[16] It shows a scattered distribution of Jews over the different economic sectors: every section comprises at least one Jew. At the same time the Jewish distribution mirrors the Polish one. Whereas Jews prevail in trade, Poles dominate the industrial and agricultural sectors. In other words, Jews were mainly engaged in commerce, whereas Poles were mainly active in crafts and crop production.

Naturally, the disparity in the Polish and Jewish occupations affected the contributions to land and income tax paid by both groups. Whereas the Jewish townsmen contributed 61 percent of the total income tax paid by the town to the Austrian treasury, the Poles contributed 92 percent of the total land-tax. Apparently the small number of Jewish taxpayers (9 percent of all taxpayers) easily outnumbered the Poles with their contributions to the town's total income tax. Moreover, Jewish taxpayers contributed almost one

Figure 3.3 Distribution of Poles and Jews in the Different Economic
Sectors in 1870.

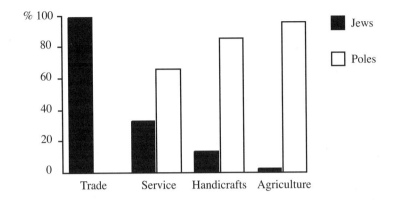

quarter of the town's total tax (21 percent). All in all, the Jews' tax per head
amounted to 2.5 times the tax paid by the Polish taxpayer (WAPK 1867a;
WAPK 1867b). These figures indicate not only that townsmen who had an
income paid on an average a higher tax than those who had land, but more
significantly, the figures display the Jews' predominance (or Poles' absence)
in the local cash economy of the small town.[17]

There have been at least two explanations for the settlement of the Jews
in the town's centre. First, the Jews' dependence on income-generating
activities induced them to reside in the social and economic centre of the
town. As the owners of shops, taverns, and holders of the rights to propination, Jews settled in the market square and immediate surroundings. However, the Jews' interest went beyond the centre alone. The cadastral
registers show that Jews also owned lots on the periphery of Jaśliska. Likewise, the administrative registers of 1870 mention four Jews who were full-
time farmers.[18] At least 10 percent of the Jews in Jaśliska owned one or two
gardens (mostly attached to the houses), while at least 18 percent of the
Jews owned some agricultural land, ranging in number from one to twenty-
one plots.

Second, the Jews' main asset in their attempt to settle in the small town
was their economic strength. They owed their economic authority to their
predominance (or the Poles' virtual absence) in the local cash economy.
Thanks to their relatively large financial resources, Jews were more flexible
and more mobile than were their Polish counterparts, who mainly had their
capital invested in land. Hence, informants stressed the character of the
rich(er) Jewish settler and the poor(er) Polish vendor:

If a person owned a lot he just built his house on it. But if there was a person who wanted to settle here [in Jaśliska], and if this person had money, and if there was a lot for sale, because sometimes there were, then this person had to buy a lot [...] One had to buy, for example Jews, because they came from outside. And they [Jews] bought lots here. They came here with money and if there was a poor town dweller, or if somebody had a second lot somewhere outside the town and wanted to build a house there, he sold his lot in town. The market square was almost exclusively inhabited by Jews. They lived there because they had money. (Andrzej F., 72)

Still, the Jews' potential mobility was limited for they did not have access to all parts of the town. Jewish holdings, for instance, were completely absent on the northeastern part of the market square. A closer look at the Austrian registers might explain why: Poles inhabiting the northeastern part of the market square on average belonged to the small group of high taxpayers.[19] Despite their better means, the Jews' opportunities to settle were clearly limited by the existing social structure. Indeed, informants claimed that members of the petty nobility were not good partners for the Jews. Better off Poles had no need to sell their houses. Moreover, tradition and pride would prevent the nobility from leaving their family lands. In like manner Jan S. (65) explained why his grandfather had not given in, despite firm Jewish insistence:

I once asked my grandmother: 'Why did you stay on this lot?' And she answered: 'Jędrek was made to stay on this place by his mother.' You know, first noblemen were living here, they were called Mezglewski, Magierowski and so on. They were very noble and they had patriotism in their blood. They would never leave their homes. They [Jews] tried to make them leave but they did not succeed.

Acquisition of Land: The Gossip about Jewish Arson

The Rumour of Jewish Arson

In Jaśliska, a persistent rumour makes the rounds with regard to the first Jewish settlers who started to inhabit the town. The most popular version is summarised below:

During the nineteenth century, Jews thrice set fire to the houses of the local petty nobility (*szlachta*)[20] who used to live in the market square. In those days, fires were disastrous because the houses were made of wood and closely built together. To make things worse Jews would throw oil into the well from which the water was extracted to extinguish the fire. As nobody noticed, the fire would spread quickly. In the end, the repeated Jewish attacks on the material reserves of the nobility proved to be successful. One after another, Jewish families bought the houses and properties of the impoverished and bankrupt nobles.

Different versions of the rumour exist. Sometimes the victims of fire are said to be ordinary Polish dwellers instead of impoverished nobles. Other informants claim that repeated Jewish arson took place in the twentieth century, as is clear from the following excerpts recorded by Polish students in 1979:

> Karol J. (born in 1899): [...] from 1907 onwards, Jews started to flock to Jaśliska from Dukla and Slovakia from where they were expelled for reasons unclear to the informant [...] The Jews, for this purpose taking advantage of bribed vagrants, set fire to the town, and thereafter bought the lots of the bankrupted victims of the fire. The latter moved behind the [town] walls where they built new farms, while the Jewish newcomers settled on the places left by them. In this way the situation changed to such an extent that between the two wars only a few tens of Poles lived in the market square, while the whole trade was in the hands of the Jews.[21]

> Józef P. (born in 1904): [...] the legend holds that the town burned down twenty-five times, always following the inspection of the bishop, providing that he came dressed in a red mantle and red cap. Very often the town was plundered by the Tartars, Turks, and Russian armies during the periods of war. Inhabitants from the neighbouring villages also assaulted the town many times. In the beginning of the twentieth century the town was tormented by fires. These fires were probably started by Jews who wanted to settle on the market square, from times immemorial inhabited by Poles only. In addition, many buildings burned to the ground during the last war.[22]

The accounts bring three new elements into the picture. Karol J. said that Jews started the fire with the help of vagrants who roamed the district. Józef P. claimed that after the Tartars, Turks and Russians, the Jewish arsonists added to the many plagues that had swept the town. Karol J. and Józef P. further stated that Jews set fire to Polish houses in the beginning of the twentieth century. Two of these elements, the Jews bribing vagrants and the manifold disastrous fires, also return in the following selection:

> Bolesław W. (born in 1904): [...] in the memory of the informant the town was swept by three fires: the first took place in December 1914 on Saint Stephen's Day, when invading Russians set fire to several houses on the market square. In autumn 1917, twenty-seven houses burned to the ground, the fire spreading from a Jewish bakery. Only a few of them were rebuilt. Finally, in 1944 Soviet planes bombed the town [...] The informants' father had once told him that Jews hired seasonal forest workers, so-called *grenerów*, who came from the south to work here, to set fire to the houses of Poles. After those repeated arsons, the ruined Poles, who mostly did not have money to pay for a fire insurance, sold their lots to the Jews.[23]

In the account of Bolesław W. we find several fires connected with Jews. The first series of fires, taking place during the lifetime of the informant's father (that is, any time during the nineteenth century) were started by henchmen of the Jews. In contrast to Karol J. and Józef P., Bolesław W. did not explain the fire of 1917 (which started in a Jewish bakery) as Jewish arson. All in all, the accounts claim that in the course of the last three centuries numerous fires had struck Jaśliska. The accounts also claim that some of these fires had been ignited by Jews (or henchmen of the Jews) in order to expel the Polish inhabitants from the town's centre. The accounts, however, are far from clear about the period in which the Jewish arsonists operated. The differences between the accounts invite a closer look at how the rumour has been transmitted in the course of time and what it tells us about the Polish-Jewish past in Jaśliska.

On Oral Traditions and Historical Gossip

The persistent local rumour about the way Jews acquired areas of the market square is a classic example of what Vansina (1985: 27) describes as an *oral tradition:* a verbal message which is a reported statement from the past beyond the present generation. According to Vansina (1985) rumours which are not contradicted survive. They first become part of the reserve of oral history, and at a later stage they become part of oral tradition. The inconsistent and imprecise temporal references made by the informants point to the status of the rumour as an oral tradition. As we have seen, informants traced the fires to the nineteenth and twentieth centuries. In the first case, the news of Jewish arson originated from a period before the lifetime of the informants. As such, the news eventually reached this generation in the form of generalisations made by contemporaries. In the second case, the fires are said to have taken place during the lifetime of the informants. This means that the rumour reached the informants as a contemporary form of hearsay. The small margin between oral history (news and hearsay transmitted by contemporaries) and oral tradition (reported statements from the past beyond the present generation) is made explicit by Katarzyna P. (88). Although she and her neighbour were contemporaries and thus potential eyewitnesses of the events, Katarzyna P. presents the story as a form of oral tradition:

> One woman, she is a little older than I am, she told me that she could remember the times when only one Jew lived here [...] They [Jews] bought houses from Poles, paid for that and Poles built houses outside the town. They [Jews] settled here in the market square. When a Pole had a house they paid for it and he went to the outskirts, because Jews liked to live in town. The houses were closely built together and they were often in flames. One used to say that Jews soaked rags in kerosene and then threw fire into the houses and after that they bought the lots and built a house there.

Oral traditions become historical gossip when there is a clear link between the record and the observation. Vansina (1985: 29-30) presents two models through which record and observation are linked. The first model assumes the existence of a chain of transmission in which each of the parties is linked: a first party (the observer who reported his experience orally, casting it in an initial message) with a second party and a third, with the last performer acting as informant. The other model holds that a next single line of transmission often does not exist. Here transmission is seen as communal and continuous, since most oral tradition is told by many people to many people:

> News, such as the birth of a boy, gets about and is transmitted by many people as gossip which in time becomes historical. Even in the generation after and later, messages do not go from one link in one generation to a link in the next one in an orderly way. People hear performers and all the auditors have heard that message. Some tell it in turn to still others. Some who tell it have heard it several times from different people, and fuse all that they heard together in a single statement (Vansina 1985: 30).

The last model explains a great deal about how the rumour of Jewish arson came into existence and how it has been transmitted over time. The accounts unmistakably relate to a set of specific events, namely, the repeated fires that destroyed the town's centre. The accounts further show that one or two generations earlier, eyewitnesses of the fires spread the news among contemporaries and later generations. Indeed, it is possible to trace the original message of the events to two specific sources: the town's chroniclers, father Garbaszewski, priest of Jaśliska, and Zygmunt Bogdański, headmaster of the local primary school. Both the priest and the headmaster witnessed the fires that plagued the town and kept diaries of the events in their chronicles. In 1885 father Garbaszewski wrote:

> A real disaster happened to Jaśliska. On October 18 during the mass in church, people began shouting: 'It is burning! It is burning! Fire!' Everyone quickly left the church. A Jewish house situated near the church was burning. A very hard wind blew the fire in the direction of the church. Bundles of burning hay were blown towards the church. There was no rescue for the church. The people in church cried and begged on their knees and prayed to the Lord to rescue the house of God. And I came to this place and made a cross and lifted the holy cross of the body of Jesus. And then a miracle happened. The direction of the wind changed and the church was saved. Four houses had been burned to the ground. On 20 October, Tuesday, exactly at noon, the whole northwestern part of the town and the whole Dalejowska street burned down. This time too the fire started in a Jewish house. The losses were enormous. It was a terrible event. Also the harvest stored in the farmsteads was lost, but nobody was injured (Garbaszewski 1872-1895).

The same event is mentioned by Zygmunt Bogdański. Though he did not witness the event, Bogdański (born in 1877) wrote a similar version:

> In 1885, on a Sunday in October, there was a fire starting in the house of Natan Leiser in the market square near the church. Three houses were destroyed. The following Tuesday another fire started in the house of the same Natan Leiser (in the house where he had moved to). The Dalejowska street burned down and also the western part of the market square and all the farmsteads were destroyed by the fire (Bogdański n.d.).

According to father Garbaszewski and Bogdański, the fires in October 1885 spread from a Jewish house and caused much havoc among (Polish) farmsteads. Interestingly, however, neither the priest nor the headmaster accused the Jews of arson. Still, the chronicles play a major part in the transmission of the historical gossip about Jewish arson. This is clear from the fact that most informants traced the gossip to the chronicles and found in them evidence of truth. The informants not only claimed to have heard about the story of Jewish arson, but they also knew that the story had been written down somewhere in the numerous chronicles on the history of the town. The authority of written evidence is also discernible in the account by Jan S. (65), whose grandfather used to read to him from the chronicle written by the former guild of coopers:

> *There was a guild of coopers. Their duty was to bury the dead. They burned candles as a sacrifice, like for example, during the day of Corpus Christi (Boże Ciało). When I built my house I dug to the foundations, and I found three layers of ashes. My grandmother told me that Jaśliska was set on fire three times. Jews came here and they were suspected of having bought up Polish houses. But a lot of Poles did not want to sell their houses. The ones living here were coopers and they used to take their products to Slovakia and Hungary, far away, because Hungary was called Magyar at that time. And today Magyar is called Slovakia. They went to Mokaczów. I can't remember it myself, but it is said that Jews set fire to the houses of the coopers the first time. There was water flowing from the mountain in wooden pipes. My great-great-grandparents were to take care of the exploitation of these pipes [...] Some sixty peasants gathered in one room and they were having a discussion. When Jaśliska was in flames, they wanted to extinguish the fire with the water from this well. They took and took and soused the houses with it. To this one and to the other one: they were standing next to each other and passed the water from hand to hand. They soused, and soused, and soused, but to their surprise the fire was not extinguished but grew bigger. It was said that the Jews had been pouring oil into this well, that is what I heard. While I was digging, I found three layers of ashes, that is what I know for sure. Each layer was 30 cm thick. I can prove it and during springtime I can dig it up and show it to you. It is enough to go one meter deep. And there you will find three layers of ashes.*

According to Jan S. the first fire took place in 1717 and the last at some time in the twentieth century. He is not sure though, because he was only a child when his grandfather read the story to him. In addition, he claimed that his grandfather had been menaced by the Jews as well. But the police patrol, who had become suspicious, passed by and prevented the house of his grandfather from being burned to the ground. The account of Jan S. clearly illustrates the communal and continuous character of the transmission of the gossip about Jewish arson. Since the gossip is told by many people to many people, it is variable in detail (that is, communal), but the message stands out very clearly (is continuous): many fires destroyed the town; several fires were started by Jews in order to buy out the impoverished Poles; after the fires the Jews settled in the centre; and the Polish victims had to retreat to the outskirts of the town.

Historical Evidence

At first sight, the informants' explanations of the fires sound plausible. Many fires struck the town and since there is always an offender (most likely an outsider who in addition has a good motive), Jews were suspected of arson. Indeed, as new arrivals Jews *were* looking for places where they could settle. Moreover, in the course of time, Jews turned out to be *successful* in finding such places. Whereas the Poles were forced to leave the town because of bankruptcy or in search of better living conditions, the numbers of Jews in the small town steadily grew. Considering the conspicuous retreat of the Poles from the town's centre and the steady advance of the Jews, the explanation of Jewish arson proves to be quite convincing. Daniel S. (82), for example, explained: 'When a house had burned down, they [Jews] became so incredibly friendly. They used to visit this person offering him help: "Here you have money! Build a new house for yourself and give me this place!" They would visit the Polish victims immediately. It was a Jewish trick.'

Though the gossip about Jewish arson is corroborated by historical evidence, the oral message is not necessarily true. There is little reason to believe that, even if it were true that Jewish hands had caused the fires, Jews had done so on purpose and with the intention of seizing Polish houses and fields. First, the documents show that the fires burned the houses owned and inhabited by Jews. On 18 October 1885 the fire on the market square destroyed three or four houses in cluster A (see figure 3.2). It is in this cluster that Jews had settled already prior to 1874, which implies that arson would have harmed them more than it would have done them any good. The same applies to cluster B, which suffered from fire on 20 October 1885. Here too most of the Jewish-owned houses were inhabited already before 1874 (see figure 3.2). It is only in Dalejowska street that many lots became the property of the Jews in the years following the fires, that is, after 1886 for cluster E, and after 1891 for cluster F (see figure 3.2).

Secondly, although there is a clear time-link between the fires and Jews buying the houses and fields of the Polish victims of fire, this link does not necessarily mean the Jews were arsonists. As we have seen, Poles were less likely to have financial reserves to compensate for any big material loss. This is also confirmed by the informants who, without exception, stressed the Poles' lack of currency (Poles having no money to pay a fire insurance; Poles going bankrupt). As a result, a Polish victim of fire could not afford the materials to rebuild his destroyed house. To be able to buy the necessary materials he was forced to sell his land and settle somewhere else, most likely on grounds outside the town that were already his family's property. The highest bidder, of course, was the Jew who had an interest in settling in town *and* had sufficient funds to buy the land and build a house on it. Seeing it from that perspective, the Polish victim of fire was forced to sell his house to the Jew not because of Jewish extortion, but because of his own lack of resources.

Historical gossip does not provide us with factual evidence. What does historical gossip contribute to our understanding? Vansina (1985: 31) explains:

> Most situations and trends in oral tradition seem to be summaries of events generalised [...] [Oral tradition] usually translates an opinion also held by the community, whether the facts substantiate it or not. Therefore statements about situations or trends need not in fact relate to actual events or observations. Often they derive from generalisations made by contemporaries or later generations. Such data testify then to opinions and values held, to mentalities, and that is their value, not as testimony of fact.

Even if the stories about Jewish arson tell us little about real events, they do tell us a great deal about how the relationship between Poles and Jews was experienced. Presumably, no Polish townsman ever observed Jews putting oil into the well and soaking rags in kerosene to set fire to the houses in town. Rather, it is said that they bribed vagrants to do the dirty work. However, although unlikely, the assumed link between the fires and Jewish arson contributes to the notion of Poles being not only the victims of fire but also the victims of Jews. The accounts of the informants invariably tell the tale of the Jews, who came to exploit the Poles by seizing the land on which they could no longer afford to live. The Poles suffered from repeated Jewish attacks which resulted in poverty, and finally they were chased out of town. As such the gossip about Jewish arson testifies to the tensions that existed between the Polish and Jewish communities in the early period of coexistence. Apparently, the first Jews who settled in Jaśliska met with feelings of resentment from native Poles.

As a message with a specific content—Poles are the victims of Jews—no informant bothered about the facts or credibility of the story. In fact, the informants could accept the story and disagree with it at the same time. When asked whether he really believed the rumour on Jewish arson, Jan S. (65) responded: 'Yes and no. I would not pay a penny either way.' He then argued: 'Listen to me, I cannot believe that they [Jews] would have done something like that. We were neighbours [...] we got along very well.' He went on to tell that after the war father Rąpała, the late priest of Jaśliska, asked the villagers to forgive the Jews for the sins they had committed, for he explained to the villagers that the Jews had been punished enough during the war. Indeed, after the war the Poles had ceased to be victims of the Jews. Indeed, the trend had reversed, or as an informant (82) put it, 'later, when they [Germans] had deported the Jews [...] the inhabitants of Jaśliska started to live in the houses of the Jews.'

Notes

1. Because most such migrants left for the United States, the lots left by them were commonly called 'American grounds'.
2. Present Wola Niżna (see map 1).
3. Kalman and Mechl S. occupy respectively the second and sixth position on the list, meaning that they belonged to the small group of high taxpayers. According to a Polish administrative index of 1870, Mechl S. earned his living as a mercer. Kalman S. is not mentioned on that list (WAPK 1870a; WAPK 1870b).
4. The total population of the town in 1867 was 868 inhabitants (WAPK 1867a; WAPK 1867b). Assuming that every family contains at least five persons, the total number of Jews is estimated to have been at least 75.
5. In 1882 the total population of the town was 900, among them 30 Jewish families (Sulimierski, Chłembowski et al. 1882).
6. The census distinguishes four types of residence: towns (*miasta*), small towns (*miasteczka*), rural communities (*gminy*), and manors (*obszary dworskie*) (GUS 1924).
7. Jews inhabited all small towns in the Sanok district. The small towns numbered only seven (including Jaśliska). Hence, Jews living in small towns made up only 15 percent of the region's total Jewish population.
8. Before the establishment of the Jewish cemetery in Jaśliska Jews would carry their dead to Dukla, a town some eighteen kilometres from Jaśliska.
9. In most cases informants would refer to Jewish lots rather than to Jewish houses, as many of the former Jewish properties had burned down as a result of the front struggle during the Second World War.
10. Here it must be noted that informants used different terms to denote the different parts of the town. The term 'town' in this context means the centre (*miasto*), which contrasts

with the periphery (*za miastem* or *pod miastem*). Since Jaśliska is small in size, the term 'town' is mostly used to denote the market square and its immediate surroundings.

11. Rymanów was situated near a railway station.

12. The Lwowska street leads far down the hill, while the market square is located on top of the hill.

13. The term *gesheft* is Yiddish and Polish for business and is used by the older Polish informants to denote Jewish trade.

14. 'Gdzie Żyd tam sklep.'

15. The Jewish propinators from Jaśliska were probably engaged in the production (milling) and wholesaling of alcohol, while they employed Jewish sub-lessees (the Jewish tavern-keepers) as retailers of the alcohol. The propinators Hersh B. and Salomon B. are listed as the best taxpayers (on income), which indicates that they earned the highest income of all inhabitants of Jaśliska. For a discussion of Jews and alcohol see also the Chapters two and four.

16. Here classified as follows: merchants, mercer, propinators and tavern-keepers (trade); postman, priest and moneylender (service); craftsmen and butcher (handicrafts); farmers (agriculture).

17. This conclusion can be drawn from the fact that a numeric minority of income taxpayers contributed with a larger sum to the town's tax total than did the numeric majority of landowners. This could indicate that cash revenues were relatively higher taxed than land. (It may be noted that by 1867 the specific 'Jewish' taxes had been abolished).

18. Informants also knew of Jews who depended for their living solely on farming, but they were mostly situated in the neighbouring villages, such as Posada Jaśliska, Lipowiec and Daliowa.

19. Among them was the family of Antoni S., the famous painter and artist of the icons in the local church.

20. The Polish nobility formed the largest franchised class in Europe (8-12 percent compared with 1-2 percent in other European states) and comprised all social strata: great magnates, the middle stratum of landed nobility, and the growing mass of landless and impoverished nobles. With the last partitioning of Poland in 1773 the legal status of the *szlachta* was annulled. Although a fair number of the wealthier noblemen were able to register as members of the Russian, Prussian or Austrian nobility, the majority were excluded, thereupon sharing the misfortunes of the common people. At the same time the noble ethos (*kultura szlachecka*), with its ideas of exclusivity, equality, resistance and individualism, continued to live on (Davies 1986). Members of the szlachta in nineteenth-century Jaśliska no longer held the exclusive noble privileges and were probably landless, poor, and subject to the wealthy clergy and landlords, just like their fellow townsmen. Still, family tradition and names, as well as their membership of the local intelligentsia marked them off from the common people.

21. Quoted from the interview by Wojciech Salwa, 19 February 1979, Jaśliska. Note the statement of the informant on the origin of the first Jewish settlers. Karol J. was the only informant who located the place of origin of the Jewish immigrants in Slovakia and Dukla.

22. Quoted from the interview by Danuta Olbert, February 1979, Jaśliska.

23. Quoted from the interview by Halina Piasecka and Jan Stepek, 20 February 1978, Jaśliska.

Chapter 4

SPHERES OF INTERACTION
Economic Relations

'Is it true that the poorest Jew ate fish and meat and drank wine on Sabbath?'
'It is true, boys, and it isn't'.' Marcin nodded his head as if he was very sad
about something. 'The Jews did not come off worst, they could make a decent
living. And now? Today even the eighty-year-old Marcin has to go begging. This
is not good, children, it is not good ... But not all Jews were rich. On Thursdays
and Fridays the Jewish poor went from door to door, to beg their bread for Sabbath. At that time the streets were crowded with poor ... There were more poor
Jews than rich Jews ... Like with us Poles' (Opatoshu 1951: 316).

Introduction

While the nineteenth century was marked by a rapid increase of Jewish
economic activity and the acquisition of Polish land and property by the
Jews, at the turn of the twentieth century Jewish expansion in Jaśliska had
come to an end. Notwithstanding the initial tensions, the time had arrived
for both communities to adapt to the 'natural' economic division that
remained from the legal structure of serfdom. The abolition of serfdom in
1848 had not fundamentally changed the socio-economic relations in the
countryside. The means of production that until then had been monopolised by the nobility were now taken up by the Polish peasants and the Jewish entrepreneurs (respectively land and capital). Neither the movement to
a 'free' capitalist market, nor the attempts by the national authorities and the
leaders of the Roman Catholic Church to alter the socio-economic rela-

tions, would eliminate the Jewish predominance in the commercial and entrepreneurial niche. In spite of the proven risks, the Jews struggled to maintain their positions in familiar enterprises, including trade, money-lending and propination. In like manner, the Poles kept to the land which they had inherited from the previous generations. The consolidation of economic relations between the Polish peasants and Jewish tradesmen in the late nineteenth century laid the basis for an economic interdependence that turned out to be characteristic for most of the interwar period in Jaśliska.

New Times, Old Patterns

Jewish Entrepreneurship

The Jewish tavern continued to play a significant role in the economy of the Polish towns and villages through the nineteenth and early twentieth centuries. In 1889 the right to distil and sell liquor, which had formerly belonged to the nobility, was purchased by the state for the huge sum of 124 million *kronen*. The same nobles now leased from the state the propination rights for entire districts and the Jewish tavern-keeper became a sub-lessee, frequently from the same noble as before, but at a much higher rent (Mahler 1990). According to official statistics (presented in Mahler 1990: 127-128) over 70,000 Jews in Galicia derived their living from tavern-keeping and 22,981 Jews were actively engaged in this occupation around the turn of the century. Jewish tavern-keepers and liquor dealers comprised four-fifths of the more than 88,000 people in Galicia who made a living by selling alcoholic beverages, and they constituted nearly 9 percent of the entire Jewish population in the country. The exceptionally large number of taverns (*karczma*) and saloons (*szynk*), reflecting the alarming extent of alcoholism in the country, could not provide a livelihood for the considerable number of Jews in the villages and towns because of the intense competition existing in this field (Mahler 1990: 128).

Evidence of this competition among Jewish producers and salesmen of alcohol in Jaśliska is provided by the Austrian registers of 1870 (WAPK 1870a; WAPK 1870b). As might be expected, the first Jewish settlers in Jaśliska pursued the traditional Jewish professions that had proven to be profitable from earlier experience. The Jew Kalman S., for instance, let out on lease the town hall to Jewish tavern-keepers on behalf of the bishop of Przemyśl. Hersh B. and Salomon B., both holders of the rights to propination, produced alcohol and sold it to their Jewish sub-lessees. The latter in turn made a living by serving vodka, wine, and beer. Next to the production and sale of alcohol, the Jews in Jaśliska made a living through trade. They traded horses, cattle, cloth, garments, or products which they purchased from local craftsmen, while other Jews were involved in money-lending. This overwhelming Jewish involvement in local trade reflected the general occupational structure in Galicia.

According to the Austrian census of 1900, the largest occupational group among the Galician Jews consisted of merchants, dealers, and brokers, comprising 29 percent of all gainfully employed Jews. Poverty-stricken Galicia had proportionally twice as many tradesmen as the rich industrial provinces of Austria. According to unofficial sources (Mahler 1990: 127) in some districts there was one merchant or broker to every eight or ten families. Even in the villages the ratio was not much lower, for instance, in a village of eighty peasants there were generally six or seven dealers and shopkeepers. In 1900 about 88 percent of Galician trade was in Jewish hands. The overwhelming Jewish involvement in petty trade reflects the poor conditions of the majority of Jews in the country at that time. Reports from the end of the nineteenth century indicate that the stock of an average Jewish store in Galicia was worth about $20, and frequently stores were worth no more than four dollars (Mahler 1990).

The capitalist concentration of trade in larger district cities, the growth of modern forms of business organisation, and the declining economic importance of the fairs and market days, also cut into the business of the Jewish shopkeepers in Jaśliska.[1] Despite the worsening conditions the Jews' prevalence in local trade remained unimpaired. As Andrzej F. (72) put it: 'They [Jews] traded. They traded everything: clothes, shoes, and leather products. And they bought everything. But no pigs. They bought cows, they traded horses and we lived like that. They usually had shops.'

In the absence of documentation on local Jewish enterprise in the interwar period, the recollections of Polish informants take on increased significance.[2] The many years that have passed, as well as the age of the informants who witnessed the prewar times, contribute to a scattered picture of the Jews' economic activities in the decades preceding the Second World War. Daniel S. (82), when asked to recall the names and professions of the Jews he had known during his lifetime, was visibly disappointed when he remembered only few of them: 'I used to know the names of these people, but I have difficulties remembering them. So many years have passed now [...] I used to know their names like I know my prayers.' Yet if we put all the information together we may conclude that Jewish involvement in retail business had dramatically increased since the status quo recorded in the Austrian registers of 1870 (see the previous chapter). Table 4.1 summarises the types and numbers of stores and businesses run by Jews in Jaśliska in the last decades before the outbreak of the Second World War. The types and number of Jewish stores in Jaśliska indicate that Jews specialised in petty trade and that they mostly supplied non-farm products and services which primarily met the basic needs of the farmers.

Table 4.1   Approximate Number of Jewish Stores and Businesses in
              Interwar Jaśliska

Type of store/business	Probable number of store type
unspecified	4
mixed goods	1
mercery	2
ironmonger's	2
grocery	5
butcher	1
tavern	3-4
building materials	1
shoemaker	1
boots and clothes	1
glazier	1
kiosk	1
branch of the 'Vienna' Insurance Company	1
horses (trade) and shoes (store)	1
livestock and wheat	1
pots and pans	2
wood	1
bakery	1-2
Total	**30-32**

Sources: interviews by the researcher (1993); interview by Halina Piasecka and Jan Stepek (1978); interview by Danuta Olbert and Maria Marciniak (1985); interview by Wojciech Salwa (1979).

Jewish Prosperity

Social stratification was a fact among the Jews in Jaśliska. A Polish informant (72) put it this way: 'There were poor Jews, there were middle-class Jews, and there were Jews who were wealthy.' Informants found the rabbi (*rebbe*) to be an example of a poor Jew. His wife baked 'Jewish rolls' to earn a living, and if this income did not suffice the rabbi and his wife depended on their more affluent co-religionists. The tavern-keeper Reich, whose two daughters were severely injured by fire, was an example of a middle-class Jew:

> *The story was like this. One fat man entered the tavern where two Jewish girls sat at the table. There was an oil lamp on the table. They also had something to drink there. And my father was not a big man [...] and this fat man said: 'Who will lift me up?'*

My father was like a cock, he wanted to show off his power. And he lifted this fat man and the man felt ashamed and grabbed my father. He turned my father upside down and that is how the lamp fell down on the Jewish girls [...] The Jews took the case to court and this fat man was to be prosecuted [...] It was a very expensive thing to heal these girls, because they had to get oil from walnuts and the Jews had to bathe these Jewish girls in it. The one who was scalded all over died but the other survived. The fat man won the case, because in a tavern it is not allowed to put an oil lamp on the table. It could stand there but not on the table. They had seven court sessions because of this accident. (Daniel S., 82)

Perhaps the most prominent Jew in prewar Jaśliska was Abraham B., owner of the sawmill (*tartak*) in Jaśliska. All informants, including the younger generations, would recall him as the richest Jew in town:

Here lived the family B., and he was the owner of the sawmill. They were quite wealthy [...] The rest were poor Jews. You know, they had shops, but they were as poor as the Poles, maybe a little bit richer. All of them were poor. There were no such rich Jews. Abraham B., who was the owner of the sawmill, he was the only one. (Wojciech M., 78)

Beside the family of Abraham B., there are strong indications that a large number of Jewish families lived under extremely poor conditions. The emigration of thousands of Jewish families from the whole of Galicia (including the town of Jaśliska) signalled the poverty among most Galician Jews.[3] Samuel O. (82) and the brothers of Josko S. (75) are examples of those who left their home town in search of better living conditions. Samuel O. left Jaśliska in the 1930s to work in the factory of his uncle in Katowice. At home there was poverty since his father, who had been working as a timber-cutter, fell ill and was no longer able to work. Although the father of Josko S. (75) was a successful mercer, Josko's five elder brothers left for Antwerp, since they themselves had little prospects in Jaśliska.

Another indication of the widespread poverty was the involvement of a large number of villagers in smuggling activities across the border with Slovakia. Interestingly, Jews played a major part in these smuggling activities as brokers between the producers, salesmen, and customers of the smuggled goods (Litwak 1969; Olszański 1985). David O. (73), brother of the above mentioned Samuel O., regularly went on smuggling expeditions to Slovakia before and during the Second World War, until the German roundup of all Jaśliska's Jewish inhabitants in 1942. During these smuggling expeditions, which usually lasted for two or more days, David O. went either by horse and wagon, which he borrowed from the lessee of the local manor *Pan* Sidor, or on foot, in which case he was assisted by two Poles who helped him to carry the purchased products. While recalling his smuggling adventures of more than fifty years ago, David O. was surprised by the risks he was willing to take for a few kilos of sugar. It led him to conclude that 'these were other times': when food shortage and the lack of basic necessities were much more compelling than the fear of being sentenced to death.

To a certain extent, the poverty of the Jewish community was masked by internal cohesion. As the story goes, even the poorest Jew would never do without a Sabbath meal on Friday. A Jew who lacked the means for a Sabbath meal would be helped out by those who had more, because on Sabbath '... none must work, none must mourn, none must worry, none must hunger' (cited in Zborowski and Herzog 1962: 37). All informants agreed that members of the Jewish community were bound by a strong internal solidarity, which stood in direct contrast with the weak Polish cohesion. Whereas the Poles would let their fellow townsmen sink into poverty, the Jews would always help each other out. Jerzy F., (76) explains: 'If for example a poor Jew came from outside and wanted to settle here, they would join to collect money for him to help him start any crafts or shop. After he had started his business, he would pay this money back, step by step'.

There are no data available on income and expenditure of Polish and Jewish households during the interwar period. However, the informants' accounts suggest that the Jews were relatively better off than the Poles. This is illustrated by the fact that the Jews recovered far more quickly from the material losses suffered during the First World War than their Polish peasant neighbours. The command of the Jews over liquid and mobile resources may account for this fact. Informants (sixty years and older) gave abundant examples to illustrate the different standards of living among the Polish and Jewish families. Along with the Jews' capacity to employ servants and workers, informants observed that Jewish women baked delicate cakes and cooked extensive meals on holidays, 'a hundred times more delicate' than Poles could afford to prepare. They observed Jews wearing shoes, jewellery and white socks, while the Poles would go barefoot and did not possess any white cloths. Interestingly, informants would put these facts on record without drawing any conclusions. Emilia F. (70), who during her childhood experienced the short-lived illusion of having a pair of shoes all to herself, did not blame the Jewish owner who took the shoes from her:

People used to pick mushrooms in the forest, but only the privileged who had shoes could do so. The same was true for church visits. Every family had only one pair of shoes, so the whole family used the same pair. If someone lived far away from the church he would carry his shoes with a rope on his back. He put his shoes on as soon as he was near the church, but he first had to wash his feet [...] Once I went to the river bank and there were Jews. Jews were more wealthy because they traded, and they helped each other out. Then I saw rubber boots that just lay errant and I was eight years old. There was nobody at the river bank. I saw these boots. I put them on and I was so happy that I had found these shoes and that I could go with them! And then somebody told it, I guess, and this Jew came to get his shoes back. I felt so sorry for that. But it was nice that I had been wearing them for several days.

On the Jews' standard of living the informants held contradictory views. As they employed different measuring standards to assess the relative wealth of their one-time Jewish neighbours they arrived at very different conclusions. The disparity in views may be explained by the divergent sources of livelihood used by Poles and Jews, which generated different types of income and required a different lifestyle. If an individual's welfare is measured in terms of money or savings, the Jews can be considered relatively well-off. In this view, money is the key to survival (in case of famine and war) and the key to power (with respect to the moneyless).

However, once prosperity is measured in terms of landed property, the Jews are worse off. In this more conservative view, land is both the key to survival (in case of economic decline) and the key to accumulation of wealth (through crop production or rental). From this it follows that Poles, whether they were landowners or low-rank peasants, could count on a secure income. Even though their income consisted of natural resources, they were not forced to save up money like the Jews, who were usually totally dependent on the money economy and therefore more vulnerable to economic fluctuations. When asked whether the Jews were rich or poor, Maria M. (84), member of a one-time well-to-do Polish family, answered: 'No, Jews were not very rich [...] There were two rich Polish families who had a lot of land and nice farms, so they were called rich. For example my family. My family rented land from the priest. [...] Most Jews were poor. They had only reserves to bring up their children [...] Jews had gold as their property.'

Economic Dependence

The integration of the Jews into the peasant economy was spurred on by the decline of the peasant autarky. As a result of the abolition of serfdom in 1848, the Polish peasants became increasingly dependent on the market for both the purchase of basic necessities and income. Especially the First World War, which marked the end of Austrian rule and the beginning of Polish independence, brought considerable material losses to the peasant households. The immediate needs of the Polish peasants increased their dependence on the market. At the same time, however, the opportunities to generate off-farm income in addition to the sale of agricultural produce considerably declined. During the interwar years the opportunities for work, which had never been exceptionally high in the region, declined with the establishment of new national borders in 1921. The closure of the borders put an end to centuries of prosperous trade with, and seasonal migration to, Slovakia and Hungary. At the same time, the Great Depression of the twenties and thirties reduced the opportunities of peasant migrants to the United States and decreased the remittances from abroad (Orlik 1979). As a result of the economic disintegration, Jaśliska lost its town rights in 1934. Meanwhile, the role of the Jews in the local peasant economy took on increased significance, as the peasants now depended on the opportunities offered to them by the local, mostly Jewish, creditors and employers.

The Jewish Swindler: The Malevolent Creditor

Whatever products Jews sold, the Polish town dwellers from Jaśliska as well as Lemkos[4] from the neighbouring villages were among their best customers. The little money Poles and Lemkos earned from selling crops or handicrafts, as emigrants, peasant workers, mine workers, or, from the second decade of the twentieth century, as workers in the sawmill, they spent on products from Jewish stores and on alcohol in Jewish taverns. The products they bought were those which they did not produce themselves, such as sugar, salt, pepper, flour, buckwheat (*kasza*), nails, cloth, matches, as well as vodka and beer. Most often the expenses they made far exceeded their small earnings. The Jews therefore sold all products, be it sugar or vodka, on credit (*na borg*):

> *When a peasant woman went to a manor to work there, with the hay or during the harvest or something, she earned 70 groszy a day. She worked from dawn to night. And one kilo of sugar costs one złoty and five cents, so imagine. Then the Poles went to the Jews who had groceries and they used to take products on credit, and they [Jews] said: 'Oh, yes neighbour, come over here, and take anything you want!' (Paweł N., 67)*

Since 1848, the practice of selling on credit was extended with the practice of private money-lending, which had become particularly widespread among the Galician Jews—especially among the village shopkeepers (Mahler 1990). This aspect is confirmed by Polish as well as Jewish informants, who explained that the practice of money-lending (which in most cases would take the form of buying on credit) was prevalent in Jaśliska until the outbreak of the Second World War. If not selling on credit, Jews lent money to the Poles so that the latter could purchase the much wanted products (though not necessarily from Jews). During the interwar period official money-lending was regulated according to the rules of the institution called 'weksel'. This so-called 'weksel' system consisted of a pre-printed license on which the covenant between the debtor and creditor was fixed (such as the outstanding debt, rent, eventual pawn and terms of instalment) and signed by the debtor, the creditor, and two witnesses whose properties served as a guarantee. The 'weksel' licenses were freely available (for instance at the post office), which implied that the Jews no longer prevailed in the sector of money-lending. Although the Polish peasant increasingly dealt with Polish creditors, borrowing money was no less risky. As Jan S. (65) put it: 'Before the war it was terrible to borrow money. It was better to prepare to die instead of borrowing money. Even a drowning person is ready to catch a blade to rescue himself. He [the debtor] would be drowned anyway, precisely because he had borrowed money. It was just a matter of time.'

The low living standard of the Polish peasants, their excessive consumption of alcohol, and their need for non-farm products in some cases resulted in a life-long indebtedness to the Jews. The numerous transactions between Polish peasants and Jewish shopkeepers gave rise to local stories about the ways Jews sought to exploit their Polish customers. It is believed that the illiterate Polish peasant, who had no control over the Jews' administration, was cheated more than once. On this so-called 'Jewish swindle' (*oszustwo żydowskie*) Daniel S. (82) commented:

> *The one thing they [Jews] were interested in was to swindle, to cheat someone, and to have money. If one [Jew] was a little more clever he used to scrape somebody like a carrot. They wanted so much to have customers, and they wanted them so much to buy things. And then they wrote down everything. But in such a way that you could not see what they were writing. It was their trick. They used to write more than the real value of the product.*

While the illiterate and naive peasant was vulnerable in the hands of Jews, the drunken peasant was even more so. The skilful Jew simply sought to exploit the innocent Pole who was unable to resist temptations. It seemed to the informants that what was good for the Jew was bad for the Pole. Jan S. (65) recalled:

> *Sometimes my grandfather did not feel like buying vodka, because he felt that it was a waste of money. Once my grandfather went to buy meat and he got vodka instead. They probably added something to this vodka, so he lost his head and did not know what he was doing. He left a large sum of money. But my grandfather could not see well, so the Jew took the money and ran away.*

The Polish peasant, who never had wished to be poor and unfortunate, needed his Jewish creditor to have some prospects. Likewise, the Jewish merchant and tavern-keeper, limited in his freedom to pursue other economic activities, needed the Polish farmer to invest in his commercial enterprise. Neither the Poles nor the Jews were able to step back from the socio-economic roles ascribed to them. Despite the absolute benefits, the final interdependency of the Polish debtor and Jewish creditor was essentially compelling. The ever growing debts tied the Polish debtor to his Jewish creditor even more strongly. The Austrian traveller Demian (cited in Macartney 1970: 196) vividly portrayed the symbiotic relationship between the Polish debtor and his Jewish creditor in nineteenth-century Galicia:

> Now the peasant enjoys a few happy days in careless tranquillity, and does not mind hungering so long as he is not athirst. But before long the time arrives when he has to pay dues to his landlord, buy supplies, and pay his taxes, and he can find no means of producing money. Again, he resorts to the Jew, who pays his debts and magnanimously contents himself with the peasant's mortgaging him his growing corn, assigning him his still unborn calf for a mess of pottage or making this or that journey for him, doing this or that job. The peasant feels only his immediate need, and immediate relief of it is all he wants. So his household remains eternally in the same state of wretchedness, and the peasant's continued habit of regarding the Jew as his friend gradually engenders an unlimited confidence in the Jew which is infinitely advantageous to the latter.

Of course, the above picture of the Jewish exploiter and the Polish underdog is biased. The Polish victim was less innocent than Demian would have us believe. The Polish debtor did profit from the close relationship with his Jewish creditor and even cultivated it. In fact, both parties tried to get as much as possible out of this relationship. The Polish customer would throw himself on the Jew's mercy in the case of excessive debts, while the Jewish storekeeper would appeal to the customer's reliability in demanding land or valuables as pawn. Still, it is true that of the two, the Polish debtor was the most vulnerable. Apart from the biased picture of the mean Jew, Demian puts one thing perfectly right: in the transactions between the Jewish merchant and the Polish peasant, the latter was likely to be the first loser.

The unequal balance of power in the debtor-creditor relations started when the debtor and creditor made the bargain. The Jewish creditor took a risk by investing in a peasant enterprise with an uncertain future, but he was almost sure to gain from the bargain, unless the debtor escaped his debts. The Polish debtor, on the other hand, called in the creditor's assistance because of his poverty. Since he had no prospect of repaying his debts, the debtor lived under the constant threat of having his farm and land put up for auction. Hence, whereas the peasant depended on the financial reserves, goodwill and policy of his Jewish creditor, the Jewish creditor controlled the expenses, land and farms of his Polish debtor. At times court cases resulted in the bankruptcy of whole Polish families. On the consequences of lending money and buying on credit the local historian Orlik (1979: 27) comments:

> The Jews further enlarged their income through the practice of usury, lending money to the people at high interest rates. They also gave products without payment on so-called credit, which enabled them to sell on auction the properties of the debtor who was overdue with the payment of his instalments, and [in this way] take possession of his mortgage.

Once the debts exceeded the value of the debtor's furniture, real estate, or pawn, the creditor had no mercy. He would send a bailiff to the debtor or, if the debtor would not pay, the debtor was summoned to court. At the court his possessions (farmhouse, furniture, valuables, land) were taken out of pawn and sold at auction for the value of the debt. As an informant (65) put it, 'and then, when the Jew noticed that he had written a lot in his note book, he went to court, and he would sit on the [debtor's] properties.' The Jews' practice to 'sit on' Polish land is said to have been everyday practice in Jaśliska in the second half of the nineteenth century. Stanisława S. (82) explained: 'My parents told me that during their lifetimes it happened very often. They [Jews] did nothing but trading wine and vodka with Hungary, and people used to drink away their money. But during our times things had changed.' Likewise, Paweł N. (63) was told that '… it happened very often. Jews used to sit on the land of the poorest people. I can't remember it myself but old people used to tell about it. '

The term informants applied to the way debts were paid (Jews 'sitting on' Polish land) makes it possible to link Polish indebtedness and the Jews' settlement in Jaśliska. We have seen that informants linked the Poles' indebtedness to Jews with Jewish arson, and consequently with Jewish settlement in the town (see Chapter three). In like manner, informants claimed that Jews had been particularly eager to 'sit on' lots in the centre of the town. An informant (82) put it this way: 'They [Jews] did not want to have fields, they wanted building lots [...] They [Jews] were no farmers.' It is unlikely, though, that Jewish creditors kept the mortgaged land to live on themselves, since most land put up for auction was only part of the property and often did not include the farm house. The same informant (Daniel S., 82) explained: 'There were no such cases that one farmer lost everything. Our land is divided into many pieces. So Jews used to take the best.' Indeed, the Jews would sell the land in order to acquit the outstanding debts rather than use it for their own purposes. This meant that the primary owner could recover his property by a roundabout way, which in fact could take several generations. Mortgage deeds in the real estate registers punctually document cases of auction and pawning. The mortgage deeds show that land went from hand to hand from Poles to Poles, from Jews to Jews, from Poles to Jews, and back to Poles again. Teresa and Maciej G. (26, 23) confirmed the ready purchase and sale of real estate in the past:

Maciej:	*As far as we know every Jew had his own shop here. And they had inns. If you would ask me whether the Poles went to visit the Jews, yes, they visited their taverns for sure. There are a lot of former Jewish lots here, on our territory. If one had no ...*
Teresa:	*If they [Poles] drunk it all away, and had ...*
Maciej:	*If they drunk it all away or something ...*
Teresa:	*Then they sat on the land ...*
Maciej:	*They [Jews] took it as a mortgage pawn and registered it. So it happens that on this terrain most lots of Polish farmers have a narrow Jewish stripe (pasek żydowski), or a Jewish diamond (krateczka żydowska). That is, former Jewish, because now these belong to the community. In this way they [Poles] had to pay back their debts.*

Mortgage deeds further show that the debtors were Poles as well as Jews, and men as well as women. However, in contrast to Poles, who often were indebted to Jews (with debts sometimes amounting to over 200 złoty), Jews were rarely indebted to Poles, as richer relatives or coreligionists were quick to help a Jewish debtor out. Names of 'fortunate' Jews often appear in the mortgage deeds buying land and finally selling or giving it to indebted Jews. As a result, Jews were indebted to 'richer' Jews rather than to Poles. Cases in which Polish families lost their land and houses to Jews were an exception. Still, informants reported two Polish families, family M. and family P., who lost their farms at auction in the late 1920s and early 1930s, the years of the Great Depression. The local historian Orlik (1979: 50-51) reports another two cases, among them the family M.:

Especially hard for the village was the period of inflation and later the big economic crisis [...] The drop of prices for agricultural products with two-third [...] and at the same time the maintenance of the then applying tax levels and costs of loans raised through the crisis, extended the poverty in the village to a catastrophic level, resulting in conditions commonly called starvation supply. "This implied that a farmer did not only sell his crop surpluses, but also sold the products that were needed to sustain the family and maintain a normal household." In this difficult time some of Jaśliska's inhabitants, among them Franciszek [M.] and Maryjanna [B.], lost their farms to the Jews who bought [the farms] on auction.

Though these were rare incidents, the bankruptcy of a number of Polish families who had been indebted to Jews helped to create the notion that the poor Polish dweller did not have a fair chance to defend himself against the 'wicked' and 'rich' Jews.[5] In like manner, informants claimed that Jews could get 'whatever they wanted'. A thirteen year old informant was sure that Jews used to 'kick the Poles out of their houses.' In addition, many informants referred to the popular proverb voicing (in their view) the one-time Jewish perspective: 'The houses belong to us, and the streets are yours'.[6]

The Jewish Rescuer: The Benevolent Creditor

Of course, the creditor-debtor relationship had two-sides. Borrowing money also had its advantages. The credit provided by Jewish shopkeepers contributed to the Poles' temporary relief from poverty during the years of crisis. In the stories of the informants the theme of the Jewish creditor and benefactor of the Poles seems to be as popular as the theme of the malevolent Jew. Andrzej F. (72) explained: 'We Poles used to say: 'When there is poverty then go see the Jew'.[7] For if one did not have money, the Jew gave products on credit, or he helped you out whenever it was needed.' Andrzej F. further pointed at the Jews' readiness to assist the Polish peasants at their own expense. To illustrate Jewish goodwill he told the following story:

> *One neighbour cut his leg with an axe, up to his knee. So he was taken to the hospital in Krosno. My own brother carried him on his vehicle. One had to wake up at 11 p.m., feed the horse and leave at 12 p.m. in order to be in Krosno at the hospital at 8 a.m., which were the opening hours. My older brother brought him [the injured] and left him there. The head of the hospital in Krosno looked at him and said: 'cut off this leg'. And he [the injured] said: 'I will not allow you to cut off my leg.' 'Then you will die, so go home!' He [the injured] went home. At home the leg was aching terribly. There was no doctor and he had no medicine. So he went to the second hospital in Sanok [...] In Sanok they said: 'cut off his leg.' [The injured answered:] 'I will not allow you.' So he went back home again. And the leg was aching. So I went to Krosno with him. I parked my horse and vehicle on the side. There was no big traffic then. I helped him to go there and they said: 'You have already been here. We will cut off the leg or you go home.' So he went home and people, farmers, the more clever ones, they decided to go to Lwów, because we had the Lwów district here, and there [in Lwów] were specialists [...] But how could we reach that place? You needed money for the train. This farmer with his leg went to Poznań before the war, on foot. He went to Poznań because he had a sister there and he also had a chest with food, clothes and underwear to change. This chest was not like a backpack but it was made of wood. He went to Poznań on foot. During the fighting on the front he had been in Kiev and he was wounded there. In the Soviet Union he had been put in hospital. Our people [Poles] said: 'Let him die. What will we do with him?' But the Jews collected money among them. They collected 17 złoty. That was an enormous amount before the war. It was the price of a ticket to Lwów. Jews col-*

lected money and gave it and he went to Lwów to the clinic and his leg was cured. He
did not need to have his leg cut off.

In addition, Jews supported Polish peasants by buying farm products for private consumption such as crops, eggs, ducks, geese, hens, and milk. Almost every Polish household had its own Jewish buyers, while Polish children would earn 'a few pennies' by selling fish to the Jews which they had caught themselves. Wojciech M. (78) recalled: 'There were always two Jewish families that came to my mother to get milk, hens, and eggs. They were the only ones to whom we sold our products.' Once the relationship had been confirmed, exchange between Poles and Jews also took place on informal terms. On this Bronisław Z. (86) commented: 'I had a Jewish neighbour, Nusim. He was a good neighbour. Nusim he was called. Once he lent me one metre of flour. I didn't have money but Nusim said: '… don't talk about money! So he lent me flour. After one month I had earned enough to return him the money.'

Informants stressed the complementarity of Polish and Jewish interests: 'They [Jews] helped us out and we helped them out. They sold us products and we gave them milk, eggs, and hens. Everything we could sell to them we sold.' At the same time this exchange of products is used as an argument to explain the relative harmony in which the Jews and Poles were living: 'We respected each other. We had to because we bought products from them.' Another informant put it this way: 'We lived on good terms, because the Jew always needed milk and an egg.' Also Jan S. (65) stressed the mutual dependence between Poles and Jews on the different levels: 'Jews lived thanks to us Poles. Jews bought milk and bought meat from our cows, and they supplied us with horses.' He then continued, 'one went to a Jew to borrow money, in order to rescue himself.' He then concluded, 'we lived very well together.'

The image of the Jewish creditor as the rescuer of the Poles calls for a more carefully balanced appraisal of the Jews' role in the peasant economy. While the informants frankly showed their disapproval of the Jews' involvement in 'usurious' activities, they did not solely perceive of the Jews as usurers. Informants unambiguously accused the Jews of 'mean' practices, but they also dismissed the 'foolish' consumerism of their forebears. In the eyes of the informants the latter were inefficient investors and excessive consumers of alcohol. Even money brought from the United States was soon spent on alcohol and food. Jan S. (65) clearly disapproved of the expenditures made by his relatives: 'My aunt, she was a niece of my grandmother, they were in America and they brought a few *groszy* home. But they spent this money very fast, the money which they had been earning. It was not good.' Informants fairly admitted that they too profited from the Jews' activities. And they pointed to their own responsibility in their dealings with Jews by laughing at 'Jewish tricks' as well as at 'Polish stupidities'. Sometimes informants would relate the clashes between Polish debtors and Jewish creditors just for fun. So did Jan S. (65), the same informant as in the quotation above, who told the story of his aunt Mrs M.[8] In the beginning of the 1930s Mrs M. ran into debts and finally was summoned to court:

A Jew had a shop, so my aunt went to him and asked him for credit [...] The Jewish shop owner asked her: 'What do you want?' [She said:] 'I want some flour because the harvest was not good, and I want sugar and salt too.' [...] So the Jew gave and gave and gave. And she could not write. When she bought one kilogram he wrote two, or even three kilograms. And that was it, and so it ended. The Jew went to court and had a look at their mortgage, in order to check how many fields they had. From that time on he knew the value of the land. So the Jew made a calculation and sent an admonition to this person. He sent all the documents. Then she came the second time. It was my aunt, Czesława, the mother of Grzesiek, and he [the Jew] said: 'Oh neighbour, you cannot get credits from me any longer, because the value of your land is less then the value of the products you took.' And he [the Jew] said: 'You must give me the money back.' She answered: 'I don't have money to pay you back'. Her husband was a shoemaker, he was mending old shoes, better shoes are thrown into the litters nowadays. So she had no money to repay her debts. Then the Jew made a case at the court. They called it auction. 'Who will give more for this farm?' And then he [the Jew] sold it. [...] So the Jew sold this field. If it was a house, people were thrown on the street. And there was also another way out. They [the debtors] kissed the Jew on his feet, and begged him to leave them in peace, to let them stay in their homes. They promised to find a job somewhere, so that they could earn money and could live in their houses. So there was a case in court and this woman, my aunt, said to the judge: 'Judge, this Jew wrote me more. He wrote me more, so he swindled me.' [The judge:] 'But Mrs. M. how can you prove it?' So the aunt brought a stick with her which they called 'paliczka'. She told that she had made some notches on her stick: 'Here I have one kilogram of flour and here I had two kilograms, and here I had pepper and here I had sugar.' She had made signs for herself, and she knew which one was for sugar and how many pounds she had bought. Pounds were used as a measure before the war. Then the judge told her: 'Mrs. M., you know what? You can paint these notches on your ass.' How could he have told her differently? People didn't go to school during the Austrian times. They didn't have to. It was not compulsory.

The story of Mrs M. brings to the fore the various aspects of the debtor-creditor relationship: the illiteracy and poverty of the Poles, the alleged 'wickedness' of the Jews, the dependence of the Polish debtor on his Jewish creditor, and the ultimate power of the Jews. Moreover, the continuation of the story (not quoted here) reveals the relative indifference of the peasants towards the misfortunes of others, even if the people involved were next of kin. Mrs M.

did not receive any help from her neighbours or family. Instead of helping her, family members bought the land put up for auction just to use it themselves. The individualism of the peasant community is in strong contrast to the alleged solidarity of the local Jews.[9] Taking into account the weak Polish cohesion, the Polish peasant had reason to be cautious not only of wicked Jews but also of the indifference shown by his Polish brethren.

The Jewish Patron: The Mighty Employer

While Jews had always lent services to the Poles as creditors, from the second decade of the twentieth century Jews also became the main suppliers of jobs in predominantly agrarian Jaśliska. It was in this period that the Jewish wood industry began to prosper. In 1912 Isaac L., his two sons Natan and Baruch, and his partner in business Abraham B. started to operate two sawmills.[10] During the interwar years the Jewish sawmills employed over a hundred Polish men and women, who worked in shifts of fifty people (three shifts a day). A Jewish eyewitness, Israel B. (in Litwak 1969: 3) recalls: 'In 1912 two sawmills were opened, one after the other, of which the owners were Jews. The clerks and chiefs were Jews, whereas the simple workers were Christians. The sawmills formed a source of prosperity for the small town.'

The role of Jews as clerks and foremen in the sawmills contributed to their comparative high social standing in the local community. This is confirmed by the account of the Jewish informant David O. (73), who remembered Alter S., the foreman of the wood-drying section in the local sawmill. Alter S. lived in Daliowa (2 km from Jaśliska) and was loved by the villagers of Daliowa, because he was the man who 'hired and fired people'. Likewise, the people from Jaśliska remember the successful entrepreneur and proprietor of the local wood industry, Abraham B. As a benefactor of the Jewish community who contributed money to the House of Prayer (*shul*) and to the Jewish school (*kheyder*), Abraham B. commanded respect among the local Jews. But for the local Poles he was no less important. Polish informants recalled him as a devout and important man, who took his religion very seriously and would never fail to be present at the religious services. By way of showing their respect to him they submissively called him 'Mister Owner' (*Pan Właściciel*). Indeed, in 1935 Abraham B.'s high social standing was sealed when he received a seat in the town council. In the capacity of councillor, Abraham B. followed other prominent Jews who had been elected to the town council in earlier decades.[11] The high reputation of the Jews in Jaśliska was also confirmed by Israel B. (Litwak 1969: 4), who made the following observation:

During the first years of the First World War representation depended on the amount of the taxes one paid. Since the Jews paid the highest taxes, they obtained six of the twelve seats, in spite of their proportionally low numbers. This situation changed in 1923 when the number of seats was reduced by one-half. The political status of the Jews, however, remained unimpaired and the people took full account of their opinions. In business matters they [Jews] were renowned advisors and also Christian intellectuals would go to them for advice.

Besides employing Poles as peasant workers in the sawmills, the Jews hired Poles as servants to clean their houses and look after their children; as *shabbes goyim* who performed light domestic tasks on religious holidays; as timber-cutters in the forest; as carters who transported merchandise and wood, and finally as day-labourers who cultivated the lands owned by Jews. As an informant put it: 'When a farmer had two strong horses, he used to work in the forest, and carry wood or merchandise to the town; and the Jews paid him for that.' The extent to which the Polish residents depended on employment, which was mainly provided by the Jews, is especially telling in accounts recalled by several Polish informants For example, on Sundays, after the morning service, a large number of Polish peasants would gather in the market square and would wait for Jews to call them and give them some kind of job. It was exactly on these Sundays that Jews used to replenish their shops with merchandise and make the necessary preparations for the week. The peasant who happened to be selected by a Jew as a carter or a porter was lucky for 'he was paid for his job'. Likewise, on Sabbath Polish boys and girls prepared to light the candles and the ovens in the Jewish homes, carried the prayer books for the Jewish men, and fetched water or performed other light domestic tasks, since on Sabbath 'Jews were not even allowed to light a match'. In return for their work the children received sweets, or bread, and occasionally money. Jan S. (65), who was lovingly called 'Yankele' by his Jewish patrons, served as a regular help on such occasions:

When Sabbath began they [Jews] prayed from night until the first meal at 11.00 in the morning. On Sabbath one Jewish woman used to go to my grandmother and would say to me: 'Yankele, go and fetch me the kugel'– it was some kind of dough from potatoes, a dish made from mashed onions and fresh potatoes. I used to bring all the pots to all the families, and I had five families. The oven was walled up in one Jewish house. A Jew stood there and was guarding so that nobody would enter. It was well guarded. When I came to bring one of these pots, they gave me a hot piece of material. In that way I could transport two pots. And I had to be careful not to fall down or to leak food, because it was their holiday meal. In return I got as much as they wanted to give me. Some ten or twenty groszy per pot. So I was always waiting for the Jewish Saturday, and for this Sabbath. I sometimes collected one złoty in this way—a worker at the sawmill had to work ten or twelve hours for this money. Sometimes when I vis-

*ited these families, Jewish women offered a piece of their special Sabbath bread to me.
They said: 'Here you are, take this.' And grandmother always asked me if I had fetched
her another piece of bread and I told her: 'here you have one, granny.' And I had money
for my exercise books, and my grandmother had money for flour. Because I went to
school. I was very happy because of that. Sometimes I saved money to buy shoes. If I
managed to save four złoty I had enough to buy high quality shoes, which I could wear
the whole year through.*

Informants did show their appreciation of the Jews for giving them an
opportunity to make a decent living. Taking into account the immediate
need of the Polish peasants, this appreciation is not surprising. To be offered
a job meant immediate relief from poverty. This fact at least partly explains
why especially those informants who once worked for the Jews—or whose
parents once worked for them—kept precious memories about the Jews.
Bronisław Z. (86), who had been working in the sawmill, claimed to have
been on good terms with the Jews, as did Daniel S. (82), who served as the
private carter of Abraham B. Rozalia B. (57), whose mother had been a servant at a Jewish home, spoke with affection about her mother's former
employer. And Jan S. (65) the *shabbes goy* loved to talk about his close Jewish friends. The accounts show that Polish employees profited from the
close relationship with their Jewish employers. In return for their trustwor-
thiness and diligence they received good salaries and were granted a number of privileges. That affection was also part of the relationship becomes
clear from the fact that all these informants claimed to have been 'favour-
ites' of 'their' Jews.[12] Bronisław Z. (86) was picked up by his Jewish
employer Isaac L. from Moszczaniec who used to pass his house on the way
to the sawmill 'because he liked me very much'. The mother of Rozalia B.
(57) was easily admitted into the midst of the Jewish family she served. The
Jewish mistress of the house taught her to cook delicious Jewish dishes and
gave her milk to drink and bread to eat during her work. Daniel S. (82) was
given wood by his employer: 'I always asked him how much I owed him, but
then he would wave with his hand and would tell me to leave.' In the same
interview, Daniel S. explained how he, and only he, was able to get a few
days off from work:

*I was an honest and good worker. Once I built a stable. In those days one did not pay
for work. And somebody helped me to build this stable. I did not pay him but worked
for him in return. So I asked Mister B. to give me a few days off, from being his
carter. Because there were still so many people for whom I had to work in return. So
I told him: 'Mister Owner', because we addressed him that way, 'why do you make it
so difficult for me?' Then Mister B. said to me: 'You work fast, slowly and well'. I
asked him: 'How should I understand this, working fast, slowly and well?' Because*

when I work precisely I work fast. And he said: 'When I don't have to improve your work, it is all right.'

And yet, despite all respect and deference shown by the Poles to the Jews of 'good substance' and 'good standing', even the Jewish benefactor and *balebos*[13] Abraham B. is said to have played tricks on Poles. It is told, for example, that on the eve of a severe winter the owner of the sawmill went to the Roman Catholic Church, much to the surprise of the Polish villagers. Why would a Jew enter the church if not for something very important? When a harsh winter approached the rumour spread that Abraham B. had been praying for a cold winter to boost the sale of his wood. While on the surface this story appears to be a typical example of peasant religious superstition, the message is clearly not a religious one: it tells about a rich Jew who does everything (even enter a church) to become richer by exploiting the poor Poles. Other stories about Abraham B. reveal a similar message, such as the one told by Józef L. (62). His grandparents lost their life-savings to the owner of the sawmill:

I will tell you an unpleasant story. There was a Jewish family called B. They were the co-owners of the sawmill about which I told you before. They had a contract with my grandmother and grandfather. Grandfather had returned from America and had brought some dollars with him. He wanted to build a house from that money. In the contract they agreed that Mister B. would build a house and then give the keys to my grandparents. My grandfather had been working in the mines. He had been working there under terrible conditions for almost three years. And then they had this money. But they could not write very well. Perhaps my grandfather could write a little, or my grandmother. I can't remember exactly, because my grandfather died before I was born. And in the contract it was stated that he [Mister B.] would build the house within one year and then hand over the keys. But after this contract had been signed, he [Mister B.] wrote an annex to it, which said that my grandparents would have to find a building lot within three months. At that time this place was crowded and on every lot stood a house [...] In any case, my grandparents did not find a place to move to. And maybe they did not even know about this annex. After three months, the deadline, Mister B. laughed at my grandparents. They never built a house and they [Jews] kept the money. In this way grandfather lost his life-savings. The building lot was not found in time, because where could they have lived? [...] They would have had to move out for one year, but there was no place to move to. It was a dirty trick. This Jewish family took the money and my grandparents became beggars. This is only one example of how these people abused the poor.

This account is a clear statement of the social inequality between the poor Polish peasants and the rich Jewish entrepreneurs. Later on in this interview Józef L. discusses another aspect of the relationship linking the

Polish employee with his Jewish employer. He recalls: 'If a man wanted to work in the sawmill, he brought hens or eggs for a couple of days, so that he would get a job. It was bribe. It was a bribe because otherwise he would not be engaged, and if he was not engaged then there was terrible poverty.' Indeed, as the owner of a factory Abraham B. could dispose freely of his peasant workers. Informants confirmed that Abraham B. 'had no special servants' but instead would recruit his workers from the sawmill: 'If he needed some helpers, he just ordered them to leave the sawmill and work on his fields. For example the one who sawed the boards, or the one who joined the boards with a wire. This work could wait.' The senior position of the Jews vis-à-vis the Poles who worked for them is also documented for the period at the turn of this century. In his memoirs father Moszkowicz, who had been serving the Roman Catholic parish of Jaśliska until after the First World War, referred to the 'undignified' practice of the Poles who worked for the Jews. In his eyes, the Jews were responsible for leaving the dirty jobs to the Catholic parishioners. On the confrontation between the Jewish town dwellers and the Russian soldiers in 1915, the first year of the First World War, father Moszkowicz recalls:

> I can't remember his name. It was a Kozak anyway, and he ordered the Jews to remove all dirtiness from the market square. It was just unbelievable: the sight of all these Jews taking their tools to the forest and the fields to bury the dead. And to see them working in the market square. As I heard, they also had to clean those places where before only Catholics had worked as the Jews' slaves. These are hard times for the Jews. But everyone who is lazy and does not feel like working is severely beaten (Moszkowicz n.d.: 40).

The social asymmetry was not just typical of the relationship between the Polish peasant workers and their Jewish employers. The Jewish community also became increasingly divided into the rich and the poor, dependants and independents, the powerful and the weak. Speaking in class terms, the poor Polish sectors were more likely to be on good terms with the poor Jews than with the rich. Accordingly, Józef L. (62) clearly distinguishes between the poor and the rich: 'The poor Jews treated the Poles all right and so did the Poles. But the rich Jews were not liked at all, because they abused the poor people too much, and the people were aware of this.' Presumably, this type of class-conscious thinking gained popularity among the peasant workers in Jaśliska with the advent of the Polish People's Republic.

Economic Competition

During the late nineteenth and early twentieth centuries attempts were made to break the link between the Jewish entrepreneurs and the Polish pcasants. Although driven by divergent interests, Austrian rulers, Jewish reformers, Polish politicians, and the rural clergy joined hands to eliminate the 'unproductive' Jewish element. Whereas Austrian rulers attempted to assimilate the largely 'ignorant' Orthodox Jewish masses, Jewish reformers demanded cultural, religious, and economic reform,[14] while leaders of Polish populist parties and the rural clergy called for the Jews' complete withdrawal from trade occupations (Mahler 1985; Golczewski 1986). Although these attempts also reached Jaśliska at a certain point, they never greatly altered the existing socio-economic relations in the small town.

The Bank of Mercy: Christian Money-Lending

Polish efforts to eliminate Jewish trade had two common features. First, private initiatives had a largely communal character. Second, all initiatives were initiated, or generously supported, by the local and national authorities and the Roman Catholic Church. In the course of the nineteenth century various institutions were established which offered alternatives to Jewish money-lending. By the end of the nineteenth century inhabitants from Jaśliska went to the Communal Bank for Orphans in Rymanów (18 km from Jaśliska) which managed the estate of the deceased parents on behalf of their under-aged children. In the same period a Savings and Loan Company (*Spółka Oszczędnościowo Pożyczkowa*) was established in Jaśliska, as well as the nationally launched institution of the *Kasa Stefczyka* (Orlik 1979: 40). At the turn of the twentieth century the national authorities introduced the rural cooperative plan associations, among them the Credit-Savings Company (*Towarzystwo Kredytowo-Oszczędnościowe*) in Jaśliska, which turned out to be the most powerful competitor of the Jewish money-lenders (Orlik 1979: 40; Mahler 1990).

These banking institutions were based largely on charitable and educational principles. This might explain why Jewish money-lending activities, unrestricted by any principle but the principle of profit, remained a powerful alternative to Christian endeavours. The failure of the Bank of Mercy, founded by the bishop of Przemyśl in 1838, may serve as an example. The Bank of Mercy aimed to support the poor Catholic peasants in the parish. Rules of lending and borrowing protected the well-being of the debtors: the debtor had to repay his debts within one year, one month, and two weeks; only personal properties were accepted as pawn; it was forbidden to fix an interest rate higher than 0.06 percent. In addition, every debtor had to pray for the health of the founder of the bank, while after the latter's death he had to pray for his soul, saying three times 'Our Father' and three times 'Lord Save Your Servant'. If a debt was not repaid within one year, the pawn would be sold at auction. In that case the debt would be repaid to the bank, while the remainder from the auction was returned to the legitimate owner (Orlik, private notes).

In the course of time, the book-keeping of the bank became increasingly cumbersome. Too often the debtors would not repay their debts, which meant that the bank could not fulfil its charitable duties. Successive priests, who were responsible for administering debts, increasingly tightened the regulations on borrowing and even demanded the bishop's permission to ask debtors to pawn their land. An official inspection of the bank in April 1870 showed its impaired functioning. It turned out that the local priest had terminated the long-term loans of some twenty-three Polish debtors. The debtors, who had been indebted to the bank for more than ten years, were summoned to repay their debts at once and in cash. In order to obtain the cash the debtors turned to Jewish money-lenders, after which they lost their land, house, property, and cattle to the Jews. When the Bank of Mercy failed commercially, Jewish money-lending took on increased significance, much to the despair of the local priests. In order to prevent Polish debtors from turning to the Jews, the community council decided to allow the debtors to borrow money using land as pawn, and to raise the interest rate to 4 percent, especially during spring when poverty was most severe (Orlik, private notes).

The Agricultural Circle: Christian Joint Ventures

The establishment of the Association of Agricultural Circles (*Towarzystwo Kółek Rolniczych*) in 1882 was a sign of the attempt to diminish rural poverty and reduce the peasants' dependence on Jewish commerce. The agricultural circle was the institution called into being by Polish populists who aimed at reforming the rural economy, and fought poverty by educating the Polish peasants and stimulating Polish entrepreneurship in the countryside (Golczewski 1986). In 1896 the rural cooperative movement operated 1,220 country stores which sold goods and agricultural implements, and bought up the agricultural products from the peasants. The activity of the 'circles', as they were generally called, was not limited to economic affairs. They launched a nationalist anti-Semitic propaganda campaign which aimed at the 'Polonization of trade' by boycotting the Jewish shopkeepers. Autonomous provincial administration in Galicia supported the agricultural circles by providing them with free subsidies and low interest credit rates (Mahler 1990: 130).

In 1892 the institution of the agricultural circle (*kółko rolnicze*) was introduced in Jaśliska. The institution, which combined both educational and economic goals, comprised a library, a dairy company, a construction company, a store, and a loan and savings office (Orlik 1979: 40). The circle paid dividends and, in this way, intended to save and distribute the peasants' capital. The local peasants, who held equal shares in the circle, received their share of the interest and profits made by the circle each year. The agricultural cooperative, set up to exclusively serve the economic interests of the Polish populace, cut into the business of local Jewish tradesmen in several ways. Firstly, the rural cooperative plan associations were powerful competitors with the Jewish money-lenders. Secondly, Poles were encouraged to buy at the store of the agricultural circle and boycott Jewish shops. Finally, the number of products which could be purchased and sold by Jews had been significantly curtailed by the state authorities. The National Council of Galicia (*Wydział Krajowy*) utilised the monopoly on the sale of salt to turn over the trade in this important commodity almost exclusively to non-Jewish stores. Purchase orders made by the administration were given to Poles only. In addition, Jewish storekeepers had to pay a higher income tax than their Polish competitors, while the sale of tobacco (a state monopoly), was systematically taken away from Jewish stores and given to Christians (Mahler 1990: 130).

Polish nationalism caused a constant pressure between Poles and Jews in Jaśliska during the interwar period. Especially in the last decade of the Second Polish Republic, there was a turn towards political and economic anti-Semitism. Jan S. (65) recalls this general change in national policies in the following manner:

> *Piłsudski had a Jewish mistress. So that is why the Jews took us by the nose. He [Piłsudski] would always toady to them [Jews]. When Śmigły-Rydz came to power Jews had to put prices on their products, and they were allowed to sell a certain percent of products only. So during the Piłsudski times one went to a shop and the Jew sold products for a price three times higher than the proper price. Then the customer bargained and the price went down until they agreed on a reasonable price. Later things changed. There was a price on every product, and the Pole gave the Jew what he owed him. For the Jew it was all the same. And there was order. They [Jews] did not swindle any longer.*

Some Polish residents took advantage of the anti-Jewish campaigns. As Józef K. (born in 1904) put it in an interview with two Polish students: 'In the 1930s Poles had four stores and one tavern on the market square and they would cooperate in order to subvert Jewish business.'[15] But even during the 1930s, the period of nationwide anti-Jewish campaigns and economic boycotts, the Poles' involvement in local trade remained limited. Table 4.2 summarises the types and numbers of stores and businesses run by Poles in the last decade before the Second World War. It appears that the official anti-Jewish propaganda had little effect on the activities and interactions of the Poles and Jews at the community level. Most of the time the Poles had no choice but to frequent the Jewish shops and did not follow the national attempts to boycott Jewish enterprise, as it was simply not in their interest. Eleonora B. (67), whose father was the owner of one of the circle's stores, recalled:

> *You know, before the war there was this slogan that said: 'Don't buy at the Jews'.[16] In spite of this, all people did their shopping at the Jews. Even the well-off [panowie] went there. In this town it was not that severe. People used to go shopping here and there. To give one example: the only textile shop was in Jaśliska, and this shop was run by a Jew. There was no hate. It was not like that. When the Jews sold tobacco in their shops they first took it from us.*

The agricultural circle was the institution that remained central to local Polish private enterprise in Jaśliska. Informants who told about the prewar economy in Jaśliska always referred to the agricultural circle as the one and only Polish store in town. Indeed, the few Polish shopkeepers who started a retail business did so under the aegis of the agricultural circle. Also the father of Eleonora B. (see excerpt above) made a second start by running the store of the circle after his own store had burned down. Eleonora B. (67), who as a teenager worked at her father's store, explained what products they sold. Interestingly, she also revealed that the products were sold on credit:

> *Everything, we sold everything, we had a wholesale firm of tobacco and all sixteen villages that belonged to our municipality took tobacco from us. And we sold bottled alcohol. We did not serve alcohol, but we sold vodka and spirits and the like in closed bottles. We sold all kinds of small things such as lamp oil, note books, and so on. We sold prepared meat and bread. This we sold until the front came in September 1939 [...] They [customers] took products from us and it was written down in a booklet. It was not like they do now. Today we buy and pay in ready cash. In those days we had a booklet, and one used to write down the things one took. Then, when the war started, everything was lost.*

Table 4.2 Approximate Number of Polish Stores and Businesses in Interwar Jaśliska

Type of store	Probable number of store type
agricultural circle	1
butcher	1
leather and leather products	1
grocery	1
ironmonger's	1
tavern	1
Total	**6**

Sources: interviews by the researcher (1993); interview by Halina Piasecka and Jan Stepek (1978); interview by Danuta Olbert and Maria Marciniak (1985); interview by Wojciech Salwa (1979).

With the elimination and deportation of the local Jewish population by the German occupants in 1942 (see Chapter seven), Polish entrepreneurship experienced a momentous growth. According to the informants, Germans anxiously supported Polish commercial enterprise because it was also profitable for them. Jędrzej P., (76) explains: 'The Germans had to have their trade started and we people had to live [...] After the Jews had been taken away, Jaśliska became the main shopping centre, because there were no longer shops in the villages.'[17] The wartime village Cooperative (*Społem*) was established in the town hall and had some forty to fifty share holders. The merchandise, transported from Rymanów (18 km from Jaśliska), Krosno (38 km), and even Sanok (80 km) by cart, consisted of rationed sugar, bread, vodka, sweets, and kerosene lamps which were exchanged for coupons. The Cooperative's main competitor was the Ukrainian Cooperative (*Spółdzielnia Ukraińska*) which had its store in the same building. In general the Ukrainians would buy products in the Ukrainian store, while the Poles would buy in the Polish store.

The same individuals who had run the *Społem* during the war years went on to organise the supply of food and industrial products after the war. On the urgency of local entrepreneurship Orlik (1979: 65-66) commented: 'The relatively large distance between Jaśliska and the nearest towns (Rymanów and Dukla), as well as the lack of proper means of transport, constituted a serious problem to the local inhabitants, who were not able to purchase even the most basic products. For that reason, the *Społem* store was opened in the local town hall immediately after the liberation.' On the rapid growth of Polish trade immediately following the end of the Second World War Jędrzej P. (76) commented: 'Time passed and there came more shops in Jaśliska [...] Banks were established, so we went to get credits from the bank, which enabled us to bring more products with us. Then real business started.' With joint power and joint capital a large residence was built in which the administration, a bakery, a butcher, a store with household products, and a mineral water factory were situated. Because of the lack of space, the greengrocer, as well as the shoe and cloth store, were established in private houses (Orlik 1979). The village Cooperative formed the basis of the Peasants' Self-Help Cooperative founded in 1947. However, the commercial principle of the Cooperative was disapproved of by the socialist authorities. The capital of the Cooperative was nationalised and the chief of the enterprise, Wojciech M. (78), was arrested and deported to the western regions of Poland. The practice of shared ownership and the annual distribution of dividends ceased to exist.

Hostile Dependency

As we have seen in the previous sections, the abolition of serfdom in 1848 did not free the Poles nor the Jews from the social restriction imposed on them. Though the Polish peasants and Jewish entrepreneurs were no longer subject to the landlords, the patterns of dependence, and to a lesser extent, the patterns of exploitation, remained unchanged. The inequality between the Jewish entrepreneurs and the Polish peasants was conspicuous in two ways. First, Jews had the means and skills to accumulate capital, and therefore to influence local politics, to control the property of the Polish peasants, and to command the Poles as their work force. Second, taking into account the Jews' strong position in the local cash economy and the Poles' dependence on non-farm resources, the Jews were able to manipulate the relatively poor and defenceless peasants. The Jewish usurer was held responsible for the poverty of the Polish peasants. Not only did he benefit from the peasant's misery, he was also said to deceive him and squeeze him dry.

Presumably, abuse of power did not corrupt all Polish-Jewish interactions. In fact, a profitable outcome of the transaction in favour of the Jewish contractor did not necessarily imply Jewish fraud. From the contractor's point of view, any deal entails a risk (a debtor may try to flee his debts), which he will take only if he expects to make a profit by it. From the Jewish perspective a bargain meant business, but for the Poles any profits made by Jews were Polish losses. The Polish accusation that Jews were malicious can be seen in the light of the Poles' traditional dependence on Jewish money-brokers. This (like any other) form of involuntary dependence typically gave rise to feelings of hostility and frustration. Though informants were fair enough to admit that Jews did not cause their poverty, they clearly felt that they were the victims of a system of economic exploitation. This feeling of powerlessness was expressed in the dramatic representations of the Poles as victims and the Jews as offenders. We have already discussed two such representations in this chapter and the previous one: the Jewish usurer and the Jewish arsonist.

Notwithstanding these notions, most informants pictured the relationship between the Poles and the Jews as an outcome of natural things. This notion included the certainty that ethnic identity entailed access to a specific means of production as well as adaptation to a specific lifestyle. The group-specific values and the statuses and roles associated with it were to a large extent complementary. On the community level this resulted in a strict division of labour. While the Jews were seen as skilful entrepreneurs and tradesmen, the Poles were considered to be handy farmers and craftsmen. In the capacity of peasants and entrepreneurs, Poles and Jews provided important goods and services for each other and occupied reciprocal and therefore different niches that were in close interdependence. In this natural order of things, the reluctance to adopt new forms of behaviour was real, which is illustrated by the minor involvement of the Poles in local commerce. Thus we see that Poles who had shops also had a farm or practised a craft, whereas Jewish farmers were always active in some sort of trade. In adapting to the 'natural' roles and statuses ascribed to their ethnicity, the Polish peasants and Jewish merchants were apt to take the line of least resistance, which among all possibilities was the most secure and most familiar.

Besides social constraints, a failing infrastructure may also explain the Poles' virtual absence from local and regional commerce. The minor involvement of the Poles in the local and regional market can be traced to the lack of a Polish trade network to realise an efficient supply and release of merchandise and information. A major advantage of the Jewish merchant was that he had access to such contacts and information, and that he, as a rule, knew his customers. The importance and the extent of the local Jewish networks is clear from the accounts of Jewish informants. First, through marriage ties Jews were able to activate a family network that reached far beyond the confines of the local community. This being the case, Jewish informants gave examples of how, in setting up one business or another (in or outside of Jaśliska), mostly relatives were consulted or implicated. Second, generations of experience and involvement in trade laid the basis for numerous contacts in the professions and with the main trading centres. This explains the large number of Jewish companies specialised in the exploitation of local forests and that were run by local Jews with expert contacts outside the region (in Cracow) and even outside the country (in Slovakia).[18]

In addition to the minority status of the Poles in a predominantly Lemko area, the Poles had a hard time establishing an alternative Polish trade network, despite the support by the Roman Catholic Church and the Polish national authorities (after 1918). Only with the outbreak of the Second World War, that is, after the complete overthrow of the existing social structure, demography, and power relations, did the Polish villagers succeed in setting up the networks for a thriving commercial enterprise. But even then, local private initiative was soon stifled by the interference of the communist authorities. The Polish alternative to Jewish commercial activity was the establishment of a strictly Polish (and Christian) joint venture in the late nineteenth century. The principle propagated by this cooperative movement (to organise a joint venture for the benefit of the entire peasant community) was never entirely abandoned.[19] Since the collapse of the socialist regime in 1989, the Polish villagers have started exploring the advantages and restrictions of the 'free' capitalist market again.

Within this set of dependency relations, the Jew is not necessarily pictured as a profiteer and usurer, but also as someone with more luck and, for that matter, endowed with better brains. Yet another version pictures the Jew as a benevolent, responsive person taking a risk and lending support at his own expense. Indeed, many informants showed their admiration for the qualities which they ascribed to the Jews: learning, persistency, ingenuity, and last but not least devotion towards their coreligionists. A proverb stressing the ingenuity of the Jews says that people should 'love each other like brothers but count like Jews'. Or as an informant (23) put it, 'it is better to engage in ten grams of trading than in one kilogram of work.' On Jewish cohesion an informant (65) commented, 'they helped each other very much and they should be praised for that.' All these qualities, the informants claimed, contributed to the Jews' success in business, as well as to their swift integration in the town's community. Hence, besides his representation of the evil spirit, the Jew set an ideal example for the Polish anti-hero or *shlimazl*.[20]

Notes

1. During the first decades of the twentieth century markets were still held in Jaśliska, though less frequently than had been customary during the nineteenth century. The traditional monthly fairs (lasting three days) were held only twice a year. During the inter-war years the practice was abandoned altogether since fairs no longer attracted enough people to have 'good business'.

2. The picture of Jewish enterprise in Jaśliska that is provided by the Polish informants is confirmed by the family histories of the Jewish informants. To give a few examples, the father of Samuel, Jacob and David O. worked as a shopkeeper until bankruptcy. Thereafter the father started working as a timber-cutter. The father of Morty L. (72) worked in the lumber business, while the father of Josko S. (75) was the owner of a mercery store.

3. Mahler (1990) convincingly argues that Jewish emigration from Galician was inspired chiefly by economic reasons. In contrast to Russia, where pogroms and legal restrictions, in addition to poverty, were the main factors in stimulating Jewish mass emigration, Jewish emigration from Galicia was entirely motivated by the economic depression in the country, which affected both Jews and non-Jews.

4. Informants used different terms to denote this specific minority group in the region, calling them Ukrainians (*Ukraińcy*), Lemkos (*Łemkowie*), or Rusyns (*Rusnacy* or *Rusini*). See the notes to Chapter two for an explanation of the usage of the terms Lemko and Rusyn in the present text.

5. A precedent of this image had been propagated by the Galician *Union of the Polish Peasant Party* in the late nineteenth century, namely the idea that Jews owned fabulous riches. The name of Rothschild stood as a clear example of a mysterious Jewish financial empire, and it was calculated that if only a part of Rothschild's money were divided among the Jews of Galicia it would have made each of them an incredibly rich person (Golczewski 1986). This picture is followed by the prophecy that the Jews would one day buy up the whole of Galicia and tell the Poles: 'Take your priests and churches and get off, this is not your country!' (quoted in Golczewski 1986: 101).

6. 'Nasze kamienice a wasze ulice' (see also Kaufman 1997).

7. 'Jak bieda to do żyda.'

8. The story of the bankruptcy is confirmed by Orlik (1979) and a number of informants.

9. On the alleged solidarity of the Jewish community see also Chapter five.

10. Unlike Abraham B., Isaac L. was not a resident of Jaśliska but lived in Moszczaniec (14 km from Jaśliska). A third sawmill was owned by a Pole called 'Słoczek'. The latter is said to have purchased the sawmill from Abraham B. For unclear reasons informants did not refer to Słoczek as an employer.

11. Jewish involvement in local politics can be traced back to at least 1879. Town records of this year mention the election of four prominent Jews to the community council of Jaśliska, among them the brothers Mozes and Shulim S., Leib B., and Samuel L. (Gmina 1858-1880).

12. This claim also worked the other way around. The Jewish informant David O. (73) said he had been the 'favourite' kid of Pan Sidor who administered the episcopal lands and owned a large number of horses. *Pan* Sidor gladly lent his horses to David O. who needed them for his smuggling expeditions to Slovakia.

13. Yiddish for a man of good substance and good standing. Zborowski and Herzog (1962) give an interesting account of the social hierarchy within the Jewish community which is reflected in the allocation of seats in the House of Prayer. The men who sit along the Eastern Wall, the *mizrakh*, are the honourable citizens of the community, among them the

rabbi and the learned. Those sitting near the Western wall are the most ignorant. The *mizrakh* are known by a variety of names, all referring to their pre-eminent position in the community. They may be called *pney*, the faces of the community; *fayneh yidn*, the fine Jews; the *eydeleh*, the noble; the *erlikheh*, the honest and the pious. Among them are also the *balebatisheh*, the men of good substance and good standing (Zborowski and Herzog 1962: 73).

14. It was the Jewish reformers (*Maskilim*), rather than Gentile conservatives, who proved to be most persistent in their call for radical measures to enlighten the 'obscure' Orthodox Jewish masses (*Hasidim*). The Maskilim (adherents of the Jewish enlightenment) demanded the reform of the Orthodox Jewish masses and sought to increase their productivity. In 'Teyater fun Khsidim' Leybele the Maskil admonishes the Hasidim in an exemplary way: 'The gentile works bitter and hard/ For all his pain/ the Jew comes by/ and steals his gain' (quoted in Mahler 1985: 17).

15. Interview by Halina Piasecka and Jan Stepek, 1978 (Jaśliska).

16. 'Nie kupuj od żyda'.

17. It should be noted that all village shops had been owned by Jews.

18. There are indications that Abraham B. and his partner Isaac L. combined the exploitation of local forests with a number of other, more or less related, activities (such as construction work). The real estate registers mention the parent company 'L. and Company' (registered in 1916 in Kraków), suggesting that the two partners in business covered a broad network which exceeded the local territory and local contacts.

19. Between 1939 and 1944 Polish entrepreneurship was organised in the form of a Cooperative (*Spolem*). In the years between 1947 and 1948 a number of stores were founded under the aegis of the Peasants' Self-Help Cooperative (*Samopomoc Chłopska*), while after the political crisis of 1956 the institution of the agricultural circle (*Spółdzielnia Kółek Rolniczych*) was revived and became charged with supplying capital goods and services to the peasant sector (Orlik 1979; Hann 1985).

20. Yiddish for an ill-fated person.

SPHERES OF INTERACTION

The Social Boundary and the Image of the Jew

They all marched past the eyes of Marcin, the grandparents, the parents, the children. He knew them all by name. And he knew them all in person. There is the old rabbi, and at the home of rabbi Segal, Marcin was quite one of the family. He brought water several times a day, cut the wood, and each Saturday he ate Sabbath bread with fish in the rabbi's kitchen. And who could measure himself with Marcin on the morning of Passover when the rebbe asked him to enter the rabbinical court? The rebbe, the judge, and the sexton waited for him. The rebbe spoke Yiddish and Marcin understood every single word. The leavened bread from all over the town was sold to him, even the bread which the Jews from Melawe had not yet brought to the rebbe but which they did not trust. And he, Marcin, bought the leavened bread and paid in cash. And when he left with his purchased 'wealth' he would bend before the court and speak in Yiddish: 'A kosher and happy Pesach wishes you Marcin, the *shabbes goy*.' The face of the old Marcin cleared up with joy, his eyes brightened and his lips muttered Yiddish words that he had not heard in years (Opatoshu 1951: 313).

Introduction

*A*t the turn of the twentieth century increased social mobility accelerated economic, religious, and political differences within the Jewish community at large, which in turn resulted in wider Jewish participation in public life. It is difficult to assess to what extent these processes also affected the Jewish community in Jaśliska. Except for the accounts by Polish informants who had little insight into Jewish affairs, and a small number of accounts by Jewish informants who had not visited their home town since their departure in the 1940s, there is little material to document this highly interesting period. What we do know is that until the Shoah most, if not all, members of the Jaśliska Jewish community were Hasidim, adherents of a Jewish pietist and revivalist movement (Litwak 1969; Yad Vashem 1984; Olszański 1991). The Hasidic culture significantly influenced the social, cultural and economic outlook of the Jewish community, and for that matter, also affected the relationship between Poles and Jews.

Strangers at Home: The Mystical World of Poland's Jews in Exile

The rise of Hasidic reign in Galicia

Hasidism was founded in the first half of the eighteenth century by Israel ben Eliezer, who for his mystical teachings earned the title of Ba'al Shem Tov (Master of the Good Name). The Hasidic movement started as a reaction to oppressive institutional Judaism, to the frequent persecutions, and to the deteriorating economic conditions of Eastern European Jewry.[1] From the very beginning of Hasidism, the ordinary, unlettered man played a central role in the ideology and practice of the movement.[2] Hasidism was spread, to paraphrase Weinryb (1972: 282), by the *lumpen intelligentsia* of itinerant preachers, jobless rabbis, and ritual slaughterers, while its adherents were largely drawn from the masses of village Jews, petty traders, tavern-keepers, lessees and other sections of the mostly poor and illiterate Jewish middle class. Also Mahler (1985) stresses the petty bourgeois character of the movement, whose members occupied the lower level of the social hierarchy vis-à-vis the Talmudists and the merchant class. But Mahler adds that also prosperous elements from the feudal sphere joined the ranks of the Hasidic movement: the wealthy innkeepers, tax lessees, and the brokers at the courts of the nobility. From poor to rich, these social elements had in common that they depended on the feudal economy within both the local community and the province at large (1985: 10).

By the beginning of the nineteenth century Hasidism was transformed from a subordinate religious movement, that was banned by the Orthodox religious establishment and was strongly opposed by its ideological opponents within Jewish Orthodoxy (the so called *Mitnaggedim*), into the reigning faith of the majority of Polish Jewry. Mahler (1985) explains the rapid ascendancy of Hasidism in Galicia as the outcome of two processes: the severe oppression of the Galician Jewry by the Austrian government, and the consolidation of conservative religious forces in the face of the Jewish enlightenment (*Haskalah*).

The Hasidim responded to the oppressive policies of the Austrian government by emphasising solidarity, charity, and benevolence among themselves and the rest of the Jewish community, and by offering a form of organised passive resistance. As Mahler (1985: 18) puts it, the 'healthy social instinct of self-help and self-defence' thrust the Hasidic masses closer together and 'strengthened mutual assistance and unified resistance to the oppressive measures of the government'. Examples of such unified resistance are the violation of the governmental prohibition of the sale of liquor in the villages by cooperating with the landowners from whom the Hasidim had rented the taverns; the evasion of excessive wedding taxes by dispensing with the civil regulations and only undergoing the religious wedding ceremony; the withdrawal from military service by furnishing incorrect birth dates or, if possible, by neglecting altogether to register sons; the strong and organised resistance to the candle and kosher meat tax by producing and selling meat and candles illegally, or by imposing rabbinical bans against Jewish taxes and the tax lessees (Mahler 1985: 21-23).

Just as the Hasidim succeeded in winning over the greater part of the Galician Jewry by their solidarity and their clandestine struggle against the oppressive decrees of the Austrian government, so Hasidism 'eventually became a conservative force that carried with it the Jewish middle class because of its defence of religion and tradition against the attacks of the Haskalah' (Mahler 1985: 24). Non-Hasidic Orthodoxy, Mahler explains, discerned in the Jewish enlightenment a greater danger to the Jewish religion and to its own hegemony than in Hasidism, and therefore its struggles against Hasidism gradually gave way to the struggle against the modernisation of Jewish life. However, the gradual process of domination of Jewish religious and communal life by the Hasidim was by no means without conflict. The new Hasidic leaders or *zaddikim* established powerful dynasties, accumulated great wealth, and exercised enormous influence over their court followers at the cost of the influence of the sitting Orthodox rabbis. Indeed, the *zaddikim* attained such a position of power that opposing rabbis were forced out of the community (Mahler 1985: 25). Through their unity, the Hasidim succeeded to place their adherents in the positions of ritual slaughterers (*shohatim*), ritual circumcisers (*mohalin*), and other positions of influence (Mahler 1985: 25). By the second half of the nineteenth century the process of blending with rabbinism had reached such a stage that most Hasidic leaders also occupied rabbinical posts in the local administration of their communities (*kehillot*) (Mahler 1985: 29).

The Hasidic Community in Jaśliska

As in all other provinces in Galicia, also in the Sanok province the Hasidim were strongly represented, they even had their own *zaddikim* in the person of Rebbe Hersh 'the attendant' in Rymanów (18 km from Jaśliska) and Rebbe Hersh Meylekh N. in Dynów (80 km) (Mahler 1985: 101). The differences between these two Hasidic leaders in terms of their teachings, social attitude, and personal character, reflected the struggle between old and new notions of the social role of the Hasidic leader. This struggle began in the early nineteenth century, when the wealth of the Hasidic leaders rapidly increased, and when a number of rebbes gave up living a simple, ascetic life and instead exploited their position in order to gain more wealth and live in luxury. The lavish life-style of some Hasidic leaders, in particular of those affiliated to the Rebbe of Ruzhin and his Sadagura dynasty in Galicia and Bukovina, was reason for the Rebbe of Tsands (Nowy Sącz), Joseph Hayyim Halberstam, to start a struggle against the excesses of the Sadagura dynasty (Mahler 1985). This struggle, which broke out in 1868, caused the split of the Hasidic community into two opposing factions: the Hasidim of Tsands and the Hasidim of Sadagura.

The political and ideological split in the overall Hasidic community also had its impact on the Hasidic community in Jaśliska. As a result of the split Jaśliska had two houses of prayer: one belonging to the Hasidim of Tsands (who formed the majority in Jaśliska), and one belonging to the Hasidim of Sadagura (Litwak 1969). The event is also remembered by a number of Polish informants, who recalled that the Jews in Jaśliska 'split up somehow' and proceeded to build a new House of Prayer. Despite the division of the Hasidic community into two opposing factions, informants did not recall any serious collisions. Polish informants stressed the unity and solidarity among the members of the Hasidic community to whom they invariably referred as 'Hasidim' (*Hasydzi*).[3] From the accounts of the Jewish informants it becomes clear that the political and ideological split lost significance over the years. In a testimony, the former Jewish resident of Jaśliska Israel B. recalled that while in the beginning Jaśliska had two ritual slaughterers, during the interwar years it had only one. Israel B. and Josko S. (75) both confirmed that during the interwar years Jaśliska had only one ritual bath and one Hasidic rabbi.[4]

The predominant Hasidic character of the Jewish community in Jaśliska remained fairly unchanged until the outbreak of the Second World War. Still, there are signs that even the conservative Hasidic community in Jaśliska was affected by the overall secularisation in the Polish society at large. In the absence of local Jewish political parties or youth associations, the Jewish youth sought alternative ways to remain informed about the outside world. Two Jewish informants claimed to have been part of a network in which revolutionary (that is, secular) books were being circulated. As teenagers they felt attracted by the revolutionary ideologies of that particular era, of course much to the grief of their parents. Another impetus for change was the compulsory military service. In those days the army did not provide facilities for Jewish soldiers to live according to Jewish customs, which was the reason that in Hasidic circles military service was considered tantamount to forced conversion. Nevertheless, a number of young Jewish males from Jaśliska went through the experience of temporary internment and had to make sense of this experience somehow. Also Polish informants observed that the Orthodox Jewish community became less inhibited to 'modern ways of life'. Wojciech M. (78) explained the difference between the sons and daughters of Abraham B. (owner of the local sawmill) and their Jewish peers:

> *Those two Jewish girls emancipated themselves. They no longer wanted to live according to the Orthodox laws. Also his son emancipated himself. [...] His daughters had a lot of money and they made an effort to adopt the new cosmopolitan lifestyle. They were not dressed in these... they looked fine. They were not living according to the Orthodox Jewish laws. Because he who is rich has the means to change.*

Viewing the Other: Jewish and Gentile Reasoning

The views of the Hasidim about Jews and Gentiles were a direct outcome of what Mahler (1985: 16) calls the 'Weltanschauung of the Cabbalah'.[5] In this view the Jewish people were not simply the chosen, but were the only people of God: 'Israel and the Torah and the Holy one, blessed be He, are one' (quoted in Mahler 1985: 16). According to the *Midrash*,[6] the whole world was created only for the sake of the Jews. The Jews are dispersed in order to gather together the holy sparks that are scattered over the earth. Consequently, feelings of social involvement did not reach beyond their own people (Mahler 1985).

The positive expression of this attitude was the principle of unconditional solidarity of the Jews and the idea of love of the Jewish people, which became a main theme in the stories and legends of the prominent Hasidic rebbes in the first half of the nineteenth century. At the same time, an unavoidable consequence of this position was a negative attitude toward the 'lesser' Gentiles, who were viewed with suspicion and held in contempt. As Rebbe Mendel of Rymanów (predecessor of the earlier mentioned Rebbe Hersh) put it, 'A Gentile does not have a heart, although he has an organ that resembles the heart' (quoted in Mahler 1985: 17). The symbol for the Gentile in the consciousness of the Hasidim was the brutal landowner or the enslaved boorish peasant. But in practice the Hasidim related to the peasants with a certain sympathy. This is confirmed in the Jewish, Ukrainian, and Polish legends about the Ba'al Shem Tov and in the stories about other Hasidic rebbes, in which the peasant would sometimes come to a rebbe for help (Mahler 1985).

Polish informants observed the Jews leading a highly 'exotic', 'introverted', and strictly separate social life, to which the Poles had no access and about which they were mainly ignorant. On Sabbath, for example, informants watched the Jews marking off their houses by a symbolic 'fence' (*eyruv*). About this fence Jan S. (65) recalled: 'They [Jews] had a rope from house to house and they were not allowed to pass this rope during Sabbath. This was only one of their commandments. One was not allowed to pass this rope. The houses were joined by this rope, like today they are by a telephone wire.' The rope, which stretched around a group of houses under the supervision of the rabbi, symbolised a demarcation line between the public and the private domain. In the public domain it was forbidden to carry ritual objects such as a prayer shawl (*talis*) or a prayer book. In the private domain it was permitted to carry these objects, although it was safer not to carry them in case the 'fence' was broken (Zborowski and Herzog 1962: 50).

To the informants, the demarcation line between public and private was one of the many examples in which Jews turned their back on the profane world. Jews, an informant (72) concluded, had a fine sense of status and their sense of superiority would show when dealing with each other: 'It was impossible to speak directly to the rabbi. There had to be an interpreter. So he had to speak to the interpreter and the latter would speak to the rabbi, and than back again. Like a triangle. Because he [the rabbi] was an important man.' Because of the strict boundary between public and private, sacred and profane, and especially, between the Jewish and gentile world, Polish townspeople rarely participated in Jewish celebrations or family life. Nor did Jews participate in festivals or fraternities organised by Poles. The local Hunters Club and Soccer Club, for example, by the nature of their activities, did not attract a single Jewish member. Despite limited interaction in the social and cultural spheres, the informants' accounts of Jewish festivals, rituals and dietary laws were numerous. For that matter, informants relied on both observation and hearsay. Where observations supplied informants with facts, hearsay provided the informants with an explanatory backing. Hearsay sometimes wholly replaced the eyewitness account, as it did for Andrzej F. (72) who found himself elaborately relating the Jewish burial ceremony—the collective mourning of the deceased, the saving of money for the relatives of the deceased, the washing of the dead, and finally the burial of the dead in the sitting position—without ever having witnessed a burial, for 'it was none of my business'.

Hearsay, of course, is supplied by the elderly people who had witnessed the 'Jewish times' and had observed the Jews living through the year according to the Judaic calendar. However, even these elderly people only observed the outward expressions of Jewish life in the small town. Especially the weekly Sabbath, and the annual festivals such as Passover (*Wielkanoc*), Tabernacles (*Kuczki*), New Year (*Trąpki*), the Day of Atonement (*Sądny Dzień*), and the Festival of Lots (*Haman*), have been subject to curious inspection and are thus mentioned by all—including the young informants. It must be noted that most of these Jewish festivals, including private celebrations such as wedding parties, took place outside the homes of the Jews or had other salient traits, and therefore were publicly noticeable.

In like manner, informants watched Jewish males walking to their House of Prayer on Fridays and Saturdays wearing black caftans, black hats, skullcaps (*szabasówki*), and prayer shawls. They watched the Jews being escorted by their wives, who wore wigs and were decked out with jewellery. They also observed the absence of their Jewish friends in school. The Poles' position as the observers of a people about whose culture they were ignorant gave rise to manifold stories based on the informants' own cultural frame of reference. This predominantly Catholic frame of reference views the Jew with a sceptical eye and contrasts the Jew's behaviour with Catholic values and customs. The peasant, therefore, attempts to explain Jewish customs in his own terms, and to interpret Jewish customs as basically divergent from Catholicism. The Polish informants, for example, concluded that the Jews celebrated Sunday, but that they did so on Fridays and Saturdays.

When Two Worlds Meet: Cross-Cultural Contact and Its Limitations

Evidence of Social Contact

Dense communal infrastructure, strong social cohesion, and an exclusivist attitude toward the outside world resulted in a strict division between Jews (*yidn*) and Gentiles (*goyim*). Among other things, it limited Polish-Jewish contact on the level of both immediate communication and administration. The Hasidic community ran its own affairs through the Jewish administrative body of the *kahal*,[7] which took care of the Jewish executive affairs, the Jewish school (*kheyder*), and the Jewish cemetery (*kirkut*). Marriages, charity, and controversies were also settled by the *kahal*, while many other aspects of social and family life were regulated according to the rules of the *Talmud* (the writings that make up Jewish religious and civil law), the *Torah*, and the rabbinate. Polish informants knew little about Jewish organisational life. Still, most of them seemed aware of the fact that the Jews kept their own administration. Jan S. (65), for example, referred to the former Jewish mayor (*wójt*) Jakób D. as the one who was responsible for Jewish communal affairs. Wojciech M. (78) explained: 'In Jaśliska they [Jews] had the so-called *kahal*. There was the rabbi, who was the main chief of the *kahal*, and they had some more representatives.'

Notwithstanding the strictly separated social life, certain forms of contact between Poles and Jews always existed, at different levels and in different forms. The Jews participated in local politics and were elected to the Polish community council already in the 1870s. After the First World War Jews went to the local primary school and made friends with their Polish schoolmates. The manifold stories, especially those told by the informants who were still children at the outbreak of the Second World War, show that social contacts between Poles and Jews were widespread and real.

The children especially would move freely, regardless of the firm social boundary which regulated interactions between Poles and Jews. First and foremost, Polish and Jewish children were much more likely to meet informally than were Polish and Jewish adults. During the interbellum period all children went to the same primary school, visited each other's homes, did homework together, and even became good friends.[8] Informants recalled that their Jewish friends were extremely quick at figures. Many times the latter would help them out or do their homework. Informants also recalled their Jewish friends visiting them on Sunday to get to know their homework which they had missed the day before, since Saturday was the sabbath for the Jews. In addition, children were more easily admitted to Jewish social and family life than were adults. This might explain why it was mainly the children who served as shabbes goyim, and who in turn became experts on Jewish affairs. Finally, thanks to their age, children were able to disregard the norms of what was socially accepted without taking a serious risk.

Thus we see that it was the children who were caught in love affairs and who gave expression to the social tensions between the ethnic communities by teasing and attacking 'the other side'. The Polish repertoire of 'Jew teasing', entailed, among others, putting excrement on the skullcaps of Jews; ringing bells when Jews passed with a coffin (so that the mourning crowd had to stop every few seconds); overturning outdoor toilets in which a Jew was sitting, and pulling the earlocks (*peyes*) of Jewish boys. The interaction between Polish and Jewish children, including attempts at provocation and mischief, might very well have stimulated a certain degree of social exchange between both communities, or otherwise have pacified Polish-

Jewish relations. An informant (54) put it this way:' Look at me! A Jewish woman carried me when I was still a baby!'

Though on a much lesser scale, at times Polish and Jewish adults would socialise too. It is said that during certain Jewish festivals and wedding parties, joy among the Jews was so great that they invited the 'elite' members of the Polish community as well as their 'closest' Polish neighbours to share the pleasures and the food with them. Andrzej J. (76) recalled the Jews celebrating the Festival of Lots (*Purim*), a one-day carnival celebrating Esther's rescue of the Jews from the villainous Haman:

> *During the summer, Jews organised dancing on the fields, which they first decorated with firewood. They put the wood on the ground and danced on it. This holiday was called Haman. They used to offer food and delicacies to the police, border guard, their neighbours and the mayor. They took this food to these houses. Also during wedding parties they invited some Poles, my uncle and father among them.*

Likewise, the Jews witnessed the Poles' activities, or in one way or another became involved in Polish affairs. Wieczysław W. (28), for example, mentioned that 'before the war' Poles went to Jews for advice. If, for instance, three candidates would beg for the hand of their daughter, parents would instantly go to a Jew to ask him which candidate was most suitable, because 'Jews knew the neighbourhood and the people living in it the best.' Moreover, members of the Polish Shooting Club used to meet in a house which they rented from a Jew. Jędrzej P. (78) explained how one day the Polish shooters disturbed the peace of the Jewish house owner:

> *I will tell you an anecdote. There was Willner O., he used to sell wine. This Jew had a tavern at the place where now this stone building stands. Opposite this building he had a wooden house where he had his shop. This shop had two rooms and one of them he rented to our Shooting Club. He had shelves on the wall, and a thin old wall connected one room with the other. There were ten of us and we met in that room. We had a radio on and one of us kicked at the wall. On the other side, everything fell down from the shelves. And he [Willner O.] went outside and shouted: 'Whose shooters are you! What are you doing in my house!' Well, we were boys, and we had a lot of energy.*

Another proof of lively social contact is that both sides made efforts to overcome the linguistic gap that existed between the ethnic communities. The Poles spoke Polish and the Jews spoke Yiddish among themselves, but this did not seem to hinder the villagers in their contact.[9] As a minority, the Jews had a special interest in speaking the language of their Polish neighbours. It is unclear to what extent Jews used the Polish language during the Austrian period (education was not compulsory and the official language was German), but it is safe to assume that Polish had been the second language for most of the Jews.[10] This was certainly the case in the years after Poland regained its sovereignty, when every Jewish child had to attend public school and had to learn reading and writing in Polish.[11] The school registers (1934-1939) show that Jewish pupils had difficulties with writing in Polish, which is illustrated by their lower marks for this subject at the end of every school term. Polish informants, however, claimed that their Jewish school friends had no difficulties with speaking Polish.

Though to a lesser extent, Poles had some knowledge of Yiddish. Although they were out of practice for over fifty years, some older informants still remembered a few Yiddish words or even whole sentences. One informant was able to write his name with Hebrew characters. Needless to say, all informants were proud to display their knowledge of Yiddish. In addition, it is said that father Rąpała, the late priest of Jaśliska, was a fluent Yiddish speaker. Among the Polish as well as the Jewish informants, father Rąpała was known to have been on good terms with the Jews. Polish informants mentioned the amicable conversations of the priest with local Jewish residents. The Jewish informant Josko S. (75), for instance, recalled the evening walks of his father with the priest. While walking, both men would discuss all kinds of subjects. Harmonious contacts between the 'learned' priest and 'lay' Jews were customary in other towns and villages in the region as well. Pearl O. (82), recalled the long walks and discussions of her father with the priest.[12] She also remembered the weekly meetings at her parents' home, to which all members of the village elite were invited, among them the priest and teachers of the local primary school.

Hierarchies of Social Contact

Any discussion on the relationship between Poles and Jews in Jaśliska should take into account the existence of another ethnic group in the area, namely the predominantly Greek Catholic Lemkos.[13] Table 5.1 gives a clear picture of the ethnic composition of the population in the area during the interwar years. The figures show that Jaśliska had the largest Roman Catholic (that is, Polish) and Mosaic (that is, Jewish) communities in the municipality. Posada Jaśliska was ethnically mixed, while all other communities had a Greek Catholic (that is, Lemko) majority. On the whole, the Greek Catholics made up 73 percent of the total population, followed by 21 percent Roman Catholics, and 6 percent Jews. Poles and Jews alike had to find a way to cope with this predominantly Lemko environment.

In fact, Polish informants made a clear distinction between Jews, residents of the town, and Lemkos, residents of the surrounding villages. While

Jews were regarded as civilised people, Lemkos were sometimes seen as primitive. The difference in mentality is often illustrated with the example that wedding parties among the Lemkos would always end up with fights, or as an informant put it, 'when there was no fight on a wedding party this party was no good.' Daniel S. (82) recalled the 'weird' Lemko practice of letting their house burn to the ground if it caught fire: 'if a house was burning, a naked woman would run around the house while the house was in flames. This really helps, doesn't it? […] It was superstition.'

Table 5.1   Population of the Jaśliska Municipality (1921) according to Religion

Village	Roman Catholic	Greek Catholic	Mosaic Faith	Total
Jaśliska	642	10	224	876
Czeremcha	0	354	10	364
Daliowa	70	476	24	570
Darów	0	233	11	244
Jasiel	2	284	3	289
Lipowiec	7	562	3	572
Moszczaniec	12	418	7	437
Polany Surowiczne	0	569	14	583
Posada Jaśliska	598	235	55	888
Rudawka Jaśliska	0	113	0	113
Surowica	3	431	19	453
Wola Wyżna	0	291	0	291
Wola Niżna	2	525	5	532
Total	**1336**	**4501**	**375**	**6212**

Sources: Główny Urząd Statystyczny (1924: table 23).

The spatial segregation of the above mentioned ethnic communities had an impact on both the frequency and quality of interethnic interactions. While Poles and Jews lived in the same town and interacted on a daily basis, interactions between Poles and Lemkos were less frequent. Still, informants mentioned that Polish craftsmen, such as shoemakers, carpenters, and coopers sold their products in Lemko villages, while Lemko farmers sold wool and flax to the Polish peasants (whose wives wove clothes from it). In addition, it is said that Lemkos were regular customers at the Jewish and Polish shops. Andrzej F. (72), whose father had been working as a carpenter in Lemko villages, pointed to the spatial factor in the Polish-Jewish and Polish-Lemko relations:

> *Everyday I met with the Jews. Because we went there to buy things. There were some twenty to twenty-five shops. One time we were buying in one shop, the second time in*

another. One had these products while the other had others. They also came and bought
milk from us. And they bought eggs, milk, and hens. And we went to them to buy things.
Or to sell a cow. We were living together like one family. With these Lemkos and
Ukrainians we did not live that way, because Lemkos and Ukrainians were not allowed
to settle in Jaśliska. So some of them lived alongside the roads and in the fields. One
[Polish craftsmen] used to go to the [Lemko] villages for work, in order to earn money.
Because most Ukrainians were not craftsmen. But we lived with Jews every day.

And yet, since cultural differences between the Poles and the Lemkos were
less pronounced (they both were raised in the Christian tradition), intermarriages occurred regularly, especially in the villages where Poles lived
along with Lemkos. In Jaśliska, however, intermarriages between Poles and
Lemkos were rare. Informants gave two reasons for this. First, there was the
historical regulation which forbade Lemkos from settling in the small town.
This pattern of settlement did not change after the restriction had been
lifted, which was the reason that Poles and Lemkos had few opportunities to
meet. Second, it is said that the Greek Catholic priests refused to conduct
marriages between Poles and Lemkos in the Greek Catholic Church
(*cerkiew*). Here again, according to the informants, it was the Lemkos who
prevented the Poles from maintaining close contacts with them.[14] However,
although in practice marriages between Lemkos and Poles from Jaśliska
were rare, in theory such marriages were possible. For most of the neighbouring villages intermarriage between Lemkos and Poles was common-
place. Paweł N. (63) put it this way: 'A Pole would marry a Lemko woman
and a Polish woman would marry a Lemko. All these families were connected with each other in one way or another.'[15]

Love affairs between Poles and Jews, on the other hand, were rarely confirmed with a marriage.[16] Precisely because the ban on Polish-Jewish love
affairs was strictly observed, it strongly appealed to the imagination of many
Polish informants. All Polish informants stressed the Jews' dislike of maintaining intimate contacts with the Poles, and told about numerous attempts of
'the older Jews' to prevent their sons and daughters from having dealings with
the Poles, or as one informant put it, 'the old Jews did not want to let it happen.' The Jews had good reasons to prevent the young from having intimate
contacts with Poles. Marrying the other side meant breaking with one's own
religion and community and adopting the religion and lifestyle of the other
side. Indeed, the family of the Jewish party would not accept a Polish lover.
Only after his or her conversion to Christianity would he or she be granted
access to the Polish community. Intermarriage, therefore, in most cases
implied conversion, an act which was strongly rejected by Orthodox Jewry.
Not only did the Orthodox Jews reject conversion from Judaism to Chris-

tianity, they were also unlikely to accept a non-Jew as a new member to their community. On the Jews' reluctance to embrace Christian converts Zborowski and Herzog (1962: 153-154) comment:

> Basic to the shtetl view of itself is the acceptance of itself as a minority, not by accident but by divine intention. The Chosen People are few among the hordes of unbelievers, and this is as God willed it to be. It is not their function to proselytise until all men accept the Truth, but merely to carry their own torch and their own burden, to fulfil God's commandments until in His time Messiah shall come. There is no attempt, therefore, to convert others to Judaism. On the contrary, it is the duty of the rabbi to warn any potential convert against assuming so heavy a yoke and to discourage him if possible from joining the ranks of the persecuted.

The endogamous lifestyle of the Jews (in contrast to the exogamous lifestyle of the Poles) confirmed the social gap that existed between the two ethnic communities. It significantly reduced the possibility of intimate social contact, let alone intermarriage. Still, the taboo on intimate relationships between Poles and Jews did not reduce in any way the interest in the opposite sex on either side of the boundary. The stories claim that there have been a number of secret 'love affairs' between Poles and Jews in Jaśliska. Jan S. (65), who as a boy was involved in a love affair with his Jewish neighbour, put it this way: 'There were a lot of cases where Poles met Jews [...] But it was love in secret.' Such 'secret lovers' would think twice before they would consider making their relationship official. If they did, it always met with the disapproval of their parents. An example of such parental sanctioning is given by the same informant who unveiled the affair with his former Jewish sweetheart Ruchla:

> *I thought about marrying her, but I was only fourteen or fifteen. I asked Ruchla: 'Do you go to church?' We talked about that several times. 'You are a Jewish woman' I said to her. And she answered: 'But I know your prayers, I will pray and love your Holy Mother. I will love you very much!' [...] She said that she would change her faith into Catholicism. She liked me so much. [...] Grandmother used to say: 'Listen, this Jewish woman is making you crazy.' And I said: 'Granny, don't worry' I said 'She is also a human being, isn't she?' So granny said: 'You will see, you will see.' But she laughed at me and made jokes [...] I went there [to Ruchla] several times, but her father shouted: 'Gai weg! Gai weg! Goy, Goy!'[17] So he chased me away [...] He did not want her to meet with a Pole, to make her 'trefna'.[18] Now I think that he wanted to prevent her from making love to me. (Jan S., 65)*

The Shoah put an end to the love affair of Jan S. and Ruchla, but even without the intervention of the war Ruchla would not have been able to marry her Polish boyfriend. No love would survive the firm social boundary set between the Jewish and Polish communities unless the lovers fled from their hometown or country:

There was one [Jew] in Posada. He managed to escape just before the war. It was in 1938 or 1939. He escaped and she survived. She waited and waited for him. She was a Pole and they pastured cows together. They met that way. They went together and nobody could take them apart. It was such a hot love. Later the war came. She survived the war, and left for America after the war. They met there and got married. (Jan S., 65)

The social gap between the opposite sexes is also reflected in the way Polish informants view their one-time Jewish neighbours. Polish male informants, for example, stressed the extraordinary beauty of the Jewish girls and women who once lived in their vicinity. In contrast, female informants claimed that they were not attracted to the local Jewish boys. This is in accordance with the often repeated claim that intimate relationships between Polish boys and Jewish girls were more frequent, despite the fact that Jewish girls were much more controlled by their parents than were the Jewish boys. The following excerpt from a conversation with a sixty-seven year old (male) informant is typical.

Question: *Did Polish girls fall in love with Jewish boys?*
Zbigniew K.:   *Rather not.*
Question: *Were the Jewish boys not interested in Polish girls?*
Zbigniew K.:   *Oh yes, but the Jews (Żydkowie) were not very handsome.*

The notion of the beautiful Jewish woman versus the ugly Jew runs parallel with the extent to which Jewish girls and boys are associated with their Jewishness. Jewish boys carried the symbols of Judaism, as they dressed differently, wore earlocks, were circumcised, and attended Jewish religious school (*kheyder*). And Jewish boys were the guardians of Jewish norms and values. In other words, the cultural differences that distinguished the two ethnic communities were far more conspicuous with the Jewish boys than with the Jewish girls. This may help to explain why it was the Jewish boys and not the Jewish girls who frequently fell victim to Polish teasing. In like manner, a Polish informant would disapprove of the unfriendly and haughty attitude of her one-time Jewish (male) schoolmates, but at the same time she would judge her Jewish girlfriends as very cordial and sympathetic.

Polish Images of the Jew

To the informants, to talk about Jews meant to talk about cultural and religious beliefs and practices that differed considerably from their own. Informants, therefore, tended to stress the contrast between 'Polish' and 'Jewish' manners and practices. One may distinguish three types of stories about the 'Jewish' manners and practices. There are the 'political' stories which typically relate the hierarchical separation between the Jewish and Catholic communities. There are the 'mythical' stories which do not have a link with a past reality and primarily serve an audience of children. Finally, there are the 'positive' stories which, next to observed facts, display the narrator's sincere interest in Jews and Jewish affairs. The latter not only express admiration for the Jews, but also ridicule Jewish practices for entertainment purposes. The same narrator might employ all different registers at the same time, which not only stresses the Poles' ambivalent attitude towards the Jews, but also reflects the social gap that cut across the Polish and Jewish communities in prewar Jaśliska.

Political Stories: The Jewish Adversary

Informants say that Jews were buried in a sitting position so that they were in constant prayer to God. The sitting position would allow Jews a considerable head start in the race to the Final Court on the day of the Last Judgement. Moreover, informants say that during the rare visits the Roman Catholic bishop paid to Jaśliska, the Jews were the first to welcome him. On these occasions Jews would take a golden statue of God with them and then hurry to the bishop in order to be the first to be blessed.[19] There is an equally popular story about a Jew who cries for his baptism on his death-bed but is silenced by his (Jewish) relatives who suffocate him with a pillow. Finally, a few informants claimed that Jews paid Poles to lie on the threshold of the synagogue (*bóżnica*) as they could step and spit on the Pole before entering.

First of all the above stories reflect the political struggle and competition for power between the Polish and Jewish communities. Polish informants not only translated Jewish customs into terms fitting their own frame of reference, but many of them also stressed the competitive force of Judaism. Take, for example, the story about the Jews being anxious to be blessed by the bishop. Literally, the story reflects a Catholic doctrine in that it suggests that Jews, like Christians, were involved in the glorification of the Lord. However, Judaism proscribes idolatry and any depiction of God. Moreover, the story suggests that Jews, like Christians, desired to be blessed by the highest representative of the Roman Catholic Church. The same is true for the other stories: on the one hand they attribute values to the Jews that are typically Catholic in content. On the other hand the stories claim that Jews hold Poles in contempt, that Jews intend to win at the Poles' expense, and finally, that Jews feel superior to Poles. Thus it is said that Poles were good enough to be stepped and spit on. The supposed Jewish contempt for Catholics and the Catholic Church is voiced by Andrzej J. (76), who was taken by surprise when he witnessed some rabbis entering a church in Silesia:

> *I will tell you one very interesting story. I was in Silesia. It was on the third of May [...] and on the third of May there was a procession, with young people, shooters, and war-veterans. First, they all went to the church. The rabbis and other authorities too [...] They all went inside the Catholic Church to attend the Church mass. These rabbis wore hats and under these hats they had skullcaps. They went to the Catholic Church, although I was sure that they would not go in. I was sure that they would stay behind on the market square and wait for the others. Our people never went to their [the Jews'] church, so I was sure that they would not enter our church. But they entered and walked to the altar, where they sat down on benches. How could that have been possible, I ask you? It was difficult for me to believe that the Jews went inside the church. But when we were offered hosts Poles knelt down and the rabbis took off their hats. After that they stood with their skullcaps. Later from our church we went to the Evangelical Church and to the synagogue. The Poles went to visit the synagogue [...] When all prayers were finished they left the synagogue, gathered on the market square and held a procession past the market square. All together. The most interesting thing was that the rabbis went into the Catholic Church, this seemed impossible to me. It was not so surprising that Poles went into the Synagogue.*

The Jewish informant Josko S. (75) started his account of prewar Jaśliska with the following anecdote:

> *I once played with a ball. And I am a Jew [...] So I played with this ball next to the church. And I had bad luck because the ball rolled into the church. I thought: 'I won't fetch that ball!' But the ball was inside, and I went inside the church to fetch the ball. Can you imagine? A Jewish child, in Jaśliska. Me, fetching the ball that rolled inside [...] And then the priest passed by and he said to me: 'Josko!' He almost shouted: 'Josko, what are you doing in this church?' And I told him: 'I went to fetch my ball.'*

This anecdote reveals that the religious division between the communities was particularly strong. The division, in turn, was maintained by two religious groups that were engaged continually in a competition for political power.

Mythical Stories: The Jewish Bugaboo

Ignorance of Jewish culture and the absence of direct contacts with Jews tickled the imagination of the informants. The most creative of all generations is the youngest generation. Indeed, stories about the evil Jew turn out to be extremely popular among informants less than fifteen years old, stories which adult informants unambiguously discounted as 'slander' and 'rubbish' made up by 'jealous old grannies'. In contrast, children eagerly related Jewish misdemeanours and unambiguously held that Jews were deceitful.

They had no reserves about displaying the anti-Jewish stereotypes that perfectly suited their world of imagination. Urszula and Agata (both 13 years old), for instance, explained:

Urszula: *They [Jews] used to catch young girls and…*
Agata: *Nice and beautiful girls. They took young and beautiful girls and they got blood from them. There was a shop and once a boy and a girl went shopping. She entered and he waited outside. There were a lot of mirrors in this shop and there was a track. This boy waited and waited. And when nobody came out he finally entered this shop and asked about this girl. They said that nobody was inside. So he went to the police station and then it came out that she was kept in a cellar.*
Urszula: *She was found dead, wasn't she?*
Agata: *No, she was found alive.*

Although adult informants felt no need to tell the researcher stories of this kind, interviews with teenagers prove that they are directly exposed to the story-telling of their grandparents. The stories are then told in a very specific setting with a very specific audience, namely, that of the grandparent who relates events from a long gone past to his grandchild. Unlike the adult family members, the grandchild is not likely to question or dispute the events. When asked whether they believed the story about Jews extracting blood from Christian girls, Agata and Urszula answered 'Why, of course!' Asked on which grounds they believed this story, Agata answered: 'If grandmother said so, it must be true'. The informal and fantastic accounts, an example of which is given below, lay the foundation of the children's perception of local history and, for that matter, their image of the Jew:

The older brothers and sisters of my grandmother served at the Jews for a small piece of bread. There were a host of Jews in the village. They were mainly involved in trade. One of these Jews, he was called Icek, was famed in the whole neighbourhood. He was the terror of all young girls. He used to put them in a barrel, of which the inside was covered with sharp nails, and extracted blood from them. The blood he used for baking cakes or so-called *macki*. One day my grandmother went to the market to sell a goose in the neighbouring village Błożyna. When she passed the synagogue (*bóżnica*), the Jewish house of prayer, she stopped and saw the praying and expiating Jews. And because she hated them very much she threw a stone through the window. The stone went through the window pane and fell on the celebrating crowd. The Jews hurried out and made after the girl. The latter ran as quick as she could through the crops and the corn fields. But in the end the Jews brought her to Icek. There they designated her for the extraction of blood. She was imprisoned in a dark room, while in the room next to her another girl was dying from terrible torture, in that barrel. Fortunately, Icek had not locked the door properly. In the night, with a heart beating in fear, she sped home. She ran through the forest, she ran like a typhoon, because she was afraid of the Jews and she was afraid of her father whipping her, because she would return without money and without the goose, which she had lost during the struggle with her assailants. Her fright proved to be correct. Father beat her with a leather string. The girl slowly recovered from all this, and when she returned to health, she continued her hard work.[20]

Within this setting of story-telling, stories about the Jews tend to concentrate on their religious peculiarities. In the same stories the typical Jew takes the shape of a mythical person, completely alien to the Poles and most often endowed with demonic features. The representation of the Jew as the devil and bugaboo unmistakably serve educational goals, as do all representations of the devil in plain, old-fashioned, Catholic training. Wieczysław and Helena W. (28, 26), a married couple with four children, confirmed the role of the Jew as a bugaboo. As one of their children appeared to be very frightened on my arrival, they explained that they had told their children the following story: if a child is disobedient a stranger will arrive, put him in his bag and take him away from his parents. In fact, I carried a large bag with me. The fear of the child caused the parents to bring to my notice the role of the Jew as a bugaboo, who is told to punish disobedient children and therefore frightens the very young:

Wieczysław:	*Children were frightened that Jews would catch a child, and throw the child …*
Helena:	*Their children …?*
Wieczysław:	*Polish children from Jaśliska …*
Helena:	*I never heard about that …*
Wieczysław:	*Then listen further. They used to catch children, Christians, and they used to throw them in a barrel with nails inside, they rolled this barrel with the child, to get blood from it, during Passover. Because Jews celebrated Passover by killing a first-born ram. And they anoint the door with its blood. It is from the bible. In Egypt during Passover. There was no plague in the houses of those who had the doors anointed with the blood of the first-born ram. In all Egyptian houses every first born child died on that day. It was the day of Passover. It is all from the bible. This holy day was celebrated, but probably the story was not true. They did not catch children nor did they take blood from them to anoint the doors*
Helena:	*They only used to …*
Wieczysław:	*frighten children in that way, like we frighten our children with the bag. And other parents will try other stories. So they used to frighten children in that way, but it was not true.*

The Jew as the present-day bugaboo is part of a long-lasting Polish tradition. The eighty-four year old Maria M. recalled that during her childhood the picture of the bloodthirsty Jew was presented to her as well: 'When I was still young they told me that story. I don't know whether they told me the truth. When I was a small kid I was afraid that a Jew would catch me and take my blood. But whether or not it was true that way, I really don't know.'

Positive Stories: The Curious Poles

Of course, the Hasidic Jews with their exotic dress and customs could hardly be overlooked. Jews were unmistakably part of the local history, but they were so to a certain degree. Polish informants witnessed the outward expressions of Jewish life, but they were mostly ignorant of Jewish culture. The ethics, stories, and cabbalism of the Hasidic community remained foreign to most of the Polish villagers. Andrzej F. (71) was one of the few Polish informants who lifted the curtain of the foreign, and therefore, fascinating Hasidic world:

> *In Dukla lived a miraculous rabbi. You know where Dukla is, do you? The rabbi who lived there was a prophet. You know what a prophet is? A person who forecasts the future. So in Dukla lived such a miraculous rabbi and our people [Jews from Jaśliska] went to him. All the Jews from this region went to him. Even from Sambor, which before the First [World] War was a town during the Austrian times. Even from Sambor people came to him. He was a miraculous rabbi and he could predict the future like a prophet. Here in Barwinek there lived a widow, a Jewish woman. She had one daughter. They [Jews] had a rule that every Jewish woman had to get married. Because nobody knows which woman will give birth to the messiah. So she had to sleep with a man and conceive a child. Because she could be exactly the one who would give birth to the messiah. And they were waiting for the messiah [...] The mother of this daughter from Barwinek went to this miraculous rabbi. She went on foot. She went on foot because in the old times there were no buses and so forth. You could hire a cart and go somewhere by cart, if you could afford one. But this Jewish woman was poor. Among the Jews there was no such thing as 'love' or 'being in love', or feelings like that. Nothing like that. The most important motive for marrying was money. And the match-maker investigated the case, she had all information about who, about where, and so forth. And she knew that there was a girl, who had no money but who needed money if she wanted to have a marriage. She had no money so she could not marry. So this old mother went to this rabbi for advice. And the rabbi gave her a piece of advice. She went all the way to Dukla. She was tired because she had been walking a long way. And she spoke to the rabbi. But the rabbi did not answer, because a woman was not allowed to speak with the rabbi. The rabbi would only speak with men [...] He called somebody and she spoke with this man and this man spoke to the rabbi. So she said: 'Mister Rebbe, my daughter is so and so old, and we have no money, but she has to get married.' And this man repeated it and the rabbi started to think, and think, and think. And finally he told the interpreter: 'Gai haim, gai haim, ich hob aine waitung.' That is what he said, in Jewish [Yiddish], to the interpreter. And he said to her: 'Gai haim, gai haim, ich hob aine waitung.' It means that she should go home [...] 'And on your way home you will get stomach pain!' [...] And this rabbi shouted: 'Gai haim,*

gai haim, ich hob aine waitung'. So she had to go. She went and she went. Near the stone quarry there is a village, Lipowica, and there is a small bridge. And her stomach started to ache exactly there. She wanted to go off the road to do what she needed to do. But where? There were people all around, so she went under the bridge and shat there. She spent a long time there. And suddenly she noticed something twinkling. And there was a wallet lying with a golden clasp. There must have been another person who had gone off the road and had lost his wallet. This miraculous rabbi, he had foreseen it. He made her stomach ache and he did not tell her that she would find a wallet there and she went there just by herself. So she took this money to the matchmaker and this girl got married. And this is the anecdote of the miraculous rabbi.

It is precisely the alienness of Jewish culture that provoked the curiosity of the Poles and which in turn gave rise to stories with a positive content. Some stories, anecdotes and jokes that were told by the informants revealed a sincere interest in and, at times, even respect for the Jews. The stories are about the exceptional religiosity of the Jews, but they also mention Jewish deviation from these rules.[21] Some stories ridicule Jewish customs and rituals, others seriously unravel the logic of Jewish laws and rituals. Whatever the contents of the story, more than once I had the impression that the storyteller was proud to reveal the secrets of Jewish life, and that he considered it to be a virtue, rather than a disgrace, to be knowledgeable on the subject. Such was the case with Andrzej F., who told about the rabbi from Dukla. And such was the case with many other informants who could hardly hide their enthusiasm when they talked about the Jews; they simply loved it. On a rainy afternoon Franciszek N. (67) gave a lengthy lecture on Jewish holidays and rituals. When he was asked why he was telling all this, Franciszek N. answered 'Well, they [Jews] have been living here, haven't they? They were our Jews.' Franciszek N. was somewhat surprised by the question. Why should he not tell about the Jews from Jaśliska? Jews were part of the local history and he, like many others, finds them very interesting.

Polish-Jewish Relations and the Image of the Jew

The attitudes and views that have been discussed so far draw heavily on the collective experience of the prewar era and include both direct and transmitted experience. If we need one word to describe the Poles' attitude towards the Jews, this word is ambivalence. Polish informants credit the Jews with negative as well as positive characteristics; often their views are inconsistent and conflicting. Another remarkable point is that the views are primarily expressed with the help of stereotypes. The term stereotype will here be defined as the one-sided, exaggerated and normally prejudicial view of a group other than one's own (Abercrombie, Hill et al. 1984: 242).

The stereotypes that passed in review are manifold. There are the plain negative stereotypes, such as the stereotype of the Jewish arsonist, who conspircs with thc cncmy and poisons the well in order to take over the town (see Chapter three); the Jewish usurer, who in the person of a shopkeeper, barkeeper, or moneylender fleeces the Poles of large sums of money whenever the opportunity arises (see Chapter four); the Jewish Antichrist and eternal adversary of Christianity, who murdered Jesus Christ, intentionally violates Christian symbols, values, and norms, and attempts to murder Christian children as well (this chapter).[22] And there are the positive stereotypes which stress the admirable character of the Jews, for instance, the derisive Jew, who is the laughing-stock of the Poles; the wise Jew, who is intelligent and erudite and always assists his Polish neighbour; and finally, the pious Jew, whose piety is no match for the Poles. It should be noted that the informants credit the Jews with a number of positive features. In the eyes of the informants, Jews, on average, display more solidarity and are cleverer and richer than the Poles.[23]

Informants of different ages employ different stereotypes. Whereas the older informants use both positive and negative stereotypes, the very young use exclusively negative stereotypes. However, an assessment of attitudes and views is not the outcome of the balance between negative and positive stereotypes, but rather of the balance between the stereotypical and non-stereotypical part of the relationship. There are two trends that support this argument. First, despite their frequent use of anti-Jewish stereotypes, most informants judge past Polish-Jewish relations positively. Second, as far as the older generations are concerned, their use of stereotypes is rather an expression of a collective experience than an assertion of what they personally think about individual Jews. This is not always the case among the younger generations.

The elderly informants, who were adults at the outbreak of the war, hold ambivalent views about their one-time Jewish neighbours. On the one hand, they stress the vital link that existed between the Polish and the Jewish communities. On the other hand, their accounts clearly reflect the social boundary that existed between the two ethnic communities. The segregation policies carried out by the Germans during the Second World War only strengthened this gap, for during this period being categorised as a Jew or a non-Jew meant the difference between life and death (see Chapter seven). All in all, this generation claims that before the outbreak of the Second World War Polish-Jewish relations in Jaśliska were harmonious.

Middle-aged informants, who were still children or teenagers when the war broke out, hold positive views on the Jews as well. As children and teenagers they entered Jewish houses and had Jewish friends. This is how they penetrated many of the secrets adults no longer cared about. In accordance with their quite intimate experiences, they claim that Poles lived on good terms with the Jews, and the liquidation of their Jewish friends made the greatest impression on them.[24]

Of the postwar generations, those who have grown to maturity (young adults) give a rather authentic picture of the Jews. They are knowledgeable about historical 'facts', such as the recent settlement of the Jews in Jaśliska, their involvement in trade, overall poverty in prewar Jaśliska, and the Shoah. At the same time they employ stereotypes and ascribe to the Jews typical 'Jewish' characteristics, such as wiliness, solidarity, stinginess, and mercantilism. Though less convincingly than their parents, this generation also concludes that Poles and Jews lived on good terms with each other.

The views held by the youngest generation (girls and boys who are still in their childhood) diverge somewhat from the general pattern. The nightmare-like stories about the Jews, told to them by the older generations, not only trigger the children's fantasy but also frighten them. As a result, many children think of the Jews as devils who terrorised and murdered Polish children, stole the Poles' properties, and chased them out of their homes. Accordingly, the children generally claim that relationships between Poles and Jews in prewar Jaśliska were bad.

Notes

1. Weinryb (1972) explains Hasidism as a revolt of the 'unlearned' masses against the learned rabbinate and the Jewish upper class. In creating a 'counter culture', the Hasidim attempted to find a substitute for the strict attitudes and values of traditional Judaism. In contrast to the moral (*musar*) teaching of traditional Judaism, Hasidism emphasised the positive, ecstatic, and joyful side of the religious experience, cultivated cabbalistic traditions, and de-emphasised Torah learning and study. Meijers (1989; 1991) too concludes that the rise of the Hasidic movement cannot be seen independently of the social interests of, and ideological conflicts between, certain groups of scholars. But he adds that Hasidism was more than just a 'counter culture'. In Meijers' view Hasidism was the outcome of a structural characteristic of Judaism, whereby two religious regimes (led by mystics and rationalists) are engaged in a continuous complementary struggle for power, and whereby each alternately holds a dominant position. Seeing it from this perspective, power relations in eighteenth- and nineteenth-century Poland had changed to such a degree that it became possible for a subordinate regime to become dominant.

2. In the tradition of the teachings of the Ba'al Shem Tov, the basic idea in all Hasidic doctrine is the notion of the divine spirit, which is omnipresent in each man and in everything that exists. Since all things, including the lowest acts, have dignity, it is possible to serve God even in the most trifling of actions (Runes 1991: 27). Thus, in Hasidic doctrine every Jew, irrespective of his wealth, social standing, or education, is in a position to achieve personal perfection by leading a pious life.

3. Polish informants explained the term 'Hasid' as a Jewish term denoting a 'very religious' person. Indeed, Hasid in Hebrew means 'the pious'.

4. The fact that there were two houses of prayer in Jaśliska but only one resident rabbi did not imply that the latter served in both communities. In Orthodox Jewish circles services can be held without rabbinical supervision, provided that there are both a minyan (the minimum of ten Jewish males over thirteen required for communal prayers) and a Torah Scroll.

5. Runes (1991: 46) defines the Cabbalah as devotional literature inspired by a mystical immediacy between God and man.

6. Runes (1991: 169) defines the Midrash as homiletic commentary on the Biblical canon, divided into legal and ritual (*Halakhah*) and legendary, moralising, folklorist, and anecdotal (*Haggadah*) parts.

7. The twentieth-century *kahal* was a less elaborate form of the historical Jewish communal autonomy that had developed in Poland since the middle of the sixteenth century. In those days the kahal was responsible for the organisation of the life of the community such as communal administration, adjudication, legislation, and education. In addition, the kahal collected taxes; determined membership of the community, housing, and fiscal policies, and hired all communal employees. Its regulations extended to economic activities, religious practice, and the family and social life of the community (Rosman 1990: 38).

   Although formally many responsibilities and activities of the kahal were taken over by Polish legislation and administration, in practice its influence in twentieth-century Poland was still considerable. The story of how Samuel O. (82), former Jewish resident of Jaśliska, obtained his present family name is illustrative of the way how Jews continued to avoid the official institutions. When Samuel's father Isidor K. fell ill and had to visit a hospital in Vienna, Samuel's sister, who wanted to escort her father, had to apply for a travel permit. It turned out that she was not listed in the civil register, nor were her brothers and sisters, nor was the marriage of her parents. In order to apply for a travel permit Samuel's sister registered under her mother's maiden name. Samuel (already in his twenties) also regis-tered under his mother's maiden name.

8. During the interwar years a new primary school was established in Jaśliska (built of stones instead of wood), providing pupils from the town and neighbouring villages with seven years of primary education. Whereas the generations before had attended only two classes of primary school, the new education act made four years of education compulsory. Both Jewish and Polish children attended classes in the public school, while Lemko children went to their own schools in the neighbouring villages for the first four classes. Lemko pupils who wanted to continue their studies went to the school in Jaśliska. However, the school registers show that only few Lemko children attended school in Jaśliska.

9. Hebrew was considered a divine language and as such was used only during services and prayers, especially by Jewish males who had been taught Hebrew in Jewish school.

10. With the exception of Josko S. (75), all Jewish informants I met in the early 1990s spoke fluent Polish. Interestingly, David O. (73) and his wife Wisia O. interchangeably used Pol-ish and Yiddish when they spoke to one another in private.

11. According to Israel B. (in Litwak 1969: 3) Jewish children were given private lessons in the German language during the Austrian times. After Poland's national independence, Jewish children were given Polish private lessons by Polish teachers. These lessons were given to compensate for the lectures which the Jewish children had missed in school for religious reasons: on Sabbath Jews would not attend school and during the Christian ser-vices Jews were also absent. The interviews with the Jewish informants confirm this.

12. Pearl O. (82), wife of Samuel O. (82), was born in Królik Polski (9 km from Jaśliska). The national census shows that in 1921 eighteen Jews lived in Królik Polski (GUS 1924). According to Pearl O. (82) these eighteen Jews made up three families. Królik Polski was further inhabited by Greek Catholics (267) and Roman Catholics (391).

13. In the interbellum period Jaśliska was an islet in a predominantly Lemko environment. See Chapter two for the historical background of the ethnic Lemkos in Poland.

14. In similar ways informants blamed the Jews (who practised strict avoidance) for prevent-ing them from maintaining close contacts with them.

15. In fact, the Lemko-Polish families were the only families that were left after the cleansing of the 'Ukrainian' villages in 1947. On the post-war period see Chapter seven.

16. On Polish-Jewish intermarriage see also the next chapter.

17. Translation: 'Clear out! Clear out! You Gentile!'

18. A Polish version of the Hebrew *treyf* (impure, ritually unclean).

19. The Jewish informant David O. (73) also recalled the visit of the bishop to Jaśliska. He spoke of the event as a very rare and special occasion during which the Jewish and Polish religious elites met in public. Within the Jewish community the meeting was a topic of dis-cussion long after the event had taken place.

20. Essay written by Urszula M. (13 years). It must be noted that the grandmother of Urszula M. lived in a village situated far from Jaśliska.

21. A popular story of Jewish deviant behaviour is the story about the Jew who, after being invited by his Polish neighbour, sins by eating fresh sausages and begs his Polish neigh-bour to keep it a secret.

22. The image of the 'Jewish bugaboo' that is transmitted to the new generations clearly fits the traditional European notion of the Jewish Antichrist: the Jew who thinks he needs 'consecrated' blood to cure himself of his skin disease—a sickness which is a direct result of his felony, the crucifixion of Jesus Christ—and therefore kills innocent Christian chil-dren on whom the 'magic' of baptism still rests (see Van Arkel 1991: 55). The notion of the Antichrist is further present in the way informants seem to interpret the rituals, con-

duct, and motivations of their former Jewish neighbours. For example, the notion that Jews are buried in the sitting position (so that they are the first to appear before the Last Judgement), or the notion that Jews were quick to welcome the bishop upon his visits to the small town (so that they were the first to receive his blessings), clearly tend to depict the Jews as competitors and apostates.

23. For an overview of the wide variety of stereotypes of the Jew that feature in Polish folk culture see Alina Cała (1992).

24. Very likely, this generation also profited by the increasing integration of the ethnic minorities into the Polish nation state during the 1920s.

Chapter 6

THE ETHNIC BOUNDARY

The Case of the Converted Jewish Woman

'Are Jews also human beings?' asked the nine-year old Janek shyly. 'My mother told me that on the Jewish cemetery the murdered Jews are wailing.' 'What else should they have been?' asked Marcin a little irritated. 'Our Lord Jesus, wasn't he a Jew? And Saint Peter? And Saint Paul? They were all Jews!' 'Jesus', Wladek interrupted Marcin, 'Our Lord Jesus, wasn't he crucified by Jews?' 'Not by the Jews, not by the Jews' Marcin shook his head in firm denial. 'Mister rabbi himself told me that pagans, the Romans, did it. And the rabbi was as righteous and pious as Our Lord Jesus himself' (Opatoshu 1951: 316).

Introduction

*I*t was only at a late stage of fieldwork that I visited Alicja S., wife of 'Wysiek' and daughter of Felicja W., the converted Jewish woman. Mother Felicja (84 years old) left Jaśliska some six years ago and now lives with two of her daughters in Nysa, a town in south-western Poland. As the family tree in figure 6.1 shows, Daughter Alicja (59) and her two sons are the only offspring still living in Jaśliska. Though informants had earlier drawn my attention to both Felicja and Alicja, for a long time I was reluctant to visit 'Converted Alka'. Several informants had warned me that Alicja would not be willing to talk. I had noticed before that informants kept silent on certain subjects. Why, then, would the daughter of a convert be willing to talk? When I finally went to see Alicja she seemed hospitable and straightforward. Without prompting she recounted the story of her mother. A few weeks later I visited her mother, who welcomed me in like manner, in Nysa (south-west Poland).[1]

Notes for this section begin on page 136.

The case of the converted Jewish woman has several interesting aspects. As a teenager, Felicja transgressed the firm social boundary between the two ethnic communities, and in doing so, provoked a series of reactions and counter reactions. Since the event took place in Jaśliska, it gives us good insight into the social structure of the village before the Second World War. In addition, the social position of the woman with conspicuous Jewish roots sheds light on Polish-Jewish relations in postwar Poland. Felicja and her daughters occupy a socially distinct place in Polish society. This is not only expressed in the views others hold of them, but also in their inability to define their own identity unambiguously. Finally, the story of Felicja and her daughter Alicja shows that the problem of conflicting identities transcends the first generation.[2]

Figure 6.1   Family Tree: The Family of Felicja W.

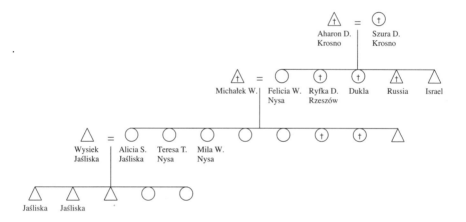

Felicja's Story

Early Childhood

In 1910, in the oil district of Krosno,[3] Szura D. gave birth to her daughter Felicja, then called by her Jewish name 'Feiga'.[4] Szura worked as a servant broker (*rajfurka*). She mediated between ladies and girls who were looking for servants and jobs respectively. She was not always paid properly for the service she offered and stopped working when her children had grown older. The mother of Felicja was a 'good woman', for she cooked and fed 'all of us children'. Only if she had money, of course, because at times father Aharon would not give his wife a penny. Aharon was not educated. He was a manual worker and a man from the village. He was taught shoemaking but since he was not good at it, he worked as a porter. He was quite successful as a porter because in Krosno 'there was nobody stronger than he was'. People envied him, so one day they caught him and threw stones at him. During this fight her father lost one eye. He was operated in Kraków and got an artificial eye.[5] During the First World War he served in the Austrian army, not as a soldier but as someone of 'more importance'. He returned in 1922. After his return he spent another eight years in Russia as a prisoner of war.[6]

When he was at home, Aharon went to the synagogue every Saturday, while Szura went on high holidays only. At home Sabbath (*shabbes*) was celebrated each Friday. Still, according to Felicja her parents were not very religious: 'They were practising, but not very much because father was a simple manual worker.' Felicja was taught Hebrew and 'Hebrew prayers' by a Jewish teacher. After she had learned reading Felicja stopped going to the Jewish school, because her father had no money to pay for her education. Moreover, it was not necessary for her to be fully initiated into Jewish law, ethics and mysticism, because 'boys had to know things like that, but girls did not need to learn.'

From early childhood Felicja had two close Polish friends with whom she sang Catholic songs and attended religious lessons: 'When I went to school, I was lucky enough to have a Polish girl always sitting on the same bench. When it was fast period she sang Lent songs. When it was Christmas they used to teach me Christmas carols. I could sing everything. I knew prayers and carols and I could sing.' It often happened that the priest would show her the door, because Jewish children were not allowed to participate in religious lessons. It also happened that her father would beat her and lift her up by the hair, because he did not like his daughter to attend Catholic services. Her curiosity did not only concern the Catholic rites. From time to time Felicja had a look in a nearby synagogue 'to see Jewish women and old Jews dancing.' She was not the only curious person. 'It was so interesting that they [Poles] came and had a look there.'

At the age of fourteen Felicja learned sewing: 'Mother made me learn sewing and I was good at it.' When her father brought her a sewing machine she started to earn a living from sewing. Felicja left her parental home when she was sixteen or seventeen years old. Her youngest sister Ryfka, who later died of tuberculosis, worked in Jaśliska as a cook in the sawmill. She took Felicja to Jaśliska, where she started to make a living. Felicja sewed for many people, Poles (among them her future godfather) and Jews alike. Besides, she made many new Polish friends.

The Baptism

At the age of eighteen Felicja converted to Catholicism, because she 'liked the Catholic faith'. Some friends had also wanted her to change her religion, especially one friend Wirginia J., a 'fine lady' whose husband was the machinist of the sawmill in Jaśliska. On the occasion of her baptism, the wife of the mayor was appointed to be her godmother, while the headmaster of the school was appointed as her godfather. The baptism of Felicja would have been a joyous event if the Jews of Jaśliska had not disturbed the celebration. The situation became so precarious that Felicja was escorted by a policeman on her way back to the church.

> *Jews threw stones. They were throwing stones, but I don't know if people got hurt because of that. It was full of people. There was such a crowd that not everybody could get into the church. Everybody was anxious to see me getting baptised. I was eighteen years old. I was still a young girl. After this celebration, my father came and pleaded with me to go home. He said there would be a good dowry for me. Suddenly they had a dowry for me and a good husband, everything to persuade me to return home. But I was already baptised, so there was no way back. I had converted. There was one friend, she was somewhat older than me and she pulled me from one side and father took me by the arm and pulled from the other side, in his direction. Although my father was much stronger, he could not possibly pull me harder [because of the large audience present]. Later Jews asked my father why he had not brought an axe or a knife with him and cut my head off, since he had been standing so close to me. Because it is a horrible thing for Jews when one of them gets baptised [...] My father came at first. Later mother came to visit me with my brothers and sisters. My brother was crying 'Give me my sister back!', 'Give me my sister back!' But I ran away and hid myself, leaving my brother in tears.*

According to Alicja, the baptism of her mother in 1928 took place because 'God wanted it that way so she became baptised and she lives till this day.' She knew that her mother had already enjoyed religious lessons in her home town, which she had attended while hiding herself under school benches. Alicja recalled that the Jews did not leave her mother in peace. They tried to stop her from entering the church and they wanted to 'kill her and stone her to death'. Somehow Felicja's parents got to know about the conversion and went to Jaśliska. At nine in the morning Felicja was baptised and at three in the afternoon her parents arrived. They were shocked and cried and spoke with her in the 'Jewish language'. But mother answered (in Polish:) 'I am not yours, I have already been baptised, my God is Jesus Christ and I believe in the Holy Mother.'

> *Then grandfather got furious. Mother was sitting on a veranda surrounded by four Polish women, among them her godmother who was the wife of the mayor. Grand-*

father, who was a very tall and well built person, started to pull mother towards him,
through the veranda and through the window. But the four women caught her and hid
her in a cellar. Thereafter mother escaped to a convent in Poznań. Rich relatives of the
godparents had helped to find her a place.

After the Baptism

After her baptism, Felicja sold her second-hand sewing machine and escaped, because 'I knew that the Jews would never leave me in peace.' A commissioner, who also lived in the house of her godmother, had a sister in a convent in Poznań. This sister found a place for her in a convent called 'The Shepherd Nuns'. Felicja continued sewing, producing twelve pairs of drawers and six shirts a day: 'There were two sewing machines and two tailors. The other tailor was older than I was. We did a kind of competition. She showed me that she was able to sew more than I did and I did the same. And the nuns were happy because we were good workers.' After five and a half years Felicja had everything prepared to go to a convent and become a nun, but a visit to the doctor interfered with her plans: 'I visited the doctor with a nun and he told me that I was not able to become a nun. I was rather slim and had too little blood. So I did not go to the convent, although I had everything prepared.'[7] Felicja returned to Jaśliska, taking her nun's costume with her.

One year after her return from the convent Felicja married Michałek W. She was twenty-four years at that time. It was not love that made her marry him: 'I had no choice. I could not marry a farmer with a large number of fields because I had had nothing to do with it earlier.' Michałek W. was a tailor and he sewed overcoats (*gunia*) and stockings for Lemkos. He also had a piece of land but 'first of all he had a profession and that is why I married him'. Felicja had eight children (among them a pair of twins), worked in the garden (in the convent she had learned how to grow carrots and tomatoes), pastured the goats, and built a small wooden house with her husband. At times, the house was full of people who had them mend or sew something: 'We sewed for everyone. For Jews, Lemkos, Poles. We even sewed for the Potockis (local nobility).'

Meanwhile the Jews had lost their interest in Felicja. They called her names and made fun of her but in a harmless way. Still, Felicja had Jewish customers with whom she spoke a few words of 'lingo' (*szwargot*).[8] After the birth of her first child, the youngest brother of Felicja paid her a visit. Also her mother visited her once, but her father never paid attention to her. Both parents 'did not wait for the war' and died a natural dead. Her youngest sister, who suffered from tuberculosis, also died before the war. She had gone to Rzeszów to work as a servant, but her health was fragile and she never got used to the hard work. Then she started to suffer from tuberculosis. She died within eight or nine days. Her sister was twenty-one when she died.

About her mother's life after baptism Alicja said that she was taken to a convent where she sewed and learned and would eventually become a nun. She never became a nun because a physician told her that she was ill and that she should get married. So her mother returned to Jaśliska and there she made many Polish friends. She regularly visited the priest who gave her religious lessons for two years. The Jews were still eager for revenge which was a real nuisance to her mother because '... there were many Jews in town'. Once grandmother wanted to visit her daughter, but the Jews would not let them meet. In the eyes of the Jews 'mother was neither fish nor flesh, she was a nobody'. Mother met father at a wedding party where they both served as witnesses. They married in 1934, after which mother gave birth to eight children, seven daughters and one son, who were all baptised. Father was a tailor and a 'very charming person' and he was loved by both 'Poles and Jews'. Still, people had something against him because he had married a convert. The conversion, however, was her luck, for 'if mother had not been baptised she would never have survived the war'.

The Second World War

When the war came Felicja was caught by the Germans: 'Germans took me and made me join the ... how is this called? They made me join the ghetto in Krosno. And then they took us to Rzeszów. We marched four abreast to the train, to the cattle wagons. In Rzeszów it was winter [...] it was freezing cold.' The first thing Felicja noticed were the piles of snow-white feathers from duvets and pillows that had been taken down from the houses: 'In Rzeszów, I tell you, there were these spoiled duvets and everything. The feathers were waist deep. There were so many feathers that there was no place to sit down. They threw everything away. They [Jewish women] had to take everything out.'[9] In Rzeszów Felicja joined the Jewish section. Jews were forbidden to wear collars and they were obliged to wear a star (*gwiazda*). Felicja, however, wore a black coat with a collar and did not wear a yellow star: 'I should have worn a star. But there was nobody to give me one. They could have shot me because of that.' One night Jews tried to persuade a tipsy Ukrainian soldier to shoot her: 'The Jews told him: "She is a convert! She has to be killed and shot!" They said so in my presence. They didn't care at all!' But the Ukrainian soldier told the Jews that he had not received an order to shoot her. He beat her instead in order to 'silence' the Jewish mob.

The next day all the people were together. Tailors were put with tailors and shoemakers with shoemakers. Felicja had no papers on her, so she joined neither group. She saw children being separated from their mothers and gathered into one room: 'They locked the doors and gassed them, because it was smelling awfully. At first, you could hear some squeals and crying. Later everything calmed down.'[10] Adults were made to pile up various things (books and dictionaries) on vehicles. Then they opened the wide gate, guarded by one German soldier. He was beating Jewish women to make them hurry. As Felicja noticed the open gate she made a cross and went through it: 'I thought, everything is the same for me, whether he will shoot me or not [...] I don't know whether he was blinded or whether he simply didn't see me. If he had seen me, he certainly would have shot me. But nobody shot me.' And Felicja safely reached the road.

On the road a woman took her by the arm. Felicja asked the woman to show her the way to the nearest church: 'Maybe I would be so lucky and reach that place, so that I could thank the Lord for having saved me [...] maybe He would have mercy on me and let me live a little bit longer.' Having paid a visit to the church she started her long trip home. On her way she gave herself out as a Polish woman who had been forced to work for the Germans and had escaped from them. Felicja could easily pose as a Pole because 'I was not like a Jewish woman and I still had all my teeth'. Though many people were afraid to help her she always found a place to stay. After some three weeks of walking, hitchhiking and hiding she reached Jaśliska. Three times on her last kilometres home she met a German truck that got stuck in the snow. The carter who had offered her a lift helped to free the Germans. When she finally reached Jaśliska late in the evening her children, who had been waiting for her, screamed: 'Mama! Mama arrived! Mama!'

Alicja recalled that Germans had taken her mother to the ghetto in Krosno. There she stayed for some two weeks, after which she was taken to the ghetto in Rzeszów: 'Mother was not caught because she was a Jewish woman, she was caught because she was a convert'. In the ghetto Jews, gypsies and converted women were imprisoned and in Rzeszów 'mother met three converted women from Jaśliska'. The women were childless but mother had children '... so they told her to escape. She took her rosary, made a cross and went through the fence while a German guard was watching her.' The guard pretended that he did not see her. She escaped through the fence and met an old lady dressed in black. Then she went home on foot. After one and a half months mother returned home: 'It was Holy Santa Claus [...] and father had some turnips and some nuts and also baked some cakes for us and he tied it on our heads, because he was very religious. Then he said: 'Children pray to Santa Claus, maybe your mother will return.' So we three children started praying. Me, Mila and Teresa."

After her return to Jaśliska Felicja had to hide herself. But soon a Ukrainian policeman came to her and asked her why she had returned. Felicja told him that she had been set free by the Germans. Then he asked her who had set her free. She answered that a good man had set her free, in fact meaning Jesus. Then they summoned her to the community office headed by the Ukrainian mayor (*wójt*) 'Iwerczuk'. The mayor said that she could never have been set free. Felicja answered that she really was and the mayor believed her, although it was common knowledge that 'a German either keeps or kills his prisoner.' As if through a miracle she survived. The late priest of Jaśliska, father Rąpała, who had baptised her used to say to her: 'You still live thanks to a miracle!'[11]

Some time after the war Polish students made the rounds and checked people for lice. They also came to Felicja (who had just arrived), her husband and daughters: 'This three-year old daughter of mine boasted: "Look at me, I have not even one [louse]!"' Thereupon the student asked: 'You don't have lice, but can you pray?' The little girl knelt down and recited the Lord's Prayer, Ave Maria, Credo, and the Ten Commandments: 'she knew everything, and this man, he was a student from the university of Kraków, he said that he could not pray that way.' In return for the prayers the student gave Felicja's daughter a small present, some biscuits and a fish made of coloured blue glass.

Alicja repeated that her mother survived thanks to a miracle. When her mother returned home the priest helped her to hide and gave her out as a lost person. Her mother would not stay at home for some two years; she even did not sleep at home. Still, she gave birth to a beautiful blond girl who looked 'like an angel', but who died before the liberation from the Germans in September 1944. Her mother's oldest sister had been shot by the Germans together with her husband and three children. They had been hiding and Poles had betrayed them. Her youngest brother had fled to Russia as a teenager immediately before the outbreak of the war. He survived in the Soviet Union, married a Russian woman[12] and died eight or nine years ago. The oldest brother had survived but had lost his wife and little daughter. He had been a tailor in the ghetto of Jasło. Several years after the war he sent a letter to Felicja in which he wrote that fifteen tailors had escaped from the ghetto, but that only four had survived. After the war he married a Czech (Jewish) woman and went to live in Israel. Alicja does not know whether her Israeli uncle is still alive. She wrote a letter to him recently, but received no reply.

The Jewish Family

After the war Felicja's brothers contacted the municipality to find out whether their sister had survived: 'The first [brother] tried to find out whether I was still alive and the second did the same, they wrote to the community office, or something.' In 1959 her youngest brother, the one from Russia, paid his first visit to Felicja. The oldest brother from Palestine, however, helped her the most. He even sent her money for a ticket to Israel. So it happened that Felicja went to Warsaw for a visa. At the embassy she had an interview with 'the highest authority', who asked her if she had been baptised. She had, like her husband and children. In that case, she was told, she would have a difficult life in Israel. So Felicja answered: 'I have a difficult life here and I will get a difficult life there, so why should I go? I was baptised here and therefore I will stay here.' She stayed in Poland and because she is old she does not need her brother's help any more. He sent a few more things to her daughter in Jaśliska. Indeed the Israeli uncle had been a great support to Alicja. He sent her parcels, sometimes even twice a month.

About her Israeli uncle Alicja said: 'He always helped me when I was in trouble [...] He helped me a lot and I think he will be rewarded for that by God.' In 1985 her uncle and his Czech wife came to visit them during a four-day trip through Poland. During this visit he complained that 'the floor was rotten and that the house was old'. He wanted her mother to live in Israel. But her mother was afraid to go and she wanted her brother to stay in Poland. At the embassy in Warsaw they asked her mother about her faith. She told them that she was baptised, '... that her husband was baptised, and that her children were baptised too.' Finally, she decided not to go because '... she was afraid of the Jews'. She had already had some difficult experiences with the Jews from Jaśliska and in Israel '... there would even be more of them.' Then her uncle wrote to her mother that she was living in a stable and that she could have had a better life if she would have come to Israel. Her mother answered that she did not care because 'Jesus Christ was also born in a stable.' Her uncle stopped sending letters, 'perhaps because he got angry.'

Alicja still remembered when her youngest uncle from Russia came to visit them in Jaśliska. It was on Whitsuntide (*Zielone Świątki*) and Alicja's mother baked rolls for her children. A group of people came from the bus, among them Wieczysław L., who guided a man towards the house. Wieczysław L. told her mother: 'I brought you a guest. I don't know whether he will make you happy but let him sit down with you.' So her uncle sat down and watched her mother baking rolls:

From early childhood mother had sewn, cooked, and baked Jewish Easter bread (maca) at the homes of rich Jewish families, so she had swift hands. I noticed tears falling from the eyes of my uncle. Mother said: 'You are similar to my brother. We have a portrait of him. We will not try to get a new one because we have his portrait already. But you are really similar to my brother'. Then they embraced and they kissed. Uncle cried and assured mother that he was her brother. But he had changed a little, because he had grown older, had been married in the meantime, and also had children.

The Russian uncle visited Jaśliska two more times. He had wanted to settle in Poland but his Russian wife did not let him go. Once he came and said: "'Glory be to Jesus Christ!" Mother was so happy that she started crying, because she had always thought that her brother did not believe in God.'

Transgressing the Ethnic Boundary

The life story of Felicja W. gives us insight in the rigidity of the ethnic boundary in prewar Poland. As will be shown below, her conversion can be explained by the marginal position she occupied in society as a child from a poor Jewish family. This is of crucial importance in understanding why the conversion took place and how Felicja became a pawn in the struggle for power by the two ethnic communities in Jaśliska.

A Social Deviant

It is sometimes said that women of all ranks of Jewish society were less likely than men to cut their ties with Judaism. Endelman (1987: 14) for example maintains that until the mid twentieth century most Jewish women 'remained at home, outside the marketplace and public life, enclosed in the private sphere of friends and family, cut off from temptations that led ambitious young men to change their religious affiliation.' In this respect the life story of Felicja is different, as she converted to Catholicism while still a teenager, the age at which Jewish girls were most restricted by the control of their parents, relatives, and elders of the community. Felicja's break with Judaism contrasts with another 'rule' pertaining to Jewish converts. Rosenthal (1954) observed that among her Jewish respondents conversion for opportunistic reasons was almost exclusively assigned to males and for romantic reasons exclusively to females. Felicja, however, did not change her faith for romantic reasons. The marriage with her late husband Michałek W. took place more than six years after her conversion.

Asked why she had converted to Catholicism, Felicja answered that she liked the Catholic faith best. Undoubtedly, there is some truth in this statement. As a teenager, Felicja had a strong sense of spirituality, but as a girl she had no access to traditional Jewish education or religious institutions. This might have disappointed her. Still, one may think of a more plausible reason why Felicja went so far as to risk a break with her family. On closer examination we may assume that religious conviction played a minor role in her decision to convert. Felicja's marginal position in the Jewish community, as well as the strong appeal of the Catholic faith community, are more likely to have prompted her conversion.

There are indications that Felicja grew up less protected and less restricted than her female Jewish contemporaries in Jaśliska. We have seen that the parental home did not set a clear example of a life strictly based on Jewish rules and practices. Though both parents were observant, they had little involvement in Jewish communal affairs, because of their poverty and the frequent absence of the father. In any event, Felicja had little affinity with the Jewish community, which is exemplified by the fact that all her friends were Poles. Moreover, the parents failed to pay sufficient attention to their daughter's activities. Through her Polish friends Felicja became acquainted with Catholicism and, because of the lack of parental control, she was able to further develop her awakening interest. In addition, we have seen that Felicja left home at an early age, which was atypical. Decent Jewish girls left the parental home only after their marriage, unless poverty forced them to earn a living elsewhere as domestics or seamstresses (Ain 1949). We have seen that Felicja and her sisters left Krosno before marriage, and that of the three sisters only the oldest married a Jew.[13]

The relative poverty and Felicja's weak Jewish identity set the conditions for her conversion. The event that turned the balance, however, was her settlement in Jaśliska. A strict division between the Polish and Jewish communities existed in this small town. We have seen that the Jews strongly marked themselves off from the Poles. The distinction between Jews (*yidn*) and non-Jews (*goyim*) reflected the Jewish fear of Gentile intrusion, as well as the Jewish disdain for the Gentile world. In communal and personal matters Jews kept strictly to Jews. Any involvement with Poles beyond what was strictly necessary (like in work or commerce) was regarded as improper, since this would blur the community boundary and endanger the traditional Jewish way of life. As Ellenson (1987: 165) observed, in the traditional world the life of the individual Jew was coextensive with the life of the community itself. The fact that Felicja had left her parental community as a single woman, was unfamiliar with the Jewish calendar and rules, and in addition had many Polish friends, made her a social deviant.

Once Felicja decided to stay in Jaśliska, where she had good prospects of making a living as a seamstress, there was no alternative for her but to make a choice. If she was to be accepted by the inhabitants of the small town, Felicja had to become a member of the Polish or the Jewish community. Since many aspects of prewar life touched on religion, this included a choice between Catholicism and Judaism. Felicja eventually chose the first option. Besides the fact that Felicja felt little affinity with the Jewish community and that the Jews themselves must have been reluctant to accept an outcast as their member, the prospect of membership of the Catholic community held several attractions for Felicja.

First, within the confines of the Jewish community, Felicja had few marriage prospects because her parents were poor and she was not a part of a Jewish community that took care of such matters. There was no dowry available for her and this might have lowered her status among the Jews. For Felicja her parent's poverty had been particularly painful. This is clear from her statement about her father's visit to Jaśliska after Felicja's baptism: 'Suddenly they had a dowry for me and a husband, everything to persuade me to return home.' But her father's petition came much too late. The decision had already been made, and since she was baptised, her decision was definite. An older informant (81) who had been a witness to the baptism also emphasised the fact that Felicja came from a poor Jewish family: 'I would not say that she was a particularly faithful person. She really had no prospects of a good life there [among Jews]. So that is why she came here, to us [Catholics].'

Second, for Felicja it turned out especially convenient to bid for access to the Polish community. Felicja's experiences in Krosno with her Polish friends and with the Catholic rites and services undoubtedly facilitated her entry into the Polish Catholic community. But most importantly, the accounts make it clear that the Catholic community in Jaśliska wanted this young Jewish girl. No less than the wife of the mayor and the director of the school were given custody of the Jewish girl and took pity on her, while father Rąpała tried his best to introduce her to the doctrines of Catholicism. The priest taught her the catechism, organised her baptism (for which he did not take any money) and risked a serious conflict with the Jewish community. Felicja: 'Jews would not let him [the priest] live in peace.' The anxiety of the Polish lay men and women certainly added to the festive excitement. And when troubles came, Felicja was carefully removed to a Catholic stronghold far away from the centre of agitation. After six years of exile her patrons decided that things had calmed down and that Felicja was ready to start a normal life with a husband and children.

Whatever the consequences, only through conversion could Felicja become a Catholic and, therefore, an accepted member of the Polish community. After this 'rite of passage', life-long security, respect, and attention were guaranteed, not only from God but also from His lay representatives. Indeed, father Rąpała rendered Felicja assistance before the war (lending her money) and during the difficult war years (seeking a safe place for her).

Alicja explained: 'Father Rąpała liked me and he also liked my mother. Because she had no parents. She had nobody. She only had the priest.' Also according to Alicja the present-day priest of Jaśliska and his assistant minister from Tarnów have a special interest in Felicja:

> *Our priest [...] liked to talk with my mother, so did priest Mariusz from Tarnów [...] Once priest Mariusz asked our priest about Mrs W. People had told him that she was a baptised woman and he became interested in her. He talked with her several times, and always when he comes here, he asks me about my mother.*

In Nysa too Felicja maintains personal contacts with the local clergy. A few days before our meeting a priest had paid her a parish visit to discuss personal matters.

The Conversion

During her years in Stoczek (1925-1938), a small Polish town fifty-five miles from Warsaw, Rosenthal (1954: 178) observed that new currents and ways were spreading among the Jewish youth who no longer were devoted to the culture of their forefathers in the same way as their parents. The most striking evidences were the decline of religious Orthodoxy and attendance at meetings of Zionist and communist organisations, and the decrease of arranged marriages. A form of deviation, however, which was never accepted and attitudes toward which remained unchanged until the outbreak of the Second World War was the act of giving up one's religion and embracing the Roman Catholic faith.

> When one changed his faith in Stoczek, it signified to all that he abandoned the Jewish community and went over to the hostile Poles. Though the saying, 'It is hard to be a Jew,' was constantly heard, there was, nevertheless, no understanding for one who stopped being Jewish. His family sat in deep mourning for seven days, as though he had died, and they never mentioned his name again. Despite the period of mourning, the community insisted that they did not recognise the act of conversion because a Jew could never be anything but a Jew. It was inconceivable in Stoczek that a Jew could come to believe in another faith. The Jew who went through conversion was, therefore, considered a *shmadnik*, an apostate and traitor, a low and spiteful character; but he never became a Gentile in the eyes of the community (Rosenthal 1954: 177).

In Stoczek the only one person to leave the Jewish faith was a young woman, the daughter of a businessman, who married a peasant from a nearby village. The conversion of the young woman left a permanent mark on her family, a blot 'which nothing could wash away and which people would never forget' (Rosenthal 1954: 178). Since the family of the convert was relatively well off, and the members of this family did not want to marry beneath their *yikhus* (lineage), the considerable decrease in status forced them to change strategies: as people of similar *yikhus* did not want to marry them, there was much intermarriage with close relatives.

In like manner, Felicja's brothers, sisters, father and mother were taken aback when they heard the news of her conversion. We have seen that the father and oldest brother were quick to visit Felicja when the rumour of the baptism had spread. We have also seen that both seemed terribly concerned with the lapse of their daughter and sister. Upon their arrival in Jaśliska, they threw themselves on the indulgence of Felicja, they pleaded with her to return home, and they promised her a decent Jewish husband. When Felicja did not show any interest, the father became angry and tried to make her change her mind by means of violence. Thereafter Felicja sought refuge with her Catholic patrons. From far she could hear the wailing of her brother: 'Give me my sister back! Give me my sister back!' After this day, the family stopped meeting Felicja. In fact, Felicja would never meet her father again. It was only after her six years' retreat from Jaśliska that her mother and youngest brother paid her some visits. Her oldest brother, however, restored contact only after the war. In short, the conversion meant a serious break with her Jewish family and Jewish background.

But Felicja was not only rejected by her own family. There was great consternation in the town when the news of the baptism reached the local Jews. Rosenthal (1954: 178) writes about a similar event when a Jewish girl from a nearby town arrived in Stoczek to be married in church. Upon her arrival almost all Jews, young and old, gathered around the town hall where she was staying and shouted insults at her. It was the same in Jaśliska, where Jews showed their disapproval by throwing stones at the celebrating crowd and shouting at Felicja. In addition, they pressed Felicja's father to take severe measures against the *shmadnik* who had brought disgrace upon her family. Felicja recalled: 'Later Jews had asked my father why he had not brought an axe or a knife with him and then cut my head off, since he had been standing so close to me.' And Alicja told: 'The Jews were chasing my mother terribly. They wanted to stone her to death. When she was baptised Jews stood near the church and they would not let her pass [...] they wanted to kill her for that.'

Though Felicja and Alicja probably exaggerated the blood lust of the local Jews, their accounts point to the strong emotions that arose because of the conversion and to the enmity that was shown towards the apostate. Presumably, the Catholic patrons suspected that Felicja would not be able to stand up to the pressure that was put on her by her family and the Jewish community. Tensions rose to such an extent that the Catholic patrons decided to send the young woman to a more quiet place. They found a sanctuary for Felicja in a convent several hundred kilometres from Jaśliska. Indeed, when Felicja returned after six years of detention, peace had returned in the small town. Although the local Jews would still think of Felicja as 'neither fish nor flesh', they did so in silence and among themselves. Nor did they bother her Gentile husband whom she married a little later. Interestingly, the convert from Stoczek found herself in a similar situation. The young Jewish woman who had married a peasant from a nearby village never visited Stoczek as did all other peasant women, but left all transactions to her husband. Those Jewish men who occasionally passed through her village would relate that she dressed, behaved, and spoke like a 'real peasant'. Her husband was known among the Jews as a just and honest man and no resentment was felt towards him.

Felicja takes the Jewish attack personally. She is right to a degree, for hatred and ridicule was directed towards her. Especially the rejection by her family had been a painful and traumatic experience. During the interview Felicja would repeatedly stress that she had felt lonely all her life and that she had raised her children all by herself, that is, without family and with a large number of enemies. More than sixty years after the baptism, the anger of her parents and siblings, as well as of the Jewish community, still appears compelling to her. Looking back at the event, Felicja doubts whether it was really worth it. If she had had a choice at that time, Felicja confesses, she would have favoured another strategy, if only to avoid the terrible conflict arising from the baptism:

> *I will tell you something, if I had known that there were three kinds of baptism … if I had been wiser, I would have waited a little bit longer. For there are three kinds of baptism. The first is 'water baptism', the second is 'blood baptism' and there is 'desire baptism' (chrzest pragnienia). I didn't know about that, I only knew about this water baptism.*[14]

Still, it is safe to assume that the anger of the Jews was not exclusively directed towards the apostate and traitor of the Jewish people; it was also a reaction to the Polish local residents who had played an active role in the conversion. The firm and active involvement of both the Polish and Jewish communities in the conversion points to a tug-of-war between the Poles and the Jews in Jaśliska. Although the immediate cause of this war was Felicja's deviant behaviour, she was never more than a pawn, in the struggle between the communities.

An Ethnic Conflict

With the conversion of Felicja the inviolability of the ethnic boundary became disputed. It was not the Jews but the Poles who intentionally violated the tacit ethnic boundary. Indeed, Felicja was perfectly aware of the fact that her conversion meant a serious assault on the strong sense of solidarity among the local Jewish residents: 'It is a horrible thing for Jews when one of them gets baptised.' As might be expected, the Jews in Jaśliska were not interested in Catholicism. On the contrary, they kept a safe distance from the Catholic residents of the town to preserve their own values and to protect these values from outside influence. Likewise, they did not recognise the act of conversion.[15] Still, despite the professed intellectual distance vis-à-vis their Catholic surroundings, they felt hurt and offended by the conversion of Felicja. The Jews' sudden anxiety in the case at hand, according to Endelman (1987: 1), can be explained as resulting from a clash between Jewish and Christian attitudes and values:

> For Jews, missionary activity expressed an ancient hostility that seemingly threatened the existence of the Jewish people and, at the very minimum questioned the legitimacy of Jewish survival in the modern world. Christians, on the other hand, saw the evangelization of the Jews in a very different light. For them, missionary work was an expression of love and concern rather than intolerance and bigotry. Whereas Jews evinced little interest in the Christian doctrine and none whatsoever in turning Christians into Jews—desiring, above all, to be left alone—Christians were unable to take such a detached view.

The Poles, and among them father Rąpała, knew that with Felicja's conversion they would risk a conflict with the Jewish residents. A possible explanation of why the Poles ventured to take that risk might be that as members of the Catholic community they derived their self-esteem from winning new souls, in particular Jewish souls, for the Gospel. Endelman (1987: 3) argues that much of the Christian rivalry with the Jews can be traced back to the intimate character of the initial relationship between Judaism and Christianity, the latter originating as a sect within first-century Palestinian Judaism. Unfortunately for the Jewish people, the younger religion chose to defend its claim—the claim that it was the new chosen people—at the expense of the elder.

> Indeed, in one sense, there was a greater satisfaction in converting Jews than pagans. The persistent refusal of Jews to admit their error, after all, was a constant affront to Christianity, since the gospel had been preached to them before other peoples and their own Scripture, so it was argued, contained the evidence for Jesus' messiahship. In this light, Jewish acknowledgement of Jesus could be

seen as a weightier testimony to Christian truth than that of heathens. Thus, the conversion of Jews was considered particularly desirable, and over the centuries an inordinate amount of attention was devoted to this objective.

The introspective observance of Judaism and the missionary doctrine of the Catholic Church also caused tensions between the Jewish and Polish communities in Jaśliska, reaching a climax with the conversion of Felicja. The 'spreading of the good news' in Jaśliska caused many Polish hearts to leap with joy, but left the Jews offended and with little trust in Polish integrity. Irrespective of the strategy each party assumed—the defensive or the offensive strategy—the objective was mainly the same: both the Poles and the Jews aimed at showing their superiority over the other, or as one informant put it, 'every side tried to show how strong it was.' The concerted efforts of the Polish local residents to win a Jewish soul, as well as the tactics they employed to avoid expected trouble, are revealed by an older married couple Stanisława (82) and Daniel S. (82):

> Stanisława: *Jews did not want to let it happen.*
> Daniel: *There were so many difficulties [...] The date of the baptism was estab-*
>   *lished and we Catholics knew about it. So we gathered, because we*
>   *wanted so much that this Jewish soul would be ours [...] At the last*
>   *moment somebody gave them [Jews] a sign. They [Jews] made her*
>   *father come here. He came from Krosno, he was a Jew [...] They [Jews]*
>   *had a law that they could only enter the first door of the Catholic*
>   *Church. Everything was lost when she [Felicja] was taken further than*
>   *the second door.*
> Question: *They could not go any further?*
> Daniel: *No, they couldn't.*
> Question: *Did she get through?*
> Stanisława: *Yes, she was baptised. His mother [husband's mother] guided her on*
>   *byways to the church, in order not to be seen. During several days she*
>   *took a few religion lessons, because she couldn't be baptised at once.*
>   *First she had to learn a bit. And the Jews did not know about it.*

Although all older Polish informants agreed about the grim atmosphere and violent outbursts at the time of the baptism, they nevertheless recalled the conversion as a joyous event. The day was theirs when the father of Felicja called her by her Jewish name and Felicja bluntly answered 'My name is Felicja Maria!' The same old married couple recalled:

> Stanisława: *She was standing on the veranda, it was our uncle's house. There were*
>   *also some other people standing next to her, one soldier among them. He*
>   *was not specially called to that place, he simply lived there. This father*

> *came up to the fence and said: 'Feiga, what have you done!' He cried*
> *and shouted so much to make her come to him. But she didn't.*
>
> Daniel: *'I will not deny Christ', she said. There were a lot of people of our faith*
> *queuing up there. I can remember it to this day.*

The painstaking efforts of the Polish and Jewish communities to claim control over the Jewish girl point to more than a clash of two different religious doctrines. The consternation during and after the conversion indicates that tensions between the two ethnic communities were real. Apparently, a persistent battle was going on; a battle between two religious, economic, and ethnic groups that sought to consolidate their position within the local political hierarchy. First, the fact that it was the elite of the Polish community who took pity on the Jewish girl supports the notion that Felicja was the main issue in a battle for political prestige. Once completed, the conversion of the Jewish girl would testify to the triumph of the Catholic community. Second, the involvement of persons and institutions outside the local community (Felicja's family and the convent respectively) indicates not only that the Polish and Jewish communities were serious about their cause, but also that in the wider society the ethnic boundary was firmly established as well. Inevitably, the outcome of the battle had an impact on the socio-political balance in the local community: victory over 'the other side' would mean an increase in political prestige. To lose the battle was an irreversible political defeat. The case of Felicja shows that latent tensions between the Polish and Jewish communities could easily catch fire when, for one reason or another, the weak political balance became disturbed.

Although delicate, the incident also shows that Polish-Jewish relations were built on a steady foundation. First, the violent upsurge of emotions following the baptism was relatively short-lived. Informants claimed that the Jews 'calmed down' after a while and that there were 'no fights' and 'no troubles' any longer. Both Jews and Poles resorted to a normal life soon after Felicja left for Poznań. And when Felicja returned, ill-feelings had softened and contacts with her mother and youngest brother were restored. The Polish local residents observed a happy young married couple, who built a new house, had many children, and lived in 'mutual agreement.' Second, the conversion did not alter customary Polish-Jewish interaction. None of the informants spoke of repercussions or discernible changes in the Polish-Jewish relations as a consequence of the conversion. Instead, it is stated, the situation readily normalised as if nothing had happened. Third, incidents like those that took place during Felicja's baptism were presumably unique in the history of the town. Informants confirm that there were no precedents to this case. Last but not least, the main character in the conflict—Felicja—

was not indigenous to the town and therefore took a neutral stance in the local situation. One may doubt whether the Catholic community, headed by a priest who spoke Yiddish and is said to have had close contacts with the rabbi, would have tried to convert a native Jewish woman.

Poles and Jews in Present-Day Jaśliska

In prewar Jaśliska, Poles and Jews lived up to the rule that one should keep to the ethnic community into which one was born. As a consequence, it was hard for a Jew to become a member of the Polish community, while it was virtually impossible for a Pole to become a member of the Jewish community. This explains why Polish informants considered Felicja's conversion a unique example of a fortunate union between Poles and Jews. Polish informants claim that intermarriages of that kind would have been more popular if the Jews had let the Poles date them. In spite of—or perhaps because of—all the restrictions there was a strong curiosity about the other side. The stories claim that Polish boys were anxious to meet Jewish girls. The alleged beauty of the Jewish women originates from these intimate friendships. Felicja too was praised for her beauty, and the man who married her was considered lucky. On her first arrival in Jaśliska, Felicja was warmly received by the Polish community, converted, married and gave birth to her children. The children too were baptised, married and gave birth to their children. Like most Polish local residents, Felicja and her children survived the war and enjoyed life-long support from the church.

But Felicja and Alicja did not feel like 'Poles', mainly because they had not been regarded as such in their environment. We have seen that the Jews of Jaśliska blamed Felicja for having betrayed her family and the Jewish community. She was considered an apostate, but still a Jew, and they never recognised her conversion. Although in a different manner, the Poles also laid stress on Felicja's Jewishness and that of her daughter Alicja. Like everyone else in Jaśliska, Felicja and Alicja carry the nickname bearing the characteristics of the family's history: Felicja and Alicja are nicknamed 'the converts' (*wychrzcianki*).[16] Although nicknaming is common practice in any village setting, the fact that the villagers brand the two women as 'converts, or worse 'Jews', sets them apart from the rest of Polish society. Even more painful, two generations of in-laws have treated Felicja and Alicja as outcasts. This experience made Felicja reconsider her identity:

I feel like a Catholic [...] I am a Catholic because I am baptised. I believe in Jesus, because Jesus came here to save me [...] But I do not feel like a Pole. Because they used to call me a Jewess (żydowica) or this or that. My own daughter-in-law used to call me that way. So why should I tell you that I am a Pole? My own daughter-in-law used to call me a Jewess.

Clearly, Felicja's admission of her Jewish identity is inspired by negative incentives ('they [Poles] will never stop reminding me that I am Jewish'). At the same time, however, she accepts her Jewish self and even seems to find some dignity in it ('I was born a Jew, so why should I deny that I am one?'). This is different for Alicja. It seems the stigma of her mother has passed on to her in an even more intense form. Having no affinity with the Jewish culture at all, and being raised in a Catholic and Polish environment, the stigma is particularly painful for her. The Polish identity to which she is strongly attached and about which she has never had any doubts ('I was brought up in a Polish and Catholic way') is simply denied to her. She experiences any reference to her person as a convert or a Jew as unjust and a personal assault on her self-respect and dignity. As a grown-up woman and mother of five children she claims the right to be called by her husband's nickname:

> *To my mother they said 'convert' […] To her child, to me, they said 'converted Alka'. That is what they keep calling us. When I was a child they called me 'converted Alka'. I have been married now for almost forty-four years, and they still call me 'converted Alka'. If they would call me [by my husband's nickname] 'Alka Wyskowa' nobody would understand.*

This experience of rejection is not specific to the lives of Felicja and Alicja. There is a clear parallel between their stories and the tales and songs told and sung by the Jews of Stoczek. The stories about female Jewish converts who gave up their religion for love usually ended with the convert being mistreated by the family into which she married because they continued to consider her a Jew. An alternative ending was to have her husband beat her: 'In any event, thoroughly chastened, she returned home and to the Jewish faith. There was such a song about the convert of Stoczek, and it was sung as long as the Jewish community existed' (Rosenthal 1954: 178). The message of the songs and tales is clear enough: '"To be a Jew is not something one chooses but something to which one is born" was the usual saying in Stoczek. The Jews of Stoczek believed that one could never hide Jewishness successfully, for if it did not show in one's face, it would come out in his or her speech or behaviour' (Rosenthal 1954: 177). Looking away from Stoczek and Jaśliska, we find that Jewish converts who lived in other European contexts and who were members of the higher social stratum had similar problems in escaping the stigma of being born a Jew:

> What ever the motives that lead Jews to abandon Judaism, they frequently found that the formal act of conversion was insufficient to convince Gentile society that they had ceased to be Jews. The best known apostates of the modern period—Rahel Varnhagen, Heinrich Heine, Karl Marx, Benjamin Disraeli—were all regarded by their contemporaries as Jews, even when, like Marx and Disraeli, they had been baptised as children. Popular opinion in most countries accepted the notion of the immutability of Jewishness (Endelman 1987: 16).

It is precisely this notion of the 'immutability of Jewishness' which helped shape the complicated, ambivalent self-identities of Felicja and Alicja. Because they are part of an environment that questions their Polishness, both women obsessively stressed their Catholic identity and explicitly cut ties with their Jewish roots. The extent to which they have adopted the views and attitudes of their Polish neighbours is remarkable, especially in the ways they view the Jews and Jewish customs. Their frame of reference is typically Polish and typically Catholic, in which few traces are left of their Jewish background. Like other Polish villagers Alicja learned that Jews crucified Jesus Christ, that Jews used blood from Polish children for baking their Easter bread (*maca*), and that a Jew was buried in the sitting position, 'so that he first reaches the Final Court on Judgement Day, for it takes ages for a Catholic to get to his feet.' Asked what she thinks about the story of Jews using Polish blood for baking *maca*, Felicja answered (emphasis mine): 'No, I should not blame any one as far as this story is concerned. It is not true, you know. I never saw *them* doing it. I spent a lot of years together with *them*, but I never saw anything like that.'

At the same time, however, because they are regarded as Jews by their Polish environment, Felicja and Alicja made no effort to wholly conceal their Jewishness and at times even showed pride in their common Jewish descent. This led to the curious scene of an old woman preaching the gospel and singing Yiddish songs. During the interview Felicja elaborated on Jewish customs at Sabbath and Easter and Alicja recalled her mother singing 'beautiful' Jewish songs in a language she could not understand. According to Alicja her mother did not hide her musical talents from her Polish neighbours and even taught one of her neighbours a number of Jewish folk songs. Still, Alicja's position is different from her mother's. Alicja has no knowledge of her Jewish past, nor does she feel any affinity with that past. She has been raised as a Polish child and has adapted herself to a Polish environment. If not for her mother and her Jewish uncles, Alicja would have lost all connections with her Jewish background. Alicja thinks of herself as a Pole, although her Polishness has constantly been under attack. To compensate for her injured sense of belonging, she clings to her Jewish family that gives her emotional and material backing.

Felicja and Alicja are deadlocked in a contradiction. Their inability to define a positive self-image is because people think in prewar categories. Religion and ethnicity are irrevocably bound together in their minds. In this context, conversion to Catholicism implies they change their ethnic identity which by the nature of their birth is impossible. The case of Felicja and Alicja clearly demonstrates the incompatibility of the ethnic categories 'Poles' and 'Jews'. In order to become a member of the Polish community Felicja adopted a Catholic identity. As a true Catholic she (and her children) had to abandon her Jewish identity and also repudiate the qualities of being Jewish.[17] As Polish Catholics with Jewish roots Felicja and Alicja are trapped by a persistent self-denial. Despite their common Jewish roots and presumed familiarity with Jewish traditions, they view the Jewish world with the eyes of sceptical non-Jews. Felicja's and Alicja's uneasiness is typical of those who have left their own community, or as Hertz (1988: 70) writes, who have left their own 'caste':

> The shadow of the caste forever dogs their heels. Their peculiar oversensitivity, touchiness, and constant mental tension stem from the fear that they will still be treated as members of the caste: this is all the more painful to me because I am *no longer* a member of the caste, do not wish to consider myself one, and want to flee as far as possible from the caste. But do others see me like that? Aren't they still treating me like a man belonging to the caste? And aren't they letting me know it? Constant uncertainty, constant suspicion.

To conclude, it may be stated that although in the past Polish-Jewish relations in Jaśliska were quite distant, relations were based on a firm foundation. The ethnic differences, tangible in almost every aspect of life, did not result in an armed peace between both communities. However, they did limit customary contacts between Poles and Jews, who would respect the social boundary whenever possible. This former boundary left a considerable imprint on present-day Polish-Jewish relations. In the minds of the Polish villagers, the cultural and social differences between the Jews and the Poles still prevail. Though not necessarily valued negatively, these differences hold that Jewishness is inconsistent with Polishness. Indeed, despite her conversion to Catholicism, the Polish villagers still regard Felicja and her daughter as Jews. As for Felicja and Alicja, they have not yet found peace of mind on the matter.

Notes

1. The interview with Alicja S. was conducted in Jaśliska, the interview with Felicja W. was conducted in Nysa. Her two daughters Mila W. and Teresa T. were present during the interview with Felicja W. (see also figure 6.1). Mila had introduced me to her mother, and Teresa lived with her mother in the same apartment.

2. It may be noted that the 'facts' recounted by mother (Felicja) and daughter (Alicja) have mainly been derived from the same source, that is, from 'Felicja-and-her-life story'. Presumably, both Felicja and Alicja 'know' the same 'facts', but the accounts sometimes diverge considerably. Personal differences (age, experience, interest, etc.) may account for the contrasts in views and explanations. The similarities, however, display the unique experience of two women of two different generations who have no clear Polish identity.

3. Krosno is situated at some 30 kilometres from Jaśliska. In 1921 the Jews of Krosno made up some 27 percent of the town's total population, which numbered 6,389 at that time (GUS 1924).

4. After Felicja's conversion her Jewish name 'Feiga' was changed into the Christian name 'Felicja'.

5. Felicja did not explain who attacked her father. The attack, however, may be indicative of her father's marginal position in either the Polish or Jewish community (see also later in this chapter).

6. The Austro-Russian war in Galicia (1914-1918) was followed by the Polish-Soviet war (1919-1920). Felicja probably confuses the two wars. It is possible, though, that Felicja's father had been caught as a prisoner of war during the Polish-Soviet war and had been released from prison long after the end of this war (in 1922 or even later).

7. Felicja probably means that she suffered from anaemia. This is a remarkable excuse for not being admitted to the convent. Presumably, Felicja was rejected for reasons other than her weak physical health. One may assume that as a Jewish woman she has never been considered a serious candidate for the holy convent. Indeed, after six years of education and work she was sent home to live a life of her own.

8. Lingo is the word Felicja uses when referring to Yiddish.

9. The feathers from spoiled duvets and pillows mentioned by Felicja symbolise the shattering impact of the war, for duvets and pillows were valuable objects in poor Polish and Jewish households. Other informants used the symbol of whirling snow-white feathers to describe the damage caused by Soviet bombs in Jaśliska in September 1944.

10. Here Felicja probably confused common knowledge about German atrocities—such as the gassing of Jews—with her personal experiences. It is not likely that Germans gassed these Jewish children in ordinary houses in the ghetto. Nor is it likely that she experienced such an event at any other point on her trip home.

11. 'Pani tylko cudem żyje!'

12. Interestingly, Alicja refers to the wife of her Russian uncle as a Russian woman, while Felicja refers to her as a convert, that is, a Jewish woman who like herself had converted to Christianity.

13. Felicja's younger sister died from tuberculosis in Rzeszów, where she worked as a servant.

14. Felicja was baptised in the Roman Catholic Church by means of a water baptism (performed by a priest or a deacon). Exceptions can be made under certain circumstances, for example in cases of emergency. Blood baptism and desire baptism are such exceptions, but they apply especially to the early Christian period when the Christian movement was weak, and when the Christians were being oppressed and persecuted. Blood baptism, then, refers to a catechumen who had not yet been baptised but was caught and tortured

to death. Desire baptism refers to a situation when a person has already decided, confirmed, or attempted to be baptised, but dies before the baptism has actually taken place. In both cases the wish of the martyr or applicant will do (J. Rotteveel, personal communication). The kind of baptism which Felicja had in mind, was probably the desire baptism. In that case she would have postponed the baptism to a later date, and if she died in the meantime, her soul was saved anyway.

15. In Stoczek conversion was so little recognised that a returning convert had to be taken back into the fold and there was no special ceremony to mark his or her return (Rosenthal 1954: 178).

16. From the noun '*wychrzta*' (convert), which is generally used to denote a Jew who converted to Christianity.

17. This hypothetical 'incompatibility' runs parallel with the thesis put forward by Endelman (1987: 2), who states that Christian self-definition came to be based on the disparagement of Judaism, so that from the earliest centuries Christian doctrine incorporated an attack on Jews and fundamental Jewish beliefs.

Chapter 7

THE DESTRUCTION OF THE COMMUNITIES

'Will you talk about Szczekac, when his horse fell down on the old Jewish cemetery?' asked a boy who had heard this story already many times from the old Marcin. 'Yes, yes, children,' said Marcin who liked to tell his stories over and over again. 'When was it? It must have been when our troops chased the Germans, the wolves, out of Poland. It was, children, a restless and hurried time, with quarrels and fighting. Everyone wanted to secure a place that belonged to a perished Jew. On a Monday, when the farmers were working on the fields, I entered the Jewish cemetery. I watched and saw Szczekac on the cemetery with a plough. People approached. I asked: "Szczekac, what are you doing with that plough?" And he answered: "I am ploughing the earth". "Aren't you afraid of the dead buried here?" I asked him. "No," he answered again, "I should be afraid of the living, not of the dead, not of these bad ones" [...] Szczekac put his horse to the plough, drove it on, the horse took a few steps, strained his ears, blew through his nostrils and just stood there. Szczekac took his whip and hit the legs of the horse, the sides, the neck. Then the legs of the horse gave way, the horse fell down, cried and lifted his head a last time. I saw locks and bones rolling, and there, where the plough had scratched the earth, lay a skull of a human being. The bystanders crossed themselves and proceeded to attack Szczekac: "Don't you see that this place is haunted? Take your horse and clear out!" You should have seen, boys, how Szczekac flung himself on the crowd, screaming and growling like a wild dog.' 'And the horse?' asked the two boys suddenly. 'The horse was brought home dead by Szczekac,' spoke Marcin with a sigh. 'With that God punished him right then and there. One should not stand up to the dead. This German, the son of the devil, had turned the cemetery into a horse market. Do you know how he came to his end? We don't even know where the bones of Hitler have gone. The people who live near the old cemetery say that they hear wailing at night. I could swear to it, this is the wailing of Hitler and his henchmen, who murdered all the Jews from Melawe, hundreds of our Jews. And God will never forgive them' (Opatoshu 1951: 315).

Introduction

*W*ith the border so close, signs of the approaching war did not go by unnoticed. The annexation of Slovakia by the German Reich in March 1939 gave rise to dark expectations. Divisions of the Polish army were sent to Jaśliska to lay mines and supply the border posts with extra munitions and soldiers. The efforts were to no avail. In September 1939 Hitler's armed force crushed the Polish army within a week, aided by the Slovaks in the South and the Soviets in the East. The policies introduced by Nazi-Germany had an enormous impact on the lives of the people in the research area: the exploitation of human capital and natural resources, the racial segregation, and the Final Solution. The segregation and elimination of the Jewish and Gypsy population by Nazi Germany was followed by large-scale population resettlement policies in the area. Despite the enormous input of human energy and state funds in the postwar period, the area never recovered from the severe losses suffered during the Second World War and during the years immediately following the war. In the early 1990s, at the time when capitalist Europe commemorated its victory over socialism, most of the (agricultural) industry in the area had already been liquidated. Half a century after the end of the Second World War, the villagers have to start anew and find themselves in a situation which in many respects reminds them of the interwar period.

Hitler's Era: German Rule in Southeastern Poland

The General Government

On the first of September 1939 the Wehrmacht attacked Poland, soon followed by the Soviets on 17 September. The so-called September Campaign was fierce and brief. On the eve of the war a few dozen males from Jaśliska were called to arms, but this act was merely symbolic. The battle was lost beforehand and soldiers were imprisoned even before they had reached the front. Local jokes tell the tale of soldiers who had been called to arms, but had no time to properly dress themselves with their uniforms. By 6 September the evacuation of the Polish municipal office, border guard station, and post office started. On 8 September detachments of the Polish army retreated through Jaśliska, leaving behind blown up bridges and mines. The Jewish sawmill went up in flames too.

By the end of September 1939, the Ukrainian police, which established its headquarters in Jaśliska, was permanently supported by a division of the German border guard (*Grenzschütz*). By that time, the whole of Poland had passed under the occupation of Nazi and Soviet forces. On the western side of the Nazi-Soviet demarcation line along the Bug and the San rivers, the Germans established a General Government (*Generalgouvernement*) which had its headquarters in Cracow. The General Government was considered German-occupied territory, while the western districts of prewar Poland were directly incorporated into the Reich. On the other side of the demarcation line, the Soviet armies annexed western Byelorussia and western Ukraine. Operation Barbarossa, Hitler's attack on the Soviet Union on 22 June 1941, ended the Nazi-Soviet Pact. After the outbreak of the Soviet-German war eastern Galicia was added to the German-occupied territories (Davies 1986).

Jaśliska was incorporated into the German-occupied territories right from the start. German occupation in Poland was extremely severe as a result of the racial conceptions held by the Germans, who made an absolute distinction between Jews and Slavs on the one hand, and nations of western Europe on the other. Furthermore, the quality of the German personnel employed in the administration was low. As Gross (1979: 54) puts it, 'There were exceptions, of course, but it seems that better qualified people, as a rule, were sent to the West. Hitler insisted that 'strong personalities', that is, fanatic Nazis, go East.' The General Government was backed with special units of the SS and the Gestapo, which could freely operate, beyond the law of the Reich and free from the influence of the Wehrmacht active in the front-line military zones (Davies 1986).

The General Government had to accomplish two residual goals. The first was to prevent the Polish intelligentsia from taking a leadership role. This goal was carried out in the so-called Extraordinary Pacification Campaign (*AB-Aktion*) in which some 15,000 members of the Polish intelligentsia (e.g., clergy, teachers, writers, journalists, medical doctors) were exterminated. Second, communication lines were to be kept in good condition so that the occupied territory could later be used for mobilisation of the armed forces in anticipation of future conquests. Along with German expansion the administration of the General Government was to support the Reich with unlimited exploitation of a non-German slave labour force and to help the Reich authorities in their task of 'cleansing' the Reich of all non-Germans subjects by means of Germanisation, expulsion, and extermination (Gross 1979). Apart from numerous labour camps and forced labour services, there were penal investigation camps and, from the end of 1941 onwards, the extermination camps.[1]

According to the outlines of the *Generalplan-Ost*, the Nazis aimed to redistribute the entire population who were on occupied territory. Already, in the first year of the German occupation, some two million Jews were consigned to closed ghettos (*Reservaten*) to separate them systematically from the rest of the population. The Aryan population was divided into German citizens born in the Reich (*Reichsdeutsch*), German nationals (*Volksdeutsch*), and all others (*Nichtdeutsch*) (Davies 1986). The Poles, like all Slavic nations, were assigned to the group of racially alien peoples (*Fremdvölkischen*) (Gross 1979). Where suitable, the Poles were destined for Germanisation (*Wieder-eindeutschung*). Since German-occupied territories were largely inhabited by *Fremdvölkischen* (an estimated 80 to 85 percent) and in addition was used as a dumping ground for 'undesirable elements' from the Reich (e.g., Jews, gypsies, invalids, political dissidents, prisoners of war, criminal elements), only a small part of the population was fit for Germanisation.[2]

Jaśliska Under German Occupation

The retreat of the Polish authorities from Jaśliska left the local residents unprotected from pillage and spurred on interethnic hostilities. Tensions grew to such an extent that a large number of villagers cleared their way to Rymanów, including practically all the Jewish families from Jaśliska.[3] Lemkos from the neighbouring villages plundered the shops that had been left vacant by the Jews and threatened the Poles who had stayed behind (Stączek 1944-1951; Orlik 1979). The Polish and Jewish refugees returned when things had quietened down (Stączek 1944-1951; Litwak 1969; Yad Vashem 1984). By that time, a 'Ukrainian' (that is, a pro-Ukrainian Lemko) from the neighbouring village Daliowa had assumed leadership in Jaśliska.[4] Polish sources claim that the new mayor put a Ukrainian flag on the town hall and proclaimed Jaśliska the capital of the Lemko district (*Lemkowszczyzna*) (Stączek 1944-1951; Orlik 1979). Bogdański (n.d.: 182), the then retired head of the primary school in Jaśliska, described the inauguration ritual performed by a Ukrainian teacher. He watched the Ukrainian teacher blessing the water of the well in the market square and encouraging his children to kiss the so-called 'Lemko grounds'.

Indeed, Ukrainian rule in Jaśliska was a fact throughout the German occupation.[5] The fact that a considerable part of the local Lemko population were enthusiastic supporters of the anti-Polish and anti-Jewish Nazi policies made the position of the Polish and Jewish minorities in the area especially vulnerable. Jan S. (65) explained: 'We were so obedient and quiet because there were 20,000 of them, of those Lemkos, and we were only 700. So we had to be obedient. During the Polish times they treated us politely. We went to supper together, they had late suppers. But then the Germans came, and they divided us and ruled.' German authorities supported Ukrainian nationalism by abolishing the Polish primary school in Jaśliska and establishing a Ukrainian primary school, which was also attended by Polish children. Jewish children were forbidden to attend public school altogether. However, it is said that Jewish children continued to learn in secret. It is also said that Polish children were unwilling to take up to the Ukrainian language that was taught in school. Protests from the side of the children and teachers proved successful. By the end of the school term 1940-1941 the Ukrainian school was moved to Posada Jaśliska, while the Polish school was upgraded to five classes (Stączek 1944-1951; Orlik 1979). After 1940 all Polish school-leavers received a bilingual *Schul-Entlassungszeugnis* printed on paper provided by the *Generalgouvernement*.

From the start Polish and Jewish civilians were put to work in industries and labour camps set up by Germans. The healthy and strong were taken to the Reich to do some type of manual work there. The men, women, and children that stayed behind were put to work in labour camps specialised in the exploitation of minerals and forests.[6] In 1942 a German firm called 'Olbrycht' started to exploit large amounts of beech wood from the forests surrounding Jaśliska. Civilians, Jews and Poles alike, were employed to cut the wood and take it from the forest to the small town. From there German lorries transported the wood to the nearest railway station (Stączek 1944-1951; Orlik 1979). In order to keep the transport running during heavy winters, civilians, among them children, were made to clear the roads of snow.

The wood industry in Jaśliska greatly contributed to German revenues. Business ran so well that German officials were installed to efficiently organise the labour force and administer the wood transports from Jaśliska. An estimated 30 *sągi*[7] of wood was taken every day from the forest (Stączek 1944-1951; Orlik 1979). In the short term this resulted in a shortage of firewood. In the long term the exploitation of forests to a considerable extent changed the physical environment of Jaśliska; whole forests disappeared, of which the younger generations only know them from hearsay. Not only local civilians were put to work in the forest. In a testimony, Mordechai D. reflects on his wanderings through Poland and his exhausting short visits to various labour camps. On his way he also passed Jaśliska, where he was put to work in the forest. Mordechai D. recalls:

> We worked in the forest up the mountains. The Ukrainian guards took us eight
> kilometres up the mountains. We went on foot and it took us three hours to get
> there. Once we got there we cut down beech trees. The work was beyond human
> endurance. In no other camp was I put to such heavy work. And they also took
> contingents from us (Bauminger n.d.: 3).

Besides the heavy work, the villagers and prisoners were burdened with
compulsory levies (*kontyngent*) which had to be paid in kind. During their
frequent visits, Ukrainian or German officials took the few horses, cows,
goats, or crops still left on the impoverished farms.[8] In return Poles and Jews
received coupons which were worth far less than the contingents taken from
them. Considering the low agricultural productivity during the war years,
the contingents were particularly cumbersome. The arbitrary German rule
in taking contingents is illustrated by the following story:

> *Once there was a Lemko farmer who had a stud-bull that he set free on cows. Germans
> had been building a border station next to this farmer. One day a man went with his
> cow to the farmer and the farmer set his bull free on the cow. At this very moment some
> Germans passed by and watched the show. They talked to each other in their own lan-
> guage and continued their way. A few days later the farmer received a paper, in which
> he was ordered to give his bull as a contingent. That was how the Germans worked.
> They took everything that had quality, without giving anything in return. So the
> farmer said to his wife: 'Hey woman, do you know what this letter means? Go to the
> police station and do something about it, because they will take our bull. And who will
> jump on the cows after that?' So she went. They [Lemkos] had their own way of dress-
> ing, so she put a shawl on her arms and went to the police station. She knocked at the
> door and entered. They [Lemkos] used to bow to the ground while saying 'Praised be
> the Lord'. And a German asked: 'Was? Was?' And she said: 'Oh, they took the bull from
> us'. And he said: 'Gut. Gut.' She said: 'So who is going to jump on the cows?' And the
> German said: 'Ja, ja.'[9] In this way they communicated. So she returned home and
> when her husband asked what the German had told her, she said: 'He will jump on our
> cows himself.' This is not a joke, this story is true. (Paweł N., 63)*

In 1940 some twenty German-speaking families from Poznań who had
not signed the list of German nationals were deported to Jaśliska. They
either did not want to register or did not fit the category of German nationals. Some local families had to share their homes with the newcomers, who
quickly gained the confidence of the local inhabitants.[10] Since they knew
German they were charged with administrative work. Without exception,
the Polish informants spoke well of their 'guests' from the West. They considered them trustworthy and 'loyal' local administrators, who committed
forgery to the advantage of the villagers and warned the villagers of surprise
attacks by the Germans. The city-dwellers, who were not accustomed to the

harsh circumstances in the countryside, had a hard time surviving hunger and cold. When three immigrants from Poznań died because they accidentally picked and ate poisonous mushrooms, they were buried on the local cemetery in Jaśliska—an act which can be considered as a token of respect by the local inhabitants.

Polish Resistance to German Rule

A large number of villagers were involved in some sort of resistance activities, as Jaśliska was an important link in the vast network of the Polish underground resistance.[11] A teacher (nickname Kopacz), father Rąpała, and the forest guard Mr D. were the main contacts in Jaśliska. The local farmers who were involved in resistance activities hid Polish officers and soldiers and helped them safely across the border. Agents of the Polish underground also passed through Jaśliska. The resistance activities were dangerous because of the firm control of the Ukrainian and German police in the area. Frequent house searches and German infiltration crippled resistance activities. In March 1940 ten people were arrested, put in prisons (in Krosno, Jasło, Tarnów, and Sanok), or taken to concentration camps (Oświęcim, Dachau). Of those arrested and put in camps only two returned. Among those released was father Rąpała, who was set free thanks reportedly to pleadings of the Greek Catholic priest from Daliowa. Raids by the Ukrainian police in August 1942 dealt the final blow to local resistance, when another series of people were arrested (Orlik 1979).

During the frequent German and Ukrainian house searches Jews played an active role in helping the Polish villagers to escape. In their capacity as guides and interpreters for the German police, Jews are said to have saved many Polish lives by warning the victims or bearing false evidence. Illustrative is the story of Katarzyna L. (65), whose father was involved in resistance activities. During one of these visits a Jewish interpreter was asked to identify her father. Though he was the person the Germans were looking for, the interpreter declared that he was not that person. After this visit the father of Katarzyna L. escaped to Kraków before the Germans had the opportunity to catch him in a second round of searches. In like manner, Rozalia B. (57) recalled the spectacular escape of her father thanks to clever Jewish tactics. One night on his way home her father met a group of Germans assisted by a Jew. The Jew, seeing Rozalia's father passing, asked him (in the third person) whether *he* was at home. Rozalia's father, being alarmed, answered that *he* would arrive any minute, and took to his heels.

In the whole region participation in guerrilla warfare against the German occupants was minimal. Ukrainian dominance and collaboration was simply too dangerous and uncertain a situation. Still, by 1943 Polish partisans reached the nearby forests. Zbigniew K. (62) was still a young boy when he was kidnapped by partisans in 1944. Zbigniew K. stayed with them for one month, witnessed some heroic acts of sabotage, and finally fled. German retaliatory measures against partisans were severe. For every German soldier killed in partisan attacks ten Polish civilians were shot on the spot. In December 1943 German police battalions visited the countryside to frighten the local population. In Zawoja two farmers were shot for hiding firearms. At the same time the German police discovered the hiding places of some Jews who hid among the local population. All of them were taken out of their hiding places and shot on the spot during daytime (Stączek 1944-1951). It is unclear what happened to the Poles who had helped them to hide.

The Destruction of a Jewish Community

Prelude

Polish and Jewish sources claim that the Jewish villagers lived a quiet life during the first years of German occupation (Stączek 1944-1951; Yad Vashem 1984). The earlier mentioned Jewish involvement in the smuggling expeditions to and from Slovakia during the first years of the Second World War shows that business went on as usual. This is confirmed by Israel B., who stresses the relatively untroubled position of the Jews in Jaśliska:

> During the first three years of Nazi rule the Jews from Jaśliska suffered less than those in the other communities. There were no actions carried out to limit their freedom and they did not starve, because they still had transactions with the peasants in the neighbourhood. Many of them were put to all kinds of work, but there were no executions (Litwak 1969: 4).[12]

In like manner, Polish informants claimed that Jews were not treated better or worse than the Poles. The special restrictions imposed on Jews (of which the exclusion from public school is one example) did not significantly change this notion. Still, there were signs of the evil German intent that also reached the Polish villagers. Józef L. (62), whose mother fell ill during the war and had to be taken to hospital in Krosno (30 km from Jaśliska), watched the impoverished Jews in the Krosno ghetto. Other informants recalled that the Jews were made to sing songs on their way to work that ridiculed the Polish nation and stressed the Jews' inferiority.[13] On other occasions, the local Grenzschütz would organise 'special exercises' for the Jewish population on public grounds. Andrzej F. (72) recalled:

They [Grenzschütz soldiers] took them, sometimes in the morning. They took all Jew-
ish men. And they did exercises with them. They led them to the fields. Everyone had
to find a stick for himself. And then they had to move as if they were cutting grass or
grain. It was winter, there was snow and everybody had to cut [...] Jewish women had
rakes and they had to scrape. Then they ordered them to kneel on the grass and eat
grass. They had to pasture like cows. Then they chased them to the river, because when
a cow is fed she must drink water. There is a stream, a small one, and they had to lie
down and drink water. Because a cow must drink water. They [Germans] did such
curious things with them.

Despite everything, for the Polish villagers the deportation of the Jews and
the subsequent massacre were unexpected. The head of the school in
Jaśliska who was in office during the war years recorded the German raid in
the following manner:

One day, in the second half of June 1942, all Jews were gathered on the market
square and were subdivided into groups. The men apart from the women, and
the women apart from their children. Then they were carried to the ghetto in
Dukla. Jewish property was confiscated on behalf of the German Reich, while
the smaller things were sold to the civilians. This action left a severe impression
on the local population (Stączek 1944-1951: 12).

This sober and brief account is in no way complete on the subject and it
clearly contrasts with the elaborate and detailed stories of the Polish informants.[14] However, the account voices a general attitude that characterises
all stories about the extermination of the local Jews: the event has had, and
at the same time has not had a dramatic impact on the local Polish community. Although inhuman and repellent, what happened to the Jews of
Jaśliska was not directly relevant to the lives of most of the Polish villagers.
During the difficult war years concern with one's own physical survival prevailed over concern about others. Below follows a description of the 'facts'
of the Shoah[15] as remembered by the Polish informants. It should be noted
that the presented 'facts' are a selection from the often anecdotal (that is,
incomplete) and divergent (in contents and emphasis) stories told by the
informants. In only a few cases was it possible to corroborate these so-called
facts with other sources.

The Forecast

For some informants the Shoah commenced with the Jews predicting their
own fate. The stories about the Jews who anticipated their own death have
two things in common. Firstly, the Jews read their future in 'Jewish books'
which foretold the coming of the 'messiah' or indicated the end of the 'Jew-

ish Nation'. Secondly, the message was not kept among the Jews but was passed on to their closest Polish neighbours. Bronisław Z. (86), for instance, once found his Jewish neighbour crying and when he asked for the reason the latter answered: 'I cry because I read in the books that no single Jew will be living on this earth in the near future.' The Poles, who witnessed the deportation of the Jews and later heard of their cruel death, could never forget the Jewish prophecy. The grandfather of Gabriel T. (13) told his grandson the following story many years after the war:

> When the Germans occupied this country, Jews predicted their own defeat and felt their end drawing near. They [Jews] had their prophets who read in the books about their own extermination. One day a Jew, he was called Dawid S., came to my grandfather and told him [grandfather] that the messiah Adolf Hitler was born, the one who would destroy them, and he announced that such was written in their books: it is written that when we [Jews] will be murdered birds will appear on the meadow. The birds are called 'pitpołak' and while they hide in the grass they twitter like 'fit fi lit'. At my grandfather's home this Jew said that when we [Jews] will be murdered these birds will cease to sing in the grass on the fields for five years. And so it happened. Grandfather remembered the words of this Jew till the day he died, and together with Władysław F. who is still living, we may verify the words of this Jew, which foretold us Catholics what would happen, and which proved to be correct.[16]

The Raid

The story further goes that on that 'terrible day', somewhere in the second half of 1942, the Poles were made to stay inside and not leave their homes until the police had cleared their way out. Jan S. (65), who was a teenager at the time, watched the raid from behind a small wall until he was discovered by a policeman, whose bullets chased him out of his hiding place. With the exception of a few urchins, most villagers had been inside their homes during the Jews' deportation.

It is said that the raid was unannounced and started when the first Jews returned from their work in the forest. From behind their windows villagers saw the Jews being chased out of their homes and herded together in the market square. Yet, even in the period between the raid and the gathering, transactions took place between Jewish and Polish villagers. In distress and panic, Jews tried to prepare for the journey and, at the same time, save their belongings. For this they needed the help of their Polish neighbours. It is said that Jewish women begged for bread from their Polish neighbours. Some of them gave bread, like Daniel S.'s (82) mother, who is said to have been a 'very brave woman'. How much 'courage' it took to be involved in the act of bread-giving is explained by Józef L. (62), who was still a boy when he made the mistake of giving a roll to a passing Jew. Józef L. and his father were on their way to Dukla (20 km from Jaśliska) when they passed a shift of workers from the stone quarry in Lipowica (18 km). A German guard noticed the boy giving his roll to a Jewish worker and threatened to shoot the child and his father. Thanks to the pleadings of the father, who explained to the guard that his son had made a terrible mistake and that he was too young to comprehend the gravity of the situation, they were left in peace. After the whole affair his father was angry with him and explained to him that he would not allow his son to meet Jews again.

During the little time that was left for the Jews to pack their things and prepare for departure some of them approached their Polish neighbours, gave them their cattle and valuables, which they had not hidden or given away earlier, and asked them to hide and store their possessions.[17] Among those approached was Rozalia B.'s (57) mother, a former cleaning lady at the home of a Jewish family. She was asked by her former employer, who came to her in agony and tears, to take care of the cows during her absence. If her family did not return, the mother of Rozalia B. would be the rightful owner. At that time neither of them knew that the cows would soon be taken as contingents by a vengeful Pole from a neighbouring village. Eleonora B. (67), who served in her father's shop during the raid, was also visited by Jews. They passed her shop to collect their identity cards, buy food for the journey, and hand over bags of valuables to store in the shop:[18]

> *Jews came to me, the younger ones. They were in the prime of life [...] All over the place packed bags were standing, and they [Jews] wanted to give them to me. But I told them: 'Take everything with you, I want nothing from you.' [...] You can say anything about me, but I am not mean, like the people who took money from a Jew, but never paid it back. I would never do a thing like that, even today I wouldn't [...] I could have taken everything they gave me, but I did not.*

It is unknown to whom these bags went after Eleonora B. had rejected them. A few hours after the raid, all possessions which had not been given to Poles were confiscated by the German Reich. The doors of Jewish houses were sealed and Poles were forbidden entry to them. Only later were the smaller things sold to the local population (Stączek 1944-1951).

The Deportation

After the Jews were gathered in the market square there were no more transactions between Jews and Poles. Names were called from a list in order to check whether all the Jews were present. After the checking procedure the guards divided the Jews into groups of men, women, and children.[19] At the

same time Jewish men and women were harassed and humiliated by the soldiers who guarded them.[20] Men and women were packed into lorries, children were simply thrown in. All informants recalled the screaming, crying
and wailing of the Jews. Andrzej F. (72) recalled that while all this was hap-
pening to them the Jews screamed out loudly 'The messiah is born! The
messiah is born!' According to Andrzej F. the Jews believed that it was the
messiah who made them suffer all this: 'they believed that when the messiah
is born they will be severely persecuted.' Katarzyna L. (65) recalled the Jews
begging for salvation and blessings:

> *The only thing I remember is that I returned from the fields with my mother. And they*
> *[the villagers] shouted: 'the Jews, the Jews, they are taking the Jews away! They are*
> *taking the Jews away!' So I ran to the road and saw the Jews being escorted out of*
> *town. It was like that. Some older [Polish] women were present and they proceeded to*
> *christen the Jews. They [the women] shouted 'christen them, christen them! They want*
> *to be christened!' Some of the women christened the Jews. They sprinkled holy water on*
> *them and bade them farewell. The Jews knew that they were going to meet their death.*
> *It was terrible.*

The above recollection perfectly pictures the drama of the moment. By the
time the Jews were taken from the town, all the inhabitants knew that they
would meet with death soon. Whereas the Jews signalled their own demise
by predicting the arrival of the messiah, the Poles predicted the elimination
of the Jews by supposing the Jews wished to be christened. The popular
belief holds that a Jew who is in distress and expects his imminent death will
always ask for his salvation.[21]

The Selection

Jews were taken in lorries to the ghetto in Dukla (20 km from Jaśliska),
where they spent some four to eight weeks. In Dukla, the old were separated
from the young and the healthy from the weak. On the selection procedure
used Andrzej F. (72) commented: 'Jewish men dug a hole and they poured
petrol into it. Not the old ones, but the young ones had to jump over it. Those
who dirtied themselves with petrol were put on one side. Those who jumped
over were put on the other side.' The strong and the healthy joined the ghetto
in Dukla, where they were put to work in the stone quarry. Or they were
deported to other labour camps. It is not clear what happened to this group
of Jews after they had ceased to be 'indispensable workers'.[22] The Polish villagers lost track of those who had been put to work in Dukla. Traces of the
old and the weak, however, were not lost. On 13 August 1942 an estimated
500 Jews from Jaśliska and surroundings were made to walk to Barwinek, a

village 14 kilometres from Jaśliska (see map 1). From Barwinek they were taken a few hundred metres into the Błudna forest to an empty clearing. There they were shot and buried in a mass grave. Dates and numbers are inscribed on the memorial plate located on the place of the massacre.

The Massacre

The news of the massacre in the Błudna forest soon reached Jaśliska. Although the local Polish population had been carefully restricted from the place of massacre, some Poles witnessed the event. Among these were curious Polish children (mostly boys), for whom it was a game to get as close as possible. The spectator, who is mentioned by all informants, is the forest guard from Dukla, who happened to be on the spot by sheer coincidence. The story about the killing of the Jews, therefore, is mostly traced back to the supposed eyewitness account of the forest guard. The account goes as follows: Guarded by their executioners Jews were made to dig a large hole. After they had finished digging, a board was laid over that hole. Jews were ordered to stand on that board, stripped of their clothes. In this manner one shift after the other was shot in the back. After each shift a layer of lime was put on the bodies. Informants stressed that the Jews were shot randomly and that only a few were killed instantly. Many of those who dropped down, were not dead but only hit in the arms or legs, which, from the informants' point of view, made the whole event even more inhumane. It is said that the earth moved for three weeks after the shooting. Then, after three weeks, life ceased for all those who had been buried.

Opinions vary on the identity of the executioners. Some informants claimed that Poles or Ukrainians were used for the killing, yet others thought that it was Jews (*Junaki, Haudeken*) who did the dirty job. One informant suggested that the Jewish executioners were stupefied with narcotics. Informants unambiguously claimed that the whole event made a tremendous impression on the forest guard. Some informants said that his hair turned grey upon seeing the slaughter. Others held that he was marked for life and lived with a terrible fear (*lęk*) which he was not able to get rid of.

Escape and Rescue

Jews who followed the retreating Red Army after Hitler's attack on the Soviet Union in June 1941 were more likely to survive the Nazi genocide, but they had to endure the Soviet internment camps instead. In fact, a recurrent theme in the accounts of Jewish survivors is that before the outbreak of the Nazi-Soviet war in 1941 Jews on either side of the borderline were made to choose on which territory they wanted to stay; on German or on Soviet territory. The choice made at that time would be decisive for a person's fate later in that war. This is clear from the story of Israel B., who was 'lucky' enough to find himself on Soviet territory in the summer of 1941. The cynical note of his interviewer Josef Litwak (1969: 2) is striking and reveals the contrasting world views of the eye-witness (Israel B.) and the interviewer (Josef Litwak):

> After the consolidation of Soviet authority [in Russian occupied territory] the refugees were compelled to register and to declare that they were willing to take on the Russian citizenship, or, as desired, to return to their hometowns which had fallen under German rule. According to the eye-witness all Jewish refugees from his region decided to return to their homes, and, to his thinking, it never entered their heads to consider the second option. Being a very devout Jew, he believes, despite the irrationality of his decision, that it was the hand of God which had guided him. For all Jewish refugees who opted to return home to German-occupied territory were deported to the internment regions in the North, and in this way escaped the massacre. The local Jews, however, were not deported and instead were murdered by the Germans between 1941 and 1942.

Only a very small number of the Jews from Jaśliska survived the Shoah. The only Jewish family that is widely known to have escaped and survived the war is the family of Abraham B. Abraham B., his wife, his married sons and daughters are said to have split up and gone different ways (Hungary, Czechoslovakia, USSR, USA). Where Abraham B. resided during and after the war is subject to speculation. One version tells that Abraham B. went to the Soviet Union and later migrated elsewhere. Another version holds that he died a natural death in Hungary or the United States. Informants claimed that the family of Abraham B. escaped because they were rich and therefore knew what happened in the world. This explanation suggests that since both money and information were crucial means for escape, most Jewish villagers perished because they were deprived of such elementary means.[23]

Of greater importance than the lack of resources was the unreliability of the non-Jewish environment. In fact, the Polish villagers distrusted their own neighbours too. A number of informants claimed that 'solidarity' and 'trust' among the villagers, conditions that were essential for the success of any clandestine activity, were lacking. In addition, the informants explained that news spread quickly in the village and was likely to be passed on to malicious Polish individuals, to the Ukrainian police, or to the German soldiers who resided in the village. We have seen that these circumstances, to a large extent, corrupted the underground network in Jaśliska. Whatever the excuses, no single Jew who escaped the transport and sought refuge in Jaśliska was rescued by the local inhabitants. This somewhat contrasts with the experiences in some of the neighbouring towns and villages.[24] Still, many informants spoke freely about one event that illustrates the Poles' failure to rescue the Jews.

It is said that a Jewish boy escaped the transport by fleeing to the forest. The stories about the wanderings of the Jewish boy after his escape vary, but informants agreed that the Jew hid in the toilet near the house of a Polish woman, a 'wrong character' and mistress of German soldiers.[25] Some informants claimed that upon noticing the Jew the Polish woman handed him over to the Germans. One informant stated that she had done so out of fear, others found her guilty of the cowardly and immoral act of betrayal. Yet other informants held that the Jewish refugee was spotted by a German soldier visiting the Polish woman. In any case the Jew was caught, was ordered to dig his own grave, and was then shot in public during daytime.

The handful of Jews who survived the genocide left Poland immediately after the war. Recent attempts to locate the survivors prove that they have found their new homes in Canada, the United States, Belgium, and Israel. The Jewish survivor Samuel O. (82) explained that some Jews who survived the war returned to their native villages. However, many of them met with hostility and were murdered. Their enemies and murderers were local criminals, bandits and soldiers who had taken control in the countryside and in the towns. Samuel O. (82) and his wife Pearl O. (82), who resided in Rymanów after the war, left helter-skelter after a Polish friend tipped them off about a planned murder. Polish informants recalled that the three sons of Isaac L. (partner in business of Abraham B.) returned to their native village Moszczaniec to take what was left from their former homes. According to the informants, they got 'lost' on their way back, suggesting that they were murdered.

Still, it is said that in the period following the end of the Second World War Jewish (male) survivors visited Jaśliska two or three times to dig up the valuables which they supposedly had been hiding in their former homes. These short visits too were veiled in silence. For safety reasons, neither the Jewish visitors nor their Polish hosts, would make their presence public. It is said that in two cases the Jewish visitors left during the night without even informing their hosts. The secretive nature of the visits is indicative of the distrust and fear among the Poles and the Jews at that time.[26] Except for the very few villagers who happened to meet the Jewish visitors, or those who had travelled to the United States, no villager would ever see 'their Jews' again. After the deportation of the local Jews in the summer of 1942, Polish-Jewish interactions had ceased, or as one informant put it, 'later, after they had left, I never met with Jews again, never!'

The Dead and the Guilty

Although the events of August 1942 caused great fear among the local population, on a general level the Shoah had only a limited impact on the lives
of the Polish villagers. To a large extent the Shoah took place outside their
realm, that is, outside the village and outside the safe boundaries of the
Christian community:

> Before, during and after the Holocaust, the Jew remained outside the common
> universe of concern. His fate at the hands of the Nazis, as horrible as it was, did
> not change—for most—the basic terms of Polish-Jewish relations. The Jew was
> never a member of the same family; caring or not caring about him had none of
> the same moral implications as feelings for fellow Poles. His disappearance was
> not mourned in a way one would mourn the death of a brother. He *was* not a
> brother […] (Irwin-Zarecka 1989a: 180-181).

In like manner, few informants made a point of mentioning the deportation
and the massacre of the local Jews or only made oblique reference to them.
This reflects the enormous gap between the Polish and Jewish communities
that existed at that particular time. Because the destiny of the Jews differed
from that of the Poles, the story of the Jews is irrelevant to the lives of most
Polish informants. It follows that few Polish informants older than seventy-
five related the wartime events. The mental distance vis-à-vis the Jews which
the older generations preserve is also reflected in the attitude of the postwar
generations, who have inherited the distant attitude which is presented to
them at home and in school.[27] The informants who seemed most concerned
with the Jews and their fate during the Second World War were those who
had been children or teenagers at the outbreak of the war. Their accounts
express a sincere interest in and compassion for the Jews, among whom they
had many friends.

   Though not every informant mentioned the massacre of the local Jews,
those who did firmly disapproved of it. Most informants described the German policy as 'devilish', 'inhumane', and 'revolting'. A true sense of drama
is certainly present in the stories about the harassment, humiliation, and
finally, the extermination of the Jews from Jaśliska. Still, some informants
weighed the fate of the local Jews against their past 'wickedness' as if finding a reason for their final punishment. But even then, in the eyes of the
informants the massacre was useless, inhumane, and inconceivable. For,
unlike the Germans, the informants considered 'their Jews' as true 'human
beings'. Despite all 'tricks' they had played on them and despite their alleged
alienness, Jews had not deserved such a fate. Jan S. (65) explained:

I really felt sorry for the Jews. In spite of the fact that they were involved in trading and that they were stingy with products. That was nothing. They wanted to live in friendship. They wanted to have money. For there was an economic crisis in Poland before the war. Everybody wanted to have money. They liked to trade and they wanted to get a few grosze from that [...] But somehow we lived with them. And our boys liked their girls so much, ojojojoj ...

While expressing their pity for the Jews, informants shared a sense of guilt at not having been able to save their Jewish neighbours. The same informant confessed his failure to rescue his one time Jewish (child) love Ruchla. If only he had known what would happen to the Jews 'I would have hidden them all', he stated regretfully:

I liked this Ruchla so much. I hold her dear to my heart and she was crying so much. She cried like a baby. And so did I. I said to my grandmother: 'Let us keep my Ruchla, let us hide her.' But she answered: 'They will shoot us. Nothing bad will happen to them. They will work and will be fed. And then, when the war is over, they will set them free.' And I said: 'Where do they take them?' And she said: 'I don't know.' It did not even occur to us. It would not come into our heads, of us simple people, what they would do with these Jews. That they would kill them and gas them ...

Most of the informants did not so much express their own inability to provide help, as the inability of the collective to intervene. It is said that the Polish villagers were unable to give a helping hand to the Jews, because the Poles had a hard time surviving too. This being the case, the tragedy and misery of one's own fate diminishes the suffering of the Jews.

We felt very sorry when Germans took them [Jews] from here. But we did not know what would happen to us. We also stood with our backs to the wall. At that time, when they took the Jews, the Ukrainian police ruled over us. There was no Polish police, but a Ukrainian police. And they told the Gestapo that Poles were destroying houses. They called the Gestapo. And the Gestapo came here. They sent a messenger and he ordered with his drums: 'Everybody to town, everybody to the market square!' They had automatic rifles and they were about to shoot. Because the Ukrainian police had called and told them that Poles robbed the Jewish houses. But this Grenzschütz officer said that it was not true. He was good and he said to the Gestapo: 'They didn't do it. It is not true.' So they gave up, because we were already at the wall. We were really moved by the fact that they took the Jews from here. But we did not know what to expect, whether they would take us. It was a terrible thing. Terrible. There was no pity and no mercy from the German side. There was no pity and no mercy, there was nothing. We lived on good terms with the Jews. (Andrzej F., 72)

The above excerpt is also typical for the way it explains the genocide of the Jews as solely the responsibility of the Germans. In the accounts of the Polish informants, Hitler is presented as the evil spirit and the brain behind the 'Final Solution'. The murder of the local Jews is clearly blamed on Nazi policies which the informants claim the Germans put into effect all over Europe and in the local areas as well. And yet, their own accounts of the Shoah never went beyond the local setting. Only one informant employed the term 'Holocaust' when referring to the extermination of the Jews from Jaśliska. Indeed, most informants have come to define the Shoah as an exclusively local experience (*'they* killed *our* Jews'). This fact has one important implication. To talk about the Shoah in terms of local opportunities, omissions, action, and inaction, is to talk about direct responsibility. Accordingly, informants tried to find answers to questions like: what did I do to support my Jewish neighbour, what did others do (or not do), and how could I have done better? Where most informants attempted to clear themselves from any direct responsibility, and pointed out the guilt of others (including fellow Poles), they denied (whether consciously or unconsciously) any moral responsibility for what happened to the Jews.

The alleged 'impassivity' of the Jews who submissively underwent their fate is another recurrent theme in the informants' accounts on the Shoah. According to the informants, Jews went 'like lambs to the slaughter' and in this way gave credit to German policies. On the docility of the Jews, Gabriel T. (quoting his grandfather) writes:

> When the Germans gathered the Jews from all over this place, the Jews went almost voluntarily, on their faces dumb sounds and tears. They neither rebelled nor tried to escape, but clung to the message that was written for them. They went like cattle to the slaughter, though they were a people of culture. Because they claimed that such was their fate.[28]

And yet another question is raised: if *we* did not save the Jews (which was impossible anyway), why did not *they* rescue themselves (since they knew perfectly what would happen)? In this way the responsibility is handed back to the victims. Poles would never have allowed themselves to have been put to death like cattle as the Jews. Poles are different and therefore they would have acted differently—less passive and more courageous. In any case, this purported 'courage' of the Poles had not helped the Jews. Despite concerted efforts to clear themselves of guilt, even Polish informants realised that it was not through their efforts that a small number of Jews managed to survive the war.

The Destruction of a Polish Community

The Aftermath of the German Occupation

In the summer of 1944 Jaśliska was 'on the move'. German armies passed through the town and troops were quartered among the inhabitants. Civilians up to the age of fifty were taken to dig trenches four kilometres away in the direction of the Slovakian border, among them children below the age of ten years. As the front approached, the German armies retreated north, taking food and crops with them. When on 8 September 1944 divisions of the Soviet and Slovakian armies approached Jaśliska from the northern and eastern side, a bloody front battle started (Stączek 1944-1951).[29] Soviet planes proceeded to bomb the locations where retreating German armies had concentrated. As a former German quarter, Jaśliska was subject to repeated Soviet phosphor bombings that destroyed the whole western and northern part of the village and killed one adult and two children. During the bombings villagers sought refuge in the nearby forests. On 24 September 1944 divisions of the Soviet Army took possession of Jaśliska, but it would take some three more months before the Red Army had cleared the area of the Germans (Stączek 1944-1951).[30] In the meantime the German armies employed the scorched earth tactic, leaving fresh mines, blown up bridges, and burned villages behind.[31] Presumably, the pro-German Ukrainian authorities got out together with the Germans.

When divisions of the Soviet army left the area in December 1944 the war was over and the villagers were eager to return to a normal life (Stączek 1944-1951; Orlik 1979). Informants made no statements on reprisals against people found guilty of collaboration with the Germans.[32] War losses were assessed by the newly established community council,[33] while so-called 'war services' were introduced that aimed at 'deleting the war losses'. All villagers had to contribute to them. All in all, in the period from October 1944 to November 1945 the local population invested some 1,100 working days in so-called 'reconstruction labour' (Orlik 1979: 62). The severe bombings resulted in 'one house to every three families'. Apart from the civilians, also the newly formed communal committees and municipal council had to contend with a shortage of housing. In the first three years of its existence the Village People's Council (*Gromadzka Rada Narodowa*) dealt with three major problems: the shortage of public buildings, offices, and capable personnel. Part of this urgent problem was solved by a gradual integration of Jewish grounds and Jewish houses in the administration of the village. A *Committee for Housing Affairs* listed all former Jewish properties.[34]

As soon as people had left their shelter in the forest, an uncoordinated hunt for houses started. Families that had lost their entire property during the bombings went to look for 'the best they could get', including former Jewish properties that were still intact. Informants mentioned two cases in which transactions took place between a Jewish survivor and Polish inhabitants who were already using the formerly Jewish-owned property. Both transactions took place in 1946 and were settled in the court of law in nearby Rymanów. On the part of the Polish purchasers it involved one private person and one village representative. They each bought one Jewish holding from the Jewish survivor Natan L. for respectively private and communal ends. The attempts of Abraham B. to sell his property to his former Polish employees Daniel S. (82) and to the father of Jędrzej P. (75) failed, because there were no ready buyers and because from a distance it was hard to put anything in motion.[35]

In the period between 1958 and 1960 the Polish state nationalised all Jewish properties that had not yet been claimed by the few Jewish survivors or bought up by the Poles. After the confiscation had become a fact, legal ownership passed to the community and to the house-seeking villagers, who now bought former Jewish properties from the state. By that time, some villagers would leave the Jewish houses and move to the houses and fields left by the Lemko deportees in Posada Jaśliska and Daliowa (see next section). Other villagers extended their lots by buying former Jewish properties adjacent to their own. At the same time, the community council started to discuss the development plans for the town centre, comprising several hectares of formerly Jewish-owned land. Within years, the People's House (*Dom Ludowy*), the health care centre, the residence of the village physician, and the state-owned Cooperative Shop (*Społem*) were built on former Jewish grounds.

Interestingly, the informants were not at all reluctant to admit that they have lived or still live on former Jewish properties. They were reluctant, however, to explain how they had obtained the properties. In fact, land ownership, including the ownership of former Jewish properties, has been the subject of a number of village disputes. Informants mentioned one case in which two families publicly denied each other's rights to a Jewish dwelling, a conflict which occurred right after the war. Some of the village disputes about former Jewish properties are still significant today and point to the existing village factions.

The Civil War: Anarchy and Policy

In the first half of 1944 a transition took place from German-occupied Poland to Soviet-imposed People's Poland.[36] In fact, as the front lines advanced, the Red army arrested and disarmed 'illegal' Polish resistance groups. Still, on the local level the political and military void left by the Germans gave plenty of room to numerous military factions that had come into existence during the war. Another two years of war started, though this time the enemy was not so clearly defined. Unlike the relatively stable period of the German occupation, the years to follow are commonly described as a period of 'real war'. Indeed, the military and political games that were played during these years left a significant impact on the region, and this time involved mainly the local Lemko people.

To the informants the new enemy had different faces. There were the soldiers of the Ukrainian Insurrectionary Army (UPA—the informants called its members *banderowcy*) who started their destructive struggle for an independent Ukraine. There were sections of the Polish Home Army (AK— also mockingly called *banda krajowa* or Home Gang) who fought for an independent Poland and against Soviet control. There were the infiltrators of the Polish and Soviet Secret Police Forces (UB and NKVD) who undermined the military activities of the Polish army. And last but not least, there was the undefinable group of plain criminals and bandits who roamed the countryside. Unfortunately, this last and most unreliable hostile group of people often consisted of natives (*nasi ludzie*). Paweł N. (63) commented on this highly confusing situation, '… all these organisations, the AK, UPA, UB and so on, it was all mixed, like peas with cabbage.' Whatever their identity, the enemies operated in bands, established their 'own' territories, and terrorised the population living in these territories. Jewish, Polish and Lemko civilians were threatened, robbed, and killed randomly. Villages were raided and burned to the ground. Individuals and entire communities were subject to extortion. In short, the numerous political factions fought a dirty war over the heads of the civilians.

Jaśliska was also subject to repeated fire threats and extortion. It is said that children and adults slept with their clothes on to be able to escape upon any sign of danger. Informants stressed the extreme fear they felt at that time. People could not move around safely, nor did they know what the next day would bring. Thanks to the (more or less permanent) presence of the Polish army in the village and thanks to the manifold clandestine smuggling connections, Jaśliska came out relatively intact. Paweł N. (63), whose father was killed by bandits (whose identities are supposedly known but still kept secret), was still a child when he served as an intermediary between the village representatives and the bands who threatened to burn Jaśliska. Paweł N. stressed the importance of careful negotiation and personal contacts during the years of guerrilla warfare:

In Jaśliska we had a Lemko teacher, who taught us the Lemko language during the German occupation [...] This teacher came here unmarried. Then he got married to a Polish woman. He saved us from many troubles. As a teacher he had contacts with popes[37] and so on. These Lemkos wanted to murder all Poles living in Jaśliska and Posada, just like it happened in the East [...] This teacher tried to bring them together, because the older generation used to live on good terms. They knew each other very well [...] All these families were connected with each other in one way or another. So the old ones tried to calm down the young ones, the bandits. And they said: 'Stop it! Give us peace because we lived on good terms for so many years!' So they [the bandits] said: 'Give us ransom!' 'What should this ransom be?' 'The ransom should contain spirits, cigarettes, sausages and bread!' Usually these kind of things. We gave heaps of it, tons of it. Most of this ransom I carried myself. It was a family affair. Not everybody could go there with this ransom and keep it in secret, because it was connected with my family. The chief of the Village Cooperative married my cousin. The Village Cooperative was called Społem at that time. He was from my family and I had to go. So I went. Even my mother did not know where I went. I had to go to a fixed place. And there they surrounded me, took the things from me, thanked me, and they said: 'Nothing bad will happen to you.' I was caught three times by these bands. I saw with my own eyes how they hanged three people in Surowica, on a pear tree, these UPA bands. Once they caught me in Szklary on the top of the hill, at noon. It was springtime, a beautiful day and the sun was shining. They lay in the ditches with rifles on both sides. With automatic rifles. They ordered me to go to the forest. I was carrying products to the shop. There was nobody near, so I had to do it. They took me three kilometres inside the forest. They had their staff and headquarters there. They asked me: 'How many soldiers, how many police and so on.' And I told them the truth. So they took the products from me and set me free.

By the end of 1944 Jaśliska formed a local civilian militia that patrolled and controlled the area. From early spring 1945 until the autumn of 1947 divisions of the Polish army were quartered among the inhabitants of Jaśliska. From May 1946 until the summer of 1947 the Polish army enforced a military campaign to restore law and order in the area. Soon the region was divided into pro-Ukrainian and pro-Polish villages, which increased the tensions between the Polish and Ukrainian army units and the civilian population. The closest serious UPA attack took place in Jasiel, where a division of the Polish army, consisting of an estimated 50 to 120 men, was completely annihilated. In 1965 a monument was erected to commemorate the massacre. Today, informants overtly challenge the official explanation that blamed the UPA for having attacked and murdered the Polish soldiers. Edward G. (52), for example, argued, '... what happened in Jasiel and surroundings was just a result of big state Politics [...] Stalin patterned his policy on that of Tsar Peter I.'

In May 1946 the first resettlement operation forced many Lemko families to leave the neighbouring villages. After the murder of General Świerczewski in March 1947, the military operation Vistula (*Akcja Wisła*) definitively cleansed the area of unreliable anti-communist and anti-Polish elements.[38] Before the enforcement of the operation the Polish army proceeded to register the local population, Lemkos as well as Poles. When in May 1947 the Lemko people received an order to leave their villages within two hours, Poles from Jaśliska and Posada Jaśliska started to pack their things too. Unlike the Lemkos, the Poles were spared this time. Still, letters from the State Bureau of Repatriation (PUR) show that Poles also fell victim to the political cleansing. A letter by the PUR dated 1949 states that 38 Polish families had left the Sanok region in 1948, including 106 persons, two horses, eight cows, two goats, and five pigs. In that same year 217 Ukrainian families had left the region, including 943 persons, 87 horses, 234 cows, 142 goats, and 100 pigs. The people and cattle involved were forcibly resettled in the so-called 'reclaimed grounds' in western and northern Poland.[39]

Polish Texas

As a result of the extermination of the Jews during the Second World War as well as the subsequent deportations of the local Lemko population (and some Polish families) between 1945 and 1947, the total number of inhabitants in the area decreased dramatically. Table 7.1 shows the impact of the war and deportations on the population count of the area. It can be seen that the region never completely recovered from its losses, and even in 1988 the population size is still well below the figures of 1921 (see also map 2). In the course of time some villages have been repopulated with migrants from the towns and villages of the low lands, including several hundred convicts employed in the State Farm in Moszczaniec (Hann 1985). Looking at the table it may be noticed that Jaśliska, Posada Jaśliska and Daliowa have the highest population figures after the war. The number of Roman Catholics as well as the number of mixed marriages with Roman Catholics (before the war) largely account for this fact.[40] In any case, the ethnic composition of the area changed from a largely multi-ethnic to a mono-ethnic Polish and Roman Catholic one. In other words, the former Polish minority changed into a majority.

Not only was there a serious decline of the population, the area also underwent a dramatic change in material terms. A letter by the State Bureau of Repatriation dated 21 January 1948 lists the material damage in the whole Sanok district after the major military operations had become a fact. In the whole Sanok district 719 houses were seriously damaged and many more had been burned to the ground. From the municipality of Jaśliska four villages were burned, while of the ten other villages 295 houses were seriously damaged. Map 2 shows the impact of the war and resettlement policies on the region. Considering the deserted character of the region, the

Table 7.1   Population Size of the Former Jaśliska Municipality
(1921-1988)

Village	1921	1950	1960	1970	1978	1988
Jaśliska	876	524	598	547	546	513
Czeremcha	364	0	0	0	0	0
Daliowa	570	217	272	346	310	264
Darów	224	0	«	«	«	«
Jasiel	289	0	«	«	«	«
Lipowiec	572	9	41	28	39	20
Moszczaniec	437	0	65	200	194	193
Polany Surowiczne	583	0	«	«	«	«
Posada Jaśliska	888	660	811	870	871	795
Rudawka Jaśliska	113	0	«	«	«	«
Surowica	453	0	«	«	«	«
Wola Wyżna	291	0	0	26	38	30
Wola Niżna	532	130	185	185	195	248
Total	6192	1540	1972	2202	2193	2063

Notes: an («) indicates that the number of inhabitants is very low, likely to be less than five persons.

Sources: population censuses of the years 1921, 1950, 1960, 1970, 1978 and 1988 by *Główny Urząd Statystyczny* (Warsaw).

term 'Polish Texas' (*Polski Teksas*) employed by many informants to denote the area of the Beskid mountains makes perfect sense.

Peoples' Poland or the Reign of Communism

After the resettlement, peace returned to the Poles. In fact many people benefited from the resettlement policies. As one informant put it, 'people moved around and changed their homes. From Posada they went to live in Wola Niżna, while other villages remained empty'. Wojciech M. (78) stresses the fact that life changed for the better after the Lemkos had left:

> *The situation improved simply. Suddenly people had enough hay and grounds. As much as they wanted and anywhere they wanted. Before one used to have such narrow strips of land that one had to guide one's horse with a rope. It was a tremendous change [...] If before someone wanted to have more land, he simply could not get it. Because there were thousands of people and thousands of cattle. It was a tremendous change, one which was unparalleled in history.*

In the years directly following the Second World War, the Polish Communist Party enforced a policy generally known as the socialisation of agriculture (Van Hulten 1962). The State Fund for Agricultural Land (*Państwowy Fundusz Ziemi*) distributed the nationalised land among the Polish peasants, while State Farms (*Państwowe Gospodarstwo Rolne-PGR*), state-run shops and restaurants (*Społem*), and a number of Rural Cooperatives were introduced. Between 1947 and 1948 a Peasant Self-help Cooperative (*Samopomoc Chłopska*) was established in Jaśliska, to which many members of the local elite (including the priest) were enlisted. In 1948 the Cooperative for Agricultural Machinery (*Spółdzielczy Ośrodek Maszynowy*) was established. In 1952 the Commune Committee for Clearing Fallow Lands (*Komitet Gminny do Likwidacji Odłogów*) installed numerous Village Cooperatives in Jaśliska and neighbouring villages, comprising workshops such as the sawmill. In the same year two State Farms were founded in Szklary and Moszczaniec (both former Lemko villages) (Orlik 1979).

Perhaps the best result of the socialisation of agriculture was the emancipation of the Polish peasantry from poverty and isolation. Thanks to the large-scale investments in rural infrastructure, extreme poverty disappeared from the lives of the peasants. At the same time opportunities to earn off-farm income significantly increased social mobility and the living standard. In the course of decades the villagers have become more dependent on off-farm employment. As can be seen in Table 7.2 this process took some thirty years. However, after the abolition of the municipality in 1976, Jaśliska lost much of its economic and administrative authority to the benefit of Dukla (20 km from Jaśliska).[41] Since then Jaśliska's economic and administrative life has been marginalised. The informants feel that attention to their problems has diminished. In any case, lack of investments made local institutions less viable over time. In 1978 the local cinema went bankrupt and at present there are not sufficient facilities for the 230 pupils of the primary school.

Table 7.2   Population according to Main Source of Income

Activities	1950	1960	1970	1978	1988
Agriculture	418	464	318	227	184
Off-farm employment	106	134	229	319	329
Percentage in agriculture	*78*	*76*	*58*	*41*	*36*
Total	**524**	**598**	**547**	**546**	**513**

Sources: population censuses of the years 1950, 1960, 1970, 1978 and 1988 by *Główny Urząd Statystyczny* (Warsaw).

The Post-Communist Era

After the abolition of communism in 1989, all rural social and economic organisations were dissolved, such as the Women's League (*Liga Kobiet*), the Circle of Rural Housewives (*Koło Gospodyń Wiejskich*), the Association of Rural Youth (*Związek Młodzieży Wiejskiej*) and the Farmers Circle (*Kółko*

Rolnicze). These originally non-political organisations organised excursions, (national) festivities, shows, folk music and dancing, courses, etc. Also the local political committees of the Polish United Workers Party (PZPR—until 1990) and the United Peasants Party (ZSL—until 1989) ceased to exist. The Peoples House (Dom Ludowy), a relic from the communist times, and the Roman Catholic Church are the only viable social institutions left at the village level. Marian N. (36), mayor (*sołtys*) of the village, is seriously worried about the decrease in social contacts among the villagers, especially among the young inhabitants, as he draws a direct parallel between the young people who have no occasion to meet and the drop in the number of young married couples in the village.

The end of communism brought about increasing unemployment. In September 1990 the Polish parliament issued a law which enforced the liquidation of the State Farms. Shortly after, the local restaurant, the state shop, and the sawmill went bankrupt. The State Farms were the most important employers in this agricultural area. The villagers who slowly got used to their status as wage earners, have recently been thrown back onto working their agricultural fields. Current prospects for off-farm employment in the area are nil, while full-time farming is not considered profitable. This is often illustrated with the example that ten litres of milk buys 'only half a bottle of beer'. Many hectares of land lie fallow and prices of land have dropped. Still, the peasants have no intention of buying additional land, for there are no young hands to cultivate it. Andrzej F. (72) commented on the recent introduction of the free-market system in Poland:

> *One day a lady borrowed money to start a shop. I read it in the newspaper. And now there are ten shops in the village and there are no customers any more. This lady had to pay her debts back. She had to repay the interest on her loan within three months. It [the interest] was one million złoty or something. She had to pay back 6 percent, that makes sixty thousand złoty interest. So she went bankrupt [...] One should not take money on credit under any conditions. No one will buy our pigs and there is no one who buys our cows. The new year is approaching and nobody knows if they will buy our milk, because the milk factory in Krosno went bankrupt. I have three cows and we are three in one household. If they don't take our milk, one cow is sufficient.*

In addition to the limited marketing possibilities, retirement pensions and unemployment benefits are low, agricultural products are of little value, while prices in the shops are rising. To some of the informants the features of poverty so characteristic of prewar Jaśliska have returned in their lives: unemployment; indebtedness; low returns; low social benefits; negligence and disintegration of the peasant class.

Notes

1.   Whereas the Jews were destined to be exterminated, Poles were destined either for Germanisation or for expulsion beyond the Ural. The residual Slavs were to be turned into a pool of half-educated slave labourers (Davies 1986: 68).

2.   During the first year of the occupation about 1.5 million Poles who were not eligible for German national status were resettled to the General Government from the areas incorporated into the Reich. These individuals accounted for about 10 percent of the General Government's population by 1940. It is estimated that, not counting the Jews, 1.65 million people were resettled in Poland during the war (Gross 1979: 72). Furthermore, between 1.3 and 1.5 million people were shipped from the General Government to Germany in order to work in German labour camps (Gross 1979: 78). The German resettlement policy as well as the extraction of Polish labour also affected the Polish community in Jaśliska.

3.   The sources do not agree on the immediate cause of the departure of the Jews from Jaśliska. Whereas Polish sources claim that Polish as well as Jewish residents left Jaśliska in fear of the inevitable war (Stàczek 1944-1951; Gajewski 1996), the *Encyclopaedia of Destroyed Jewish Communities* (Yad Vashem 1984) holds that the Jews from Jaśliska were forced to leave the military sensitive area since they were regarded as disloyal Polish citizens. It should be borne in mind that this 'encyclopaedic' information is based on the testimony of Israel B. (Litwak 1969), who had not witnessed the destruction of the Jewish community of Jaśliska himself, but who had been informed about it by a relative, and whose account had been recorded by a third party, his interlocutor Josef Litwak. The latter (1969: 4) reports: 'Following the outbreak of the war on the first of September 1939 the Polish authorities expelled the Jews from Jaśliska to Rymanów on the pretext that this section of the population was disloyal to the Polish state and, therefore, were not allowed to reside near the front.' However, it may also have been that the Polish and Jewish inhabitants of Jaśliska had learned from the experience of the First World War when the absence of law and order had spurred on hostilities in a similar way. Not only in September 1939, but also in August 1914, Jewish residents from Jaśliska, and a small number of Poles, sought refuge at the homes of their urban brethren in Rymanów.

4.   When talking about the Second World War informants commonly referred to the Lemkos as Ukrainians. The term Ukrainian by no means refers to all members of the neighbouring Lemko communities. In this context, the term Ukrainian is used to denote pro-Ukrainian Lemkos, as well as Ukrainians who had been brought in from western Ukraine by the German authorities. In return for their voluntary cooperation Ukrainians were granted the right to establish a sovereign Ukraine. Unfortunately for the Ukrainians, the German support for Ukrainian sovereignty was only short-lived (Davies 1986).

5.   It should be noted that the majority of Ukrainian officials and policemen who settled in Jaśliska were non-locals, drawn from the western Ukraine or *Ruś-Zakarpacka*. Informants recalled that, besides Ukrainians, other nationalities served in German police and army units as well. These recruits (called 'Mongols' and 'Tartars') from far away were considered less civilised and more cruel than the Germans.

6.   Germans started a stone quarry near Dukla (Lipowica). Other labour camps were set up too, for example in the ghetto of Rymanów. The main labour force in these labour camps was supplied by local Jews. Some informants claimed to have recognised Jews from Jaśliska who were put to work in the stone quarry in Lipowica, after their deportation

from Jaśliska in 1942. After the war the stone quarry, set up by German planners, continued to be used by Poles. The stone quarry was taken out of production only recently.

7. A Polish unit of measurement for wood (≈3 cubic metres).

8. It is not clear whether these officials were Ukrainians or Germans. Many stories claim, though, that malicious individuals (including Poles) sometimes demanded contingents without German authorisation.

9. 'Ja' in Polish means 'I'.

10. Real friendships developed out of these encounters. Some informants still correspond with their former guests from Poznań.

11. The main underground link in the region went through Jaśliska, which was named after the hill *Kamień* located between the Slovakian border and Jaśliska. The important role of Jaśliska in the underground network can be attributed to its strategic position near the Slovakian border and the small number of German personnel in the locality.

12. Here again it must be noted that Israel B. had not witnessed the destruction of the Jewish community of Jaśliska himself, but had been informed about it by a relative. The same is true for most of the other Jewish informants; they did not witness the purge in Jaśliska themselves.

13. A translation of one of these songs sounds like this: 'While our Golden Hitler taught us how to work, our Śmigły-Rydz taught us nothing' (A nasz Hitler złoty, nauczył nas roboty, a nasz Śmigły-Rydz nie nauczył nas nic). Marshal Śmigły-Rydz was the Commander in Chief of the Second Polish Republic (1935-39).

14. The author wrote about the events after the war. This might explain the rather distant and formal tone which she employed throughout her text.

15. The word Shoah in this context refers to the deportation and elimination of the Jews of Jaśliska.

16. Quoted from an essay written by Gabriel T. (13 years).

17. Here it must be noted that some of these transactions had already taken place before the raid. The rumours about Jews having hidden and buried valuables and money inside their homes, indicate that Jews had already made some preparations.

18. Probably Jewish identity cards were stored in this Polish shop to keep the Jews from escaping.

19. Opinions vary with respect to the identity of the soldiers who supervised the raid. Some informants claimed that they were members of the Gestapo or the Schupo (*Schützpolizei*), others held that they were Ukrainians, yet others stated that they were conscripts from the far East (e.g., Tartars, Mongols).

20. Some informants related that the beards of the men were cut off with knifes, and that they were forced to kneel and eat the grass. Other informants claimed to have seen a Jewish woman giving birth to a baby. The woman was beaten and the baby was taken from her. It is further claimed that children, especially the small, were beaten and kicked. One informant claimed to have seen a small child being lifted and torn apart by his legs and arms. Although it is unclear whether the described atrocity really took place or whether it is a product of the imagination of the informant, it certainly reflects the sense of drama felt by the informant.

21. See also Chapter five regarding Polish popular beliefs in relation to the Jews.

22. According to Israel B. (in Litwak 1969: 4) on 14 August 1942 the young people (men, women, and children) were made to walk on foot to the railway station in Iwonicz (28 km from Jaśliska), where they were put on transport to the extermination camp Bełżec. Israel B. knows of five or six survivors from all the Jews who had been sent to the camp Bełżec.

23. Private connections and financial resources also affected the successful escape of Josko S. (75) and his parents from Jaśliska. Josko S. was smuggled out of Poland immediately before the outbreak of the war. His parents soon followed after they had received passports from their migrant sons in Belgium. But most Jewish families stayed in Poland. In this respect the story of Samuel O. (82) is exemplary. Samuel O., who happened to be serving in the Polish army when the war broke out, was caught by the Germans as a prisoner of war. After his release in 1940, he was always on the move, but he did not return to Jaśliska until the end of the war. Except for his two brothers David O. (73) and Jacob O. (79), his whole family perished during the war.

24. Informants mentioned several cases of Polish aid in neighbouring towns and villages. Among them was the forest guard from Posada Jaśliska who by accident found the hiding place of one Jewish refugee. The forest guard provided the Jew with food and drink until the war was over. In Królik Polski, two Jewish families were hidden and provided with food by Polish and Lemko villagers (in total an estimated six persons were rescued). In Rymanów several cases are known of Poles who sheltered Jews during the war. In addition, in some villages to the east (for example Moszczaniec) it is said that Jews successfully hid among the local population (although this has not been confirmed by other sources).

25. In former days (and even in some of the present-day farms) toilets stood in the garden.

26. On the dangers in the region in the years following the Second World War see the next section.

27. While it seems that most informants who were born after the Second World War have learned about the Jews of their hometown through their parents and grandparents, their knowledge about them is fragmentary and blend with local traditions of story-telling. To this one should add that little attention is paid to the extermination of the European Jewry during the history classes in school. For a discussion of the teaching of Jewish history in Polish schools during the socialist era see Radziwiłł (1989).

28. Quoted from an essay written by Gabriel T. (13 years).

29. This so-called *Operacja Dukielska* (in Czech and Soviet literature respectively operation Dukielsko-Preszowska and operation Karpacko-Dukielska) was named after the Dukielski region in which the battle took place. In a tourist bulletin printed in 1982, operation Dukielska is labelled as the most extensive and bloody battle fought on Polish territory during the Second World War. The heroic act of resistance against German rule is still immortalised in the permanent exhibition of the 'Museum of Brotherhood in Arms' in Dukla (*Muzeum Braterstwa Broni*), to which every generation in the region has paid at least one visit. The exhibition remained unchanged at least up to 1993.

30. According to a booklet titled *The Liberation of the Polish Communities and Towns by the Soviet Army and the Polish People's Army* Jaśliska was officially liberated by the 38th division of the Soviet Army on 20 September 1944 (Informator 1977).

31. The neighbouring village Czeremcha was burned to the ground with the exception of two sheds.

32. Two informants related that after the Germans had left, a former Ukrainian officer stood up in public and offered his apologies to the villagers.

33. According to Orlik (1979: 61-62) an estimated twenty-one persons were send as convicts to the German Reich, forty-nine villagers were killed in German concentration camps, while 40 percent of the houses were destroyed. The number of people killed during the war does not include the victims of starvation, exhaustion, or cold, nor does it include the Jewish victims of the Final Solution.

34. Since the concentration of Jews had been largest in the north-western part of the town, most Jewish houses had been burned as a result of the bombings. This meant that the

municipal council had to deal mostly with Jewish lots without or with severely damaged dwellings.

35. In a letter to Daniel S., Abraham B. offered Daniel S. several hectares of fields which he possessed in Posada Jaśliska. Abraham B. wrote this letter before the war was over. Daniel S. never replied to the letter and in this way tacitly refused the offer. He gave two reasons for his refusal. Firstly, as the war was still on he was not even sure whether he could keep his own land, so 'why take the fields of someone else?' Secondly, during the first years of Communist rule the situation was no better and foreign contacts were regarded with suspicion. Daniel S.: 'I did not respond to my friends from Czechia and I did not respond to this Jew. Because I was afraid. One was afraid at that time.' In a letter to the father of Jędrzej P. (75) Abraham B. offered his house in Jaśliska for sale. Then the front came and left the people 'completely naked'. Also the family house of Jędrzej P. had burned down, after which they moved to the house of Abraham B. Although Abraham B. seriously attempted to organise a sale contract (Abraham B.'s son in law visited Jaśliska one time, while his own son sent the papers to the town council of Jaśliska) the transaction was never fixed, because there was 'no money to buy the house'. Jędrzej P. is sure that if his father had met with Abraham B. in person, the latter would surely have given him permission to live in his house. After all, it was wartime and life was not easy then.

36. In November 1943 'The big Three' had decided that postwar Poland would fall under the Soviet 'zone of influence'. On 22 July 1944 a pro-Communist administration, the Polish Committee of National Liberation (PKWN), was installed. This Soviet-sponsored body was not connected with the Polish government in exile. On 31 December 1944 the Polish Committee of National Liberation changed its name to Provisional Government of the Polish Republic (RTRP), but was only recognised as such by the USSR. At Yalta (February 1945) the Allied leaders insisted that representatives of the parties supporting the Polish government in London should join the members of the RTRP to form a united Provisional Government of National Unity (TJRN). At Potsdam (August 1945) a declaration was made about 'free and unfettered elections' in Poland. The Provisional Government lasted from 28 June until January 1947. On 6 February the first elected government took office, but the elections were not really what one would call free. In December 1948 the Polish communist and socialist parties merged into the Polish United Workers' Party (PZPR), which from that time on became the ruling Party of Poland (Davies 1986).

37. Russian Orthodox or Greek Catholic priests.

38. Informants expressed their doubts whether this 'liberal' and 'human' general of the Polish army was murdered by Ukrainian bandits or because Stalin wanted him dead.

39. The combat against the rich peasants (*kułak*) and other 'political enemies' resulted in the deportation of at least twelve families from Jaśliska in 1949. Some families were forced to leave Jaśliska within 24 hours, while others were made to leave within a few days. Some were free to choose their new home (on the condition that it was far from their home district), others were sent to arranged places such as Nysa, Opole, Olsztyn and Biała Piska (Western Poland). Only a few of the deportees returned to Jaśliska after 1956, when the Communist policies were somewhat relaxed. The former deportees still feel distrust and grievance for the harm they were done by, as they see it, 'our people'. The national policy, which was locally interpreted in an arbitrary way, produced bitter tensions between the villagers, many of which still last.

40. Figures of ethnic or religious composition are not available for the postwar censuses because during this era that kind of information was, for ideological reasons, not considered relevant.

41. In October 1944 Jaśliska became an independent municipal centre organised in the Village People's Council (*Gromadzka Rada Narodowa*) and ruled 16 villages. In 1953 efforts were made to decentralise local administrative power. As a result the Jaśliska municipality was divided into several district councils *(Gromady)*. In 1973 Gromada Jaśliska became a municipal centre again. The people's council *(Rada Narodowa)* and presidium *(Prezydium)* in Jaśliska governed 14 villages (an estimated 1,800 people). In July 1976 Jaśliska lost its municipal status. Its eastern territories were given to the municipality of Komańcza and its western territories, including Jaśliska itself, became part of the Dukla municipality. The western territories of the former Jaśliska municipality were divided into four village administrator's centres *(sołectwo)*, i.e., Jaśliska, Posada Jaśliska, Daliowa, and Wola Niżna. Since that time four village heads *(sołtys)* have represented Jaśliska's interests in the Dukla municipal council.

Chapter 8

DISCUSSION
Physical Experience and Symbolic Representations

That there are no more Jews in Melawe, no single person to speak Yiddish with, is bad for Marcin. Each Saturday he visits the houses and he lives from what he receives. When [his wife] Jadwiga was still alive life was much easier. She would take in washing here and there, and when they made their Saturday round they would collect twice as much. Since she died Marcin is starving. Unfortunately, he had to lie in his bed the whole winter through. If not for his good neighbours, who now and then brought him a spoon of warm food, who knows whether he would have survived the winter? (Opatoshu 1951: 313)

Introduction

*I*f there is one word that aptly describes the attitudes and views of the informants regarding their former Jewish neighbours, this word is ambivalence. This distinctive aspect of the Polish-Jewish relationship, which is also sensitively described by Opatoshu in his story *The Jew Legend*, formed the thread running through the preceding chapters and will form the point of departure for the discussion below. As was hypothesised in Chapter one, actual 'physical experience' of the prewar era indeed proved to constitute a mainstay on which informants base their present-day views of the Jews. The close interdependence between the Polish and Jewish communities, as well as the ethnic competition for resources, entailed close political and economic articulation. Of crucial importance in the maintenance of the political and social equilibrium were the strict ethnic boundaries between the Polish and Jewish communities, and, as will be argued in the discussion below, the

Notes for this section begin on page 188.

patron-client relationship that had developed between the members of the two communities. It is in the light of this specific set of relations that much of the images informants use to characterise their former Jewish neighbours and to describe the local Polish-Jewish past can best be explained.

Other studies indicate the aspect of patronage in the relationship between Poles and Jews in Poland in the seventeenth and eighteenth centuries, when Jews functioned as intermediaries between the higher Polish aristocrats and the peasant serfs (Hertz 1988; Rosman 1990; Hundert 1992). In this situation, the Jews were clients of the wealthy landlords who leased out to them the management of the feudal estates. For the peasant serfs the Jews functioned as powerful brokers who had access to the goods and services required by them. In the discussion which follows it is argued that while with the collapse of feudalism the Jews largely lost their role as brokers between the landlords and the peasant serfs, they gained a new role as patrons providing access to first-order resources (jobs, funds, specialised knowledge) to their peasant clients. It goes to show that the measure of cooperation that characterised magnate-Jewish relations in the Polish-Lithuanian Commonwealth can be extrapolated to the peasant-Jewish relations that developed in the towns and villages of early twentieth-century Poland.

The fact that informants use negative stereotypes to describe their Jewish neighbours, while at the same time they present a picture of an harmonious past, points to a complex correlation between 'real life' experience and 'symbolic' representations. It has been shown, for example, that images and stereotypes are employed irrespective of how people think or talk about their former Jewish neighbours. This indicates that 'real life' experience has had a particularly strong influence on attitudes and views. In addition, among the younger generations anti-Jewish stereotypes live a life of their own. This, in turn, may be indicative of the way in which 'real life' experience gradually loses significance while 'symbolic' representations gain weight. Last but not least, the uniform positive appraisal of the relationship between Poles and Jews in the period preceding the Second World War by both Polish and Jewish informants can partly be explained by the impact of the Shoah on the way informants perceive the Polish-Jewish past.

The Physical Experience: Jewish Patrons and Polish Clients

Jewish Patrons and Polish Clients: Towards an Alternative Perspective

In an essay on patronage Burkolter (1976: 7) gives the following working definition of patron-client relations:

Two parties unequal in status, wealth and influence form a dyadic, particularistic, self-regulating (no formal normative regulations are needed) relationship of asymmetrical commitment, and face-to-face contact, and legitimated by certain values. The relationship depends on the formation and maintenance of reciprocity in the exchange of resources (goods and services) in totalistic terms (package deal), meaning that none of these resources can be exchanged separately.

Theoretically, the patron-client relationship is distinguished from other social relationships in a number of ways. To begin with, the asymmetry between the two partners to the patron-client contract is more distinct than in other relationships, which is implicit in the goods and services that they exchange. In this contract, the patron is obliged to furnish his client with some basic means of subsistence, to be a 'subsistence crisis insurance' for him, to protect him in various fields, or to act as a broker and exert his influence for the benefit of his client. The client, on the other hand, provides the patron with basic labour services, as well as supplementary services which are especially ordered by the patron. In addition, he shows deference to the 'honour' of the patron, serves as a loyal member of the patron's faction, leads new clients to the patron's clientele, and agrees to maintain the status quo, which means the hidden promise to give up all claims to autonomous access to resources (Burkolter 1976: 9). Therefore, the difference in power between the patron and the client largely depends on the degree to which the patron monopolises the flow of information, goods, and services to and between his clients (Boissevain 1974).

Another important aspect of the patron-client relationship is that it exceeds the confines of membership of the family, group, or kin (Burkolter 1976). From this it follows that entry into this patron-client relationship is mostly voluntary. A relationship may be initiated from the side of the patron or from the side of the client, both with the help of the same strategy. A patron who is looking for a client helps someone generously and apparently unselfishly through some economic calamity, in the courtroom, or in other difficulty. Thereafter that person may be obliged to reciprocate. A client who seeks to establish relations with a powerful person will voluntarily perform services for him, in order to involve the stronger party in a sort of debt relation (Burkolter 1976: 11). This links up with another important feature of the patron-client relationship: the exchange of services between the patron and the client is seldom predictable. Ideally, neither the content of an equivalent service is defined nor a specified time is set when the return service has to be undertaken, as 'it is in the interest of both parties to keep the channel open, either by underpaying or overpaying at a later date' (Boissevain 1974: 159).

Where a social group has control of the means of production utilised by another group, a relationship of inequality and stratification emerges. This was still the case for the Poles and Jews in Poland in the nineteenth and twentieth centuries. During the period of the 'Second Serfdom' (1550-1850), the Polish nobility had monopolised the means of production employed by both the Polish peasants and the Jewish merchants. After the abolition of serfdom in 1848, the Poles and Jews took control of the means of production associated with the economic sectors in which they traditionally operated, that is, the Polish farmers took control of land, while the Jewish tradesmen took control of capital and capital goods. In the late nineteenth and early twentieth centuries farming increasingly failed to provide a living for many peasant households. As a consequence, the Polish peasants became increasingly dependent on the resources (capital) that were monopolised by the Jews. Indeed, to be able to make a living, many had to turn to Jewish creditors, and, from the second decade of the twentieth century, to Jewish employers, to gain the necessary cash or goods.

A crucial aspect of the post-feudal relationship between Poles and Jews is not so much the asymmetry it implied–this had already been the case in the relationship between the Jewish brokers and the peasant serfs of the seventeenth and eighteenth centuries–but rather the type of resources that were exchanged. Here it is necessary to make a distinction between *first-order* and *second-order resources*. Boissevain (1974: 147) defines the former as resources that are directly controlled, such as land, jobs, scholarship funds, or specialised knowledge. The latter are strategic contacts with other people who control such resources directly or who have access to such persons. According to Boissevain (1974: 148) those who dispense first-order resources may be called *patrons*. Those who dispense second-order resources are *brokers*. By virtue of the resources they possess, patrons can provide limited credit for their clients, while brokers create unlimited credit for their clients (Boissevain 1974). It has been argued that the patron-client ties of pre-modern times are transformed qualitatively with modernisation and the emergence of a state. With the transformation of the system the figure of the mediator and power broker emerges, who acts as a link between national and local systems, and bridges the distance between distinct value systems (Wolf 1966; Burkolter 1976). Accordingly, small-scale patrons, whose speciality was to dispense limited credit to their clients, become brokers who, through a network of personal contacts, have specialised in creating unlimited credit. Interestingly, the case of the Polish Jews shows a reverse picture.

As we have seen in the first two chapters, the historical role of the Jews within the estate structure was that of the intermediary between the landed nobility and the enslaved peasantry. In the capacity of intermediaries or *brokers* Jews had access to persons who had a monopoly over first-order resources (such as land, funds, monopolies—the arenda—and specialised knowledge) and bore responsibility for the distribution of information (the famous 'Jewish mail'), goods, and economic services. After the abolition of serfdom, Jews lost their preferential access to law and order, which implied that their role as brokers between those who owned land and those who worked on it lost significance. Meanwhile, because of their former activities as brokers, the Jews got hold of a number of first-order resources–jobs, funds, specialised knowledge–which were in short supply and on which the peasants heavily depended in order to make a living. When we distinguish between patronage, i.e., the dispensation of first-order resources, and brokerage, i.e., the dispensation of second-order resources, then the situation of patronage applies to the relationship between the Polish peasants and the Jewish entrepreneurs in the early twentieth century.

Patron-Client Relations in Jaśliska

The question remains to what extent Poles and Jews in Jaśliska were linked by patterns of patronage. Considering the close interdependence between the Poles and the Jews and the relatively strong economic position of the latter, one important characteristic of patron-client relations—the asymmetrical commitment of two parties—certainly pertains. Many peasants in one way or another depended on Jews, who represented the most vital economic sectors of trade and industry. Likewise, many Jews maintained relations with more than one Polish client. Moreover, the small size of the peasant community, as well as the prevalence of feudal relations and certain cultural values[1] in the countryside, all contributed to the climate in which patron-client ties best flourished. The small size of the community increased face-to-face contacts, while the measure of informality of the relationships was high. In addition, as we have seen in the preceding chapters, group solidarity among the peasants was low, meaning that they employed individualistic strategies to further personal, rather than group, needs.

Patterns of patronage can also be discerned in the example of the Polish peasant who brought a chicken to Abraham B. or occasionally worked on his fields. By voluntarily giving presents to the owner of the local sawmill the peasant, in fact, applied for a job. If Abraham B. accepted the services performed by the peasant, and, in addition, employed him as a carter, timber-cutter, or domestic help, duties were still to be paid. As long as the job would last, the peasant remained indebted to 'Mister Owner', who furnished him with the basic means of subsistence. As is clear from the informants' accounts, Abraham B. had free disposal of his employees, that is, the workers of the sawmill and all others whom he employed. In return for the extra labour services paid by his employees, and to ensure such services at a later date, Abraham B. granted his employees certain privileges and acted as their 'subsistence crisis insurance'. In like manner, Jewish families who had Poles working for them as domestic helps (cleaning, serving), porters (carrying water or merchandise), or carters (transporting merchandise or wood) would grant their employees certain favours in addition to paying their regular salaries.

The outstanding example of a 'subsistence crisis insurance' was the Jewish creditor. Whenever a Polish peasant was short of cash or goods he went to a Jewish shopkeeper who in turn granted him limited credit. A proverb directly relating to this service says: 'When things are bad, go see the Jew.'[2] However, a Jewish shopkeeper not only granted credit when his client was short of money. To grant credit was to employ a strategy which tied the Polish client to his Jewish creditor, and vice versa. The ensuing debt relation enabled both parties to profit from the services and return services that went beyond regular and formal transactions. Polish debtors and Jewish creditors forged a tighter link by presenting each other gifts or by doing each other a favour every once in a while. There was no question of paying off debts until the moment the debts exceeded the financial potential of the debtor. In that case the relationship was no longer profitable and the partners would quit, and, if the worst came to the worst, the debtor was taken to court and his properties were sold at auction. The mortgage deeds witness numerous cases of land transfers from Polish debtors to Jewish creditors. Although this was rarely the case, a settlement of debts sometimes meant the bankruptcy of a Polish family.

While it is clear that the Jews were powerful in the economic arena, it is harder to assess their political influence. In the absence of data regarding the formation of political alliances (including voting behaviour) among the Poles and the Jews in Jaśliska during the interwar years, the extent to which the Jewish patrons were able to win the support of their clients vis-à-vis rival patron-client groups remains unclear. Still, the Polish and Jewish informants hinted at the special kind of prestige and authority enjoyed by the Jews in Jaśliska. The case of Abraham B., who was held in great respect by Jews and Poles alike, and who in addition was active in local politics, is a perfect example of a powerful local leader with apparent political aspirations. On the Jews' political power Wojciech M. (78), who used to be active in local politics, commented: 'When the elections took place in Jaśliska, they [Jews] were always the most important, because they were the richest, they had money, and in fact it was they who decided about everything. There were also poorer ones among them, but the Jews were better organised.' If this statement reveals one thing, it is that the Jews had a considerable influence in local politics.

Still, there were limits to the relative power of the Jewish patrons. As is argued in the literature on patron-client relationships, the relative bargaining position of the patrons and the clients may be dependent on outside forces. If the patron is backed by the state, the police, or the courts in his local domination of resources, he will be able to use coercion at little cost, and as a result, will be more successful in the political manipulation of his clients (Burkolter 1976). In spite of the relative strong economic position of the Jews in Jaśliska, as members of an ethnic minority they did not have preferential access to law and order. This limitation implied that higher political goals were probably of lesser interest to a Jewish patron than to his non-Jewish counterpart. Hence the capital of the Jewish patron, that is the network he had activated, and his credit, that is the faith his people had in him, though proper political instruments, were primarily a means to an end—to serve his economic interests.

Therefore, the bond between the Jewish patron and the Polish client was largely economic. Whereas the Jewish patron was mainly interested in economic transactions with his client, the Polish client was primarily interested in the economic protection of his patron, the latter having access to scarce resources. The Jewish patron thus committed himself to the Polish peasant when he needed a loyal customer or an efficient worker. The Polish client, on the other hand, went to the Jew when he needed economic support. Indeed, entry into a patron-client relationship was voluntary, and once a relationship was established a number of strategies were pursued which aimed at getting the other party into a debt relation. First, the return service was postponed for an unspecified period. Second, the content of an equivalent service remained unspecified. And finally, the channels were kept open by underpaying or overpaying at a later date. It was especially between Jewish employers and creditors and Polish employees and debtors that such unconditional transactions took place.

Patron-client ties characterised the relationship between Poles and Jews in Jaśliska to a degree. Not all the Jews maintained potential patron-client relations with the Poles. Most Jewish families were poor and were themselves involved in patron-client ties with their wealthier co-religionists. Moreover, not all Poles lost their autonomy in dealings with the Jews. While most Polish families needed the local Jews in one way or another (for employment, credit, or other kinds of economic support) some of them, especially the wealthier Polish families, could afford and also attempted to operate independently of the Jews. Unlike the classical patron who at all times is able to win the support of his clients, the Jewish patron was unable to maintain a certain measure of political independence. In fact, the Polish peasants depended on the Jews as individuals, but the Jews as a group depended on the political goodwill of the Polish community. The weak political position of the Jews is illustrated by the fact that the 'hidden promise' to give up all claims to autonomous access to resources, which is described as a significant obligation of the client towards the patron, was openly contested by the Poles with the establishment of the Agricultural Cooperative in Jaśliska.

The conclusion that Jews had limited political power brings us to another aspect of the patron-client relationship. It should be stressed that, beside the profitable economic returns, the social returns of patron-client ties were also considerable. The socialising of Poles and Jews turned out to be especially instrumental in reducing social conflict. Polish and Jewish informants confirm that the Jews carefully invested in the social relations with their Polish neighbours and clients. Therefore, Jews regularly and occasionally helped out their Polish townsmen in times of need–no such case was presented of Polish support for the Jews. As a minority with limited political power, engaged in stressful activities and exposed to enmities from the national authorities, Jews had good reasons to stay on good terms with the surrounding society. Hence they supported their Polish neighbours in times of need, rewarded the services performed by their Polish clients, and expressed their gratitude to local authorities by giving them presents and inviting them to participate in cheerful Jewish celebrations. In this way, social interaction served to stabilise and strengthen the ties between the Polish and Jewish communities.

On Polish-Jewish Coexistence

A number of scholars of Poland's Jewish history have stressed the authoritative role played by Jews in the village communities during the feudal period (Hertz 1988; Rosman 1990; Levine 1991). What is most striking, however, is that the Jews continued to play this role (although in a somewhat altered form) until the destruction of their communities during the Second World War. Wanda Wasilewska, a prominent communist in interbellum Poland, for example, observed during her wanderings through Polesie[3] in the late 1930s that peasants treated local Jews as people to trust and turned to Jews as intermediaries in relations with the state authorities (cited in Hertz 1988). The perspective of patronage, which is also apparent in the above observation, sheds a different light on the quality of the relationship linking Poles with Jews in interbellum Poland. The view that hostility towards the Jews is inevitable due to their pariah position in the local economy and their marginal position in local politics and culture needs a more carefully balanced appraisal. A critical observation may also be added to the view which is voiced by, for example, Foster (1974) that the marginal position of the Jews enables them to disregard the traditional social demands of the host society, which stress generosity and reciprocity, discourage profits from commercial transactions, and avoid conflict and competition.

The example of Jaśliska shows that the interests of the indigenous peasant population and the trade minority need not necessarily be conflicting and that mutual economic interests may give rise to a considerable social and political rapprochement between the two groups, rather than dissension. While there was a large measure of interdependence between the peasants and the Jews in Jaśliska, neither group commanded absolute power within the village community, which resulted in a weak political equilibrium between the ethnic communities. These conditions, in turn, induced the peasants and the Jews to be cautious and to relate to one another on sociable rather than on hostile terms. At the same time, the stable, constant, and strong contacts between the peasants and the Jews in a variety of settings laid the basis for social relations that went beyond the original utilitarian motivation. Rosman (1990), author of an in-depth exploration of magnate-Jewish relations in the Polish-Lithuanian Commonwealth, arrives at similar conclusions for the magnate-Jewish relations. By analysing the Sieniawski-Czartoryski estates Rosman demonstrates the measure of cooperation between magnates and Jews in eighteenth-century Poland. While Jews guaranteed the viability of important economic institutions and provided commercial services, magnates furnished an environment for Jews to conduct their religious and commercial activities. Rosman (1990: 209-210) concludes that within such a variety of settings, Polish-Jewish interactions cannot be conveniently characterised as utilitarian:

> Beyond economics, the Sieniawski-Czartoryski example implies that Jews could not help but be drawn in the main arena of society. Jews were not involved in the marketplace only. They had an interest in and influence on what transpired in the Sejm, the town and village councils, the church institutions, and the magnate palaces. Jews not only did business with Poles, they lived with them; social, cultural, and political associations were unavoidable [...] Marriages of convenience are still marriages. They generate a dynamic and entail responsibilities which went beyond the original utilitarian motivations. The Jewish-magnate nexus once formed—for whatever reasons—took on a life of its own and was a potent factor in society.

The large measure of economic interdependence that had been developed during the interbellum period positively contributed to the relatively peaceful relations between the Poles and the Jews at the community level. Indeed, the accounts of both Polish and Jewish informants show that Poles and Jews met on numerous occasions and that socialising between Poles and Jews was rather the rule than the exception. These meetings were not just chance encounters; they were an integral part of daily life and were approved of by both ethnic communities, as long as they did not harm the economic and political interests of the group. Hence we find numerous examples of Polish and Jewish children who became friends in school, of Polish and Jewish neighbours who shared the care of their common courtyard, of Polish clients and Jewish patrons who exchanged services on a regular basis, and of Jewish laymen and Polish authorities (secular and religious) who debated views of religion, life, and politics.

A certain level of cooperation, however, does not mean that tension between the Polish and Jewish communities was absent. Throughout the period of coexistence both communities struggled to prove superiority and determine their position in the social hierarchy in terms of economic success, control over means of production, religious supremacy, and political power.[4] However, competition and hostility between the ethnic communities was considerably reduced owing to the often close personal links of patronage connecting Jews with peasants. And yet it was precisely these close links which signalled the peasants' dependence on Jewish entrepreneurs, and which gave rise to the peasants' ambivalent attitude towards the Jews. Hostility and distrust on the one hand, affection and respect on the other, can be explained by the peasant's position as underdog and dependant of the local Jews. In fact, the widespread joke (cited in Hertz 1988) about the Polish squire who hated all Jews with the exception of his broker, his lawyer, his doctor, his banker, and so on, also applies to the Polish peasant, for the joke illustrates the tendency toward ambivalence which is inherent in the Polish-Jewish relationship.

Symbolic Representations: Polish-Jewish Relations and the Image of the Jew

The Relationship between 'Imagined' and 'Real Life' Experience

The prewar patron-client ties influence the way in which Polish informants view their one-time Jewish neighbours. Informants who had maintained relations with Jews hold predominantly positive views of them, for they had belonged to a select group of people who could count on a certain measure of protection from and preferential treatment by the Jews. The informant who positively judges his relation with shopkeeper X or employer Y not only expresses his or her gratitude for the services he had been offered, but also justifies his or her own inferior position within the relationship. To enter into a relationship with a Jew meant improvement, to be employed or to get assistance enhanced the individual's prospects, and in many cases it meant that one was simply better off. On the other hand, it is safe to assume that the villagers who had not maintained such relations held less positive views about the Jews.

Notwithstanding their positive judgement of the Polish-Jewish past, informants frequently employed anti-Jewish stereotypes to characterise the Jews. These stereotypes are clearly linked with the European anti-Semitic tradition, in that they correspond to images that found general acceptance in early Medieval Europe, that is, the theological stigma of the Antichrist and the economic stigma of the usurer and 'worshipper of Mammon' (Grynberg 1983; Van Arkel 1984; Zenner 1991). At the time when the Jews settled in Jaśliska certain prejudices found acceptance in the stereotype of the Jewish usurer and the Jewish arsonist.[5] Though certain elements of the stereotypes can be identified as reflections of 'real existing' relations, this is true only for a few of such elements, and even then the stereotypes tend to present a one-sided, exaggerated and prejudiced view of the Jews, with emphasis on the negative and distinctive features. It has been shown, however, that most informants have a more differentiated and more positive view on the Jews than the stereotypes would like us to believe. If such differentiated and positive judgements of Polish-Jewish relations prevailed, why did the informants frequently employ anti-Jewish stereotypes?

First of all, stereotypes are a suitable tool for communication. They express excessive feelings (such as feelings of frustration, impotence, admiration, triumph). Similarly, it is hard to avoid the impression that informants use stereotypes for the sake of convenience; more than once the stereotype turned out to be a suitable tool to illustrate the atmosphere of a world well-known to the informants but unknown to the researcher. In addition to being a stylistic device, stereotypes have an important socialising function: they create a sense of social solidarity, preserve social boundaries, and regulate social interaction (Barth 1969; Hertz 1988). As an instrument to organise social relations, stereotypes are often resistant to change or correction from countervailing evidence. Stereotypes therefore tend to be persistent, especially when there is no authority that disapproves of the means, and when in addition the means fit the culture of the people who employ them. This being the case, it can be argued that the current usage of anti-Jewish stereotypes by the Polish informants does not necessarily imply that they adhere to an anti-Semitic ideology.[6]

In a way, real life experiences have an important corrective function. Interaction implies the decline of social distance, and where social distance is small, it becomes impracticable to keep up certain prejudices. The seeming contradiction between on the one hand 'real life' experience, and on the other prejudice formulated as stereotypes, is confusing at times. To illustrate this point, informants whom I asked whether they really believe the story of Jews burning the houses of the Poles would not answer the question, precisely because this question forced them to make a difficult choice, that is, a choice between an image and personal experience, which in fact are units hard to compare. Whereas the stereotype tells them that Jews are arsonists, their own experience tells them that Jews are a friendly people with whom they lived on good terms. In other words, the stereotype tells a story and brings a message which can exist *next* to one's own experiences, that is, next to the experienced facts. As long as no one bothers whether the story of the stereotype is true—like the present researcher—inconsistencies do not hurt. It is precisely this paradox which Hoffman (1998: 13) finds most characteristic of *shtetl* culture, for it was in this culture that 'both prejudices and bonds were most palpably enacted—where a Polish peasant might develop a genuine affection for his Jewish neighbour despite negative stereotypes and, conversely, where an act of unfairness of betrayal could be most wounding because it came from a familiar.'

The Transition from Physical to Symbolic Experience

In reverse it may be argued that the absence of interaction stimulates the development of stereotypes, and, in the long term, even increases their credibility. This is at least what I observed among child informants. Apparently, the children easily adopt the anti-Jewish stereotypes presented to them by the older generations, and smoothly fit them into their own world view. It should be borne in mind that all informants in their childhood have been exposed to the stereotype of the 'Jewish bugaboo', as this is a traditional theme in peasant folk culture. But whereas most adult informants made an effort to place the notion of the Jewish bugaboo in its proper perspective, child informants simply pictured the Jew as synonymous with the devil— their image of the Jew is static, one-dimensional, and exclusively negative, unmodified by the experiences of direct interpersonal contact.

To a lesser degree the absence of direct interpersonal contact also affects the views of the adult informants. In fact, the informants' image of the Jew has not changed much over the last fifty years. In their minds they retain the picture of the Hasidim, members of the Orthodox Jewish community, who for them constitute the 'real Jews'.[7] In general, informants have lost track of contemporary Jewry, and as far as they are still in touch with contemporary Jews, this is in the United States, where Poles and descendants of Polish Jews come into direct contact. What is more, Polish labour migrants who do not speak English and who have access only to untrained jobs often end up carrying out the same kind of work (housekeeping, child care) for the wealthier Jewish families that their parents and grandparents had done in prewar Jaśliska. Agnieszka P. (33) explains:

> *I went to work in the USA, in New Jersey [...] I did what every Pole does there: cleaning and looking after children 'baby sitting' [...] To be more precise I cleaned in Jewish houses [...] There were two families. I cleaned for the ladies from these families, and their mothers. [They] were Poles of Jewish origin. The mothers of these ladies I cleaned for could even speak Polish [...] Generally I can tell you nothing about Jews from Jaśliska, but I can tell you a lot about American Jews. I was also at a Jewish celebration. It was my first experience in America [...] There were Jews with special caps. They had these candles of course. In Poland one cannot see this. I was cleaning on Monday, after this party. All these caps, these candles. First I didn't know what these caps were for, because I had never seen them before. Later I asked my aunt what the purpose is of these caps [...] But later I saw this picture in a shop. Real Jews (rodowici) wear these all the time, not only on holidays. One can see Jews in the shops and on the streets with these caps, the same as in the old times in our place, Jaśliska.*

For the older generations physical experiences with their one-time Jewish neighbours gradually lose significance. The more alienated they are from the original physical experiences, the more blurred the contexts of these experiences become, and the more important the symbolical content which these experiences communicate become. Since in present-day Jaśliska a contemporary frame of reference is clearly lacking, the legend of the local Jews, and the symbols which are used to bring them back to life again, have grown larger than the Jews themselves.

All this may give us new insights into the dilemma which was formulated in Chapter one—why is there anti-Semitism in Poland without Jews? On closer investigation it turns out that anti-Semitism in a country without Jews is no contradiction. It has been shown that in addition to the Jews' social and economic position, the quality of interpersonal contact between Jews and non-Jews, as well as the presence of anti-Jewish stereotypes, are also crucial in explaining the existence of an anti-Semitic ideology. I thus share the conclusions of Van Arkel (1984), who argues that anti-Semitism may occur when the following three conditions are fulfilled: (1) the existence of collective prejudice towards the Jews, which is expressed in an anti-Jew-ish stereotype (in Van Arkel's model called stigmatisation); (2) the absence of interaction between Jews and non-Jews; (3) the terror of public opinion that forces people to discriminate even when they would never do so voluntarily.

We have seen that in interwar Jaśliska the first condition prevailed. Anti-Jewish stereotypes were widely accepted in the peasant community. How-ever, the second condition (no interaction) was absent, which may explain why the stereotypes did not necessarily lead to anti-Jewish actions at the local level when during the 1930s the Polish government propagated a pol-icy which aimed at marginalising the Jews economically and politically. The terror exerted by Nazi Germany during the Second World War led not only to the third condition, but also, through genocidal policies, to the second condition. Indeed, war activities, as well as the lack of efficient central con-trol, caused an upsurge of intimidation and terror in the region, which in particular became directed against the weakest of society, such as the returning Jewish survivors. These outbursts of anti-Semitic violence, although rejected by my Polish informants, were indicative of the atmos-phere in the period immediately following the war.

In present-day Jaśliska the first two conditions prevail. Interaction between Jews and Poles has ended since the elimination of the local Jewish population in 1942. The persistence of anti-Jewish stereotypes, on the one hand, and the absence of a school curriculum which presents an unbiased reading of Poland's Jewish past (that is, until the fall of the socialist regime in 1989),[8] on the other hand, form the basis for latent anti-Semitism among the younger generations. If combined with the third condition, the force of an anti-Jewish public opinion, such ignorance is especially dangerous. It is precisely this ignorance which Opatoshu warns us about in his story of the Jew Legend of Melawe. It seems that in Jaśliska elderly men and women of the generation of Opatoshu's grandfather Marcin only stimulate the biased views of the younger generations through their story-telling. And yet, it seems that with the coming of age the impact of anti-Semitic imagery weak-ens in favour of 'common-sense' explanations; once removed from grand-parental control the generation of young adults seems to develop its own perspective on the Jews and on past Polish-Jewish relations. The fact that these young adults have had little support from the Polish educational sys-tem is a result of, and, at the same time, results in, the lack of a nation-wide critical reflection on the Polish-Jewish past. Until recently, the propagation of anti-Semitic imagery was not condemned and a shared sense of moral guilt for what happened to the European Jewry during the Second World War is only recently beginning to form.

The Impact of the Shoah: On Outsiders, Victims and Bystanders

To paraphrase Hoffman (1998: 7), the shadow of the Shoah is long, and it extends backward as well as forward. Indeed, the impact of the Shoah on our current understanding of the Polish-Jewish past is considerable. For one thing, the criteria that are currently employed to assess the extent of prewar and wartime anti-Semitism in Poland are based on definitions that were formulated in the postwar era. Understandably, the horrors which came to light after 1945 considerably reduced the level of tolerance with respect to anti-Semitism. A hundred years ago tendencies which are now defined as anti-Semitic were then tolerated in a way which for us, after the Shoah, is unacceptable. In general, what we consider decent is historically determined (Van Arkel 1991).

In a similar way, views of the past are influenced by one's individual life history. In the present context, besides the perpetrators, whose views are not discussed in this book, three categories of life histories are discerned; those of the victims, the bystanders, and the outsiders (see also Chapter one). The Jewish informants represent the first category, the Polish informants represent the second category, while the third category consists of those (Jews and non-Jews alike) who did not live through the war in Poland, either because they are from a later generation, or because they were elsewhere at the time. I believe that among the bystanders and victims there is a tendency to idealise prewar Polish-Jewish relations or to keep silent about the past. The bystanders and the victims employ strategies which according to Irwin-Zarecka (1989a) I will call 'neutralising strategies'. Such strategies 'neutralise' the memory of those people who employ such strategies and affect their view of the past.

The first two groups, the victims and the bystanders, have an interest in keeping the event of the Shoah inexplicable. A person who does not distinguish between cause and effect bears no moral responsibility; the bystander cannot be held responsible for what happened to the Jews, and the victim cannot be held responsible for what happened to his or her own family. A person who is not responsible cannot be found guilty; the bystander is not to be blamed for his or her action or inaction, and the victim is not to be blamed for the fact that he or she (and *not* his or her family, children, partner, friend) did survive. An important strategy to suppress one's private sense of guilt is to stress the positive side of the prewar relationship, and also to stress one's own inability to act. The more positive the relationship before the Shoah, the less deep is the individual's guilt ('they took our Jews away' and 'it just happened to us'). And the more convincing the individual's impotence, the less likely is his or her responsibility ('we really wanted to help, but we couldn't' and 'we didn't know what was going on').

As already noted in Chapter one, unlike the victims and bystanders, outsiders do have an interest in answering the question of what allowed the Final Solution to happen. In Western circles, a frequently heard explanation for the efficient execution of the genocide is that Poles, by virtue of their anti-Semitic disposition, had an active part in it. This premise gave rise to an extremely negative picture of Polish-Jewish relations before, during, and even after the Shoah, putting special emphasis on the deadly fanaticism and inertia of the Poles. It goes beyond the scope of the present study to explain why the notion of Polish anti-Semitism is so persistent. Still, it is worth mentioning, as Irwin-Zarecka (1989a: 181) does, that in Western and Polish circles notions of responsibility and guilt are different. Whereas Westerners accept the notion that everyone bears moral responsibility for what happened to European Jewry (since everyone is a member of the civilisation which made the Final Solution possible),[9] Poles define the problem of responsibility mainly in terms of direct responsibility. This idea of direct responsibility implies that the question of moral guilt is dealt with in a different manner:

> As victims of the Nazis and people who, even at their worst, never ascribed to the idea of mass extermination in solving the 'Jewish question', Poles felt and feel that only the Nazis themselves bear responsibility for the 'Final solution'. As people continually challenged in that view by critics from outside, Poles have come to define this matter even further in terms of direct responsibility. Because they were so close, the idea of moral responsibility speaks to them only of their action or inaction; the much larger terrain of feelings, perceptions, and attitudes towards the Jew is no consideration (Irwin-Zarecka 1989a: 181).

The impact of the Shoah on the perceptions of the bystanders, victims, and outsiders can be illustrated with the example of Jaśliska. To start with the first group, the bystanders, Polish informants who lived through the war presented a positive picture of prewar Polish-Jewish relations. According to them, interactions between Jews and Poles were on friendly, even on cooperative, terms. When referring to the period of the German occupation informants claim that most Poles behaved decently ('there are bad guys and good guys everywhere, aren't there?'). Informants unanimously pitied the Jews and claimed to have been absolutely unprepared and defenceless to oppose German actions. Under the circumstances—the Germans' superior power; Ukrainian collaboration; poor living conditions; death penalty for resistance or assisting Jews; ignorance of the Germans' evil intentions; fear for one's own destiny; the risks of betrayal in a small village community—Polish villagers were unable to rescue their one-time Jewish neighbours. Instead, my Polish informants claimed that the Final Solution was the work of the Nazis, and that the Nazis alone should be blamed for the fate of 'their Jews'. At this point the informants' positive evaluation of the past performs an important neutralising function: by presenting an idealised vision of the past they negate any form of moral responsibility for the fate of their Jewish neighbours.

As far as one may generalise from the interviews with five Jewish survivors, it is at least remarkable that all five informants hold positive views on prewar Polish-Jewish relations in Jaśliska. Poles and Jews lived on peaceful terms, which, according to my informants, was the logical outcome of the conditions that prevailed in the countryside: the small Polish and Jewish communities lived in close proximity and interdependence and therefore had no choice but to adapt to each other.[10] The predominantly positive experiences in the prewar period violently contrast with the experiences during the war time and the years immediately following the war. All Jewish informants expressed their confusion about the sudden change in attitude among the Poles and Lemkos following the outbreak of the Second World War. The murderous policies of the Germans as well as the subsequent explosion of anarchy and hostility among the local population (which was particularly directed towards Jewish refugees and returnees) came to them as a complete surprise. Within living memory relations between the different groups have been harmonious, and all of a sudden the world is full of violence, treason, and hatred. Why this sudden change? More than fifty years after the war the informants are still puzzled. In their eyes Poland has developed into an anti-Semitic country, which is very much unlike their own experience in prewar Poland. On the contrary, they stress unanimously that in their day-to-day dealings with Poles anti-Semitism was not feasible. While this vision of the past may have some truths, it certainly presents an idealised picture of Polish-Jewish relations. This idealised picture, in turn, can be explained as an (unconscious) attempt to soften and neutralise the memory of the Shoah, which in the informants' present lives still is the source of deep sorrow and pain.

Outsiders, on the other hand, have no interest at all in neutralising the past, but instead try to explain the Polish-Jewish relationships in terms of the wartime period. As a result, their views differ considerably from those of the bystanders and the victims. A vivid example of the incompatibility of views is provided by the eye-witness account of Israel B. (victim) as recorded by Josef Litwak (outsider) on behalf of the Yad Vashem archives in 1969. Israel B. (born in 1901) grew up in Jaśliska and left the town in 1936 when he married and started a new life in a neighbouring town. Until his departure from the small town, Israel B. had been a business partner in his father's drapery, grocery, and bar. When he was interviewed

Israel B. lived in Israel and had retired from his job as an official. During the interview Josef Litwak observes that his interviewee is strikingly positive about life in the small town. Indeed, Israel B.'s words are as follows (in Litwak 1969: 3):

> One hardly noticed anti-Semitism amongst the people. The relationships between Jews and non-Jews were rather good and the trading contacts were based on mutual trust. Until the outbreak of the war there were no Christian shops in Jaśliska or in the neighbouring villages. Also the officials, priests and teachers from the villages bought in Jewish shops. We did not experience anything like anti-Jewish harassment. The good relationship between Jews and non-Jews gave rise to a steady material prosperity among the Jews. Although there was one cooperative shop run by Christians in which agricultural products were sold, there was no question of competition. The merchants from Jaśliska enjoyed a good reputation and were considered to be smart and honest people.[11]

The interviewer Josef Litwak, who has not been a witness of Nazi persecution, did not hide his scepticism about the story told to him, and dismisses it as an obtuse, impertinent, and false rendering of history. In an introduction to the eye-witness account, Josef Litwak (1969: 2) comments:

> [...] The idealisation went so far that the eye-witness did not take any notice of anti-Semitic behaviour until the outbreak of the war in 1939. This is clearly unthinkable in the light of what we know about anti-Jewish sentiments, which culminated in the period between 1935 and 1938, that is, from the moment Poland became an ally of Nazi Germany and proceeded to attack Czechoslovakia, during which Poland sided with the Nazis.[12] The eye-witness presents an idyllic picture of the small town, where once a hundred Jewish families lived, who, by his report, could make a 'modest' living—at least in the eyes of the eye-witness—with trade and smuggling over the Slovakian border. All Jewish inhabitants were pious and there were no political parties or Jewish youth associations. The public political activism which characterised Jewish life between the two wars did not reach this small town, not at all. They continued living in the cultural atmosphere of the eighteenth century, unaffected by the social changes that passed Jewish life in general and life of the Polish Jews in particular in the period preceding the Shoah. It was a small community with 'weak' Jews perhaps, as we see it now and maybe also some of those who lived at that time, who were satisfied with their part, until fate came upon them, while they did not even notice that the end was approaching.[13]

Taking this excerpt as an example of the outsiders' point of view, it is typical of the way in which traditional Polish anti-Semitism is used as an argument to explain history. Here too, the collective experience of the Shoah very clearly stands in the way of an objective evaluation of past Polish-Jewish relations.

It is not my intention to pass judgement on the validity of the positive or negative view about Polish-Jewish relations in prewar Jaśliska. What matters is the extent to which the neutralising process influences the way in which the past is recalled and interpreted. The examples given above can give us some insights regarding the views and recollections of the Polish informants. For one thing, it was observed that few informants displayed any sense of guilt; most informants had no problem talking about their former Jewish fellow citizens or reflecting on the Jews' fate during the Shoah. Here the effect of the neutralising strategy is clearly discernible. In general, it was observed that informants would talk about 'their Jews' with much more ease than about certain subjects related to a more recent past. Informants related the fate of the local Jews, the villagers' failure to save them from death, and the villagers' purchase of former Jewish properties more frankly than the unresolved political intrigues and conflicts among fellow Poles. It is as if the villagers have definitely closed the Jewish chapter in local history, and sometimes feel like telling a fairy-tale about a long gone past which no longer bears any relevance to their present-day lives.

In addition, it has been shown that there is a salient contrast between the informants' evaluation of past Polish-Jewish relations and the stories that are being told. A positive judgement about a man who in the same breath has been described as a free-loader is far from consistent. Here also the effect of neutralisation is discernible. Apparently, informants have good reasons to hide ill-feelings towards the Jews. This is not to say that informants always spoke highly of the Jews, on the contrary. The best story-teller never minces matters. Still, where the neutralising effect seems present is in the evaluation of past Polish-Jewish relations. Adult informants unanimously stressed that Poles and Jews lived on good terms and that, as a rule, Jews were good people.[14] It is likely that sixty years ago the informants would have expressed themselves less cautiously. The fact that stories about 'Jewish tricks' and a cautious approach to the Polish-Jewish past easily go hand in hand indicates that in the era before the Shoah ambivalence may be the most truthful characterisation of the villagers' attitude towards the Jews.

Notes

1. See Hertz (1988), who stresses the authoritative role played by the Jews in the village community, which he traces to the legacy of feudal society, in which the peasants had limited freedom and in which the Jews took on the role of intermediary on behalf of the landed nobility. Hertz unravels the cultural values and ideologies that underpinned this relationship and that, being firmly grounded in the society's value system, survived the feudal system.
2. Reportedly, in Poland people now say: 'Though things are bad, there is no Jew to go to' (quoted in Hertz 1988: 200).
3. A region in White Russia, formerly part of eastern Poland.
4. It can be argued that tensions between Poles and Jews became particularly apparent on the religious level. First, religion was very much interwoven with the ethnic identity of the Polish and Jewish communities. Second, as an object of prestige and identity, religious difference was to be stressed and defended by both communities. Third, considering the fact that religious boundaries were indisputable, inter-communal fights over religious matters were less dangerous and, therefore, sanctioned to a degree.
5. The notion of the Jewish arsonist fits yet another ideological constant in European tradition, that is, the image of the Jew as Judas the betrayer. In the course of centuries this image took different forms: the Jew who is in league with the Muslims; the Jew who forms a fifth column among the invading Tartars, and who were considered to be the ten lost tribes coming to revenge their oppressed brothers; the Jew who conspired with heretics and lepers, and who poisons the wells with the Black Death (Van Arkel 1991: 54).
6. Zenner (1991: 50) also distinguishes between anti-Semitic imagery and anti-Semitic ideology, since such imagery may be found even among those who are not ideologically anti-Semitic. Weber, according to Zenner, was not so much an anti-Semite as a user of such imagery.
7. This conclusion converges with the observation made by Miron Gordon, then Israeli's ambassador to Poland, who in an interview (Wprost, April 1991, 11-12) stated that the Poles' image of the Jew is primarily that of the traditional Polish Jew from before the Second World War. It is this picture that abundantly prevails in Poland's traditional culture and popular jokes. The Jewish diaspora in the United States constitutes a second frame of reference, which is not surprising if one considers the large Polish and Jewish communities that coexist in the United States. Only in the last instance do Poles associate Jews with the (Jewish) citizens of Israel.
8. See for example Radziwiłł (1989).
9. Bauman (1992: 273), for example, explains the essence of moral responsibility as follows: '[t]he crimes could be individual and private; the guilt is collective and shared. The survivors are guilty, and their survival is their guilt. This is not a guilt which will be recognised in any human court of justice. But then moral conscience cannot be exonerated by human courts.'
10. It must be borne in mind that the Lemko population outnumbered both Poles and Jews in the area. As I suggested earlier in this study, this might have encouraged a reconciliation between the Polish and Jewish communities. One Jewish informant, for example, stressed the 'civilised' character of the Poles in contrast to the 'boorish' Lemkos from neighbouring villages. The opinion of this informant, however, somewhat diverges from the views of the other Jewish informants, who hold more positive views of the Lemko people.

11. Translated from Hebrew to Dutch by A. Gebhard (University of Amsterdam). Translation from Dutch to English mine.

12. Josef Litwak confuses facts in an interesting manner. In 1938 Poland annexed the much disputed town Cieszyn (a town bordering Czechoslovakia), but did so by way of precaution regarding the imminent annexation of Sudetenland by the German Reich. Poland's precaution was justified in so far as the Germans, after occupying Sudetenland, proceeded to occupy other parts of Czechia, thereby violating the agreements of Munich (September 1938). In March 1939 the German Reich annexed the whole of Czechia after which Slovakia joined the Rome-Berlin axis. In September 1939 the Slovakian and German armies invaded Poland (Hoetink, De Bruyne et al. 1956).

13. The fierce criticism by Josef Litwak of the 'weak' and 'backward' *shtetl* Jews from Eastern Europe was much in line with Israeli thought in the decades following the war. In general, European Jews who returned from the war were looked down upon. These victims of war were accused of having been disgracefully submissive and did not match the then Israeli desire for a (secular) heroism (Segev 1993).

14. This opinion, of course, also corresponds to the cultural notion that one should never say anything bad about the dead.

Chapter 9

CONCLUSION
The Jew Legend Revisited

The boys stayed in their places, some on the bench, some in the grass, and continued listening to the unusual stories; they took in Marcin's accounts on the
Jews, as if the events had taken place several hundred years ago. They listened
to the songs of the birds, which were carried from tree to tree, and rose from the
destroyed tombs. As if lifted from the collapsed graves, from the ruins of the
Holocaust, the melody of the cemetery hummed the tune of the legend
(Opatoshu 1951: 317).

*T*he conspicuous role of the Jew in Polish culture, despite the virtual
absence of a Jewish population in Poland, has led us back to the questions
with which we began: Why is it that Jews still play an important role in cultural expressions and in the consciousness of the Poles? And how exactly do
Poles perceive their one-time Jewish fellow citizens? In order to seek an
answer to these questions I have opted for a case study approach, which, as
was argued in Chapter one, allows for a more accurate and contextualised
understanding of the complex subject of Polish-Jewish relations. The interviews I have conducted with Polish and Jewish informants, as well as the
archival sources that I have used to complement the first-hand anthropological data, all relate to the case of Jaśliska, a small town like many that
existed in prewar Poland: a town in which Poles and Jews lived in close proximity, and that, as a consequence of the Great Depression and the Second
World War, has now become a peasant community of minor importance.

To most of today's inhabitants of Jaśliska, the word 'Jew' is just an
abstract term and no longer refers to any real living person—to an individ-

Notes for this section begin on page 194.

ual with whom they might meet, visit, or talk. More than fifty years ago the Nazis murdered most of the Jewish residents from Jaśliska. The few Jews who survived the labour and death camps escaped the country in the years following the Second World War. Although no Jews live in Jaśliska today, the word 'Jew' is often used by the Polish villagers and it stirs up a special kind of emotion in the person who uses it. The context in which the word is used, and the meaning it is given, directly relate to the town's local history, that is, to the experience of Polish-Jewish coexistence in Jaśliska in the decades preceding the Second World War. In Opatoshu's sense, Jaśliska's Jewish past is very much alive for the young and old generations of Poles who inhabit this community. Any sensitive listener can hear the melody of the legend chanting the tale of the town's former Jewish residents. Jaśliska has no longer an old Jewish cemetery,[1] but the melody is hummed by the living memory of the Jews' Polish contemporaries. These elderly men and women were not at all hesitant to talk about Jaśliska's Jewish past. On the contrary, they told their memories, stories, and opinions about their one-time Jewish neighbours without prompting.

Writing about Poles and Jews, one inevitably has to deal with the popular and scholarly views of Polish-Jewish relations that exist inside and outside of Poland. The most popular and perhaps most widespread view of Polish-Jewish relations is that Poles are virulent anti-Semites and that Jews are the Poles' permanent victims. The screening of the documentary 'Shoah' by the French director Claude Lanzmann in 1985 strongly influenced public opinion in the latter direction. In his film Lanzmann portrays Poles as naive, indifferent, and even guilty bystanders of the Nazi genocide of European Jewry (see also Lanzmann 1985). The fact that Poland was the place where much of the Nazi policy of mass murder was carried out inevitably raises the question as to what degree the earlier attitude of the Poles towards the Jews aided the Nazis in carrying out their genocidal plans. It explains why so many postwar scholars of Poland's Jewish history have focused on the anti-Jewish attitudes and actions in the period preceding (and, to a lesser extent, also following) the Final Solution (Heller 1977; Friedman 1980; Mahler 1985; Hirszowicz 1986; Levine 1991). In this perspective, to write about Poles and Jews is to write about a disturbed and hostile relationship.

The present study provides no ready answer to the question whether Polish anti-Semitism is special or not. By locating the relations between the Poles and Jews in a specific time and place, I have tried to suggest a more complicated relationship between cooperation and conflict, that is, between the pragmatic interests that Jews represented and the socio-cultural emotions that they evoked. In order to assess the ambivalent nature of the relationship, we have had to step back to the nineteenth century, which marked the beginning of Polish-Jewish coexistence in Jaśliska, and to the first decades of the twentieth century, during which a relationship developed that was marked by cooperative symbiosis. The structure of prewar society, I have suggested, continues to exert a strong influence on the present-day views held by the Polish informants. For most of the villagers the interwar period was a time of poverty and deprivation. The peasants, who no longer were self-sufficient, increasingly depended on Jewish creditors and employers. The relationship that developed between Poles and Jews was one between clients and patrons, the latter supporting the former in return for economic loyalty and labour services. The patron-client ties laid the basis for the Poles' ambivalent attitude towards the Jews. On the one hand, Polish informants stressed the inequality between the Polish peasants and the Jewish entrepreneurs, while on the other hand they put emphasis on the benefits resulting from interactions with the Jews. By using the stereotype of the usurer and arsonist, the informants expressed dislike of their inferior position with regard to the wealthier Jewish inhabitants. At the same time, the villagers' involvement in the acts of reciprocity gave rise to a more positive view of the Jew: the benevolent Jewish creditor and employer who rescued the Poles from bitter poverty.

The ambivalent nature of the relationship is also apparent on another level. The symbols and images the informants employed to describe prewar Polish-Jewish relations tend to present an exaggerated and generally negative picture of the Jew. This, however, does not prevent the informants from passing a positive judgement on prewar Polish-Jewish relations. At this point the impact of the Shoah on the informants' views is detectable. First, the Shoah put an abrupt end to decades of Polish-Jewish interaction. The absence of direct interpersonal contact and the persistence of certain cultural notions added to a mythical representation of the Jew. This representation, though clearly related to past 'real life' experience, remains unmodified and detached from social reality. This trend is particularly manifest among the youngest generation, where children's fantasies and transmitted stereotypes combine to produce a bizarre picture of the Jew. Second, the disturbing fact of the genocide, which eliminated all members of the local Jewish community in an unexpected, brutal manner, is likely to have contributed to a more cautious and neutral evaluation of the past, devoid of Polish-Jewish conflict and hostility.

In Chapter one it was argued that a case study approach, employing first-hand archival and anthropological sources that are connected in time and space, would allow for insights that can not be gained using secondary or macro-level sources. An important question to ask is can we generalise these findings for the Jaśliska research village to the wider Polish society and to other interethnic relations. Jaśliska is an exceptional case in at least one way. The fact that Poles and Jews lived in a predominantly Lemko environment might explain the high degree of cooperation between the two ethnic communities, as they felt, perhaps more than elsewhere, dependent on one another. However, it is becoming more and more clear that this type of peaceful coexistence is not just typical for Jaśliska. Informal conversations in neighbouring Lemko villages give a similar picture. Orla-Bukowska (1994) found a similar pattern in parts of western Galicia that have been historically dominated by Poles. Though this still has to be proven, it is likely that in the small towns and villages of certain other parts of rural Poland similar symbiotic relations existed. Finally, my conclusions support the notion which is categorically stressed by Hertz (1988: 202) that '... fundamental research toward establishing the image of the Jew in the Polish popular mind will necessarily come to indicate [the] ambivalent nature.'

However, there is no reason to assume that relations were equally balanced in larger urban settings. As we have seen, one of the reasons the relations were cooperative in Jaśliska, as in other small towns and villages, was the interpersonal contact and interdependence between the various ethnic groups in these rural and relatively isolated settings. Although a comparative study of urban and rural settings still needs to be done, it is possible that in larger towns interpersonal contacts between Poles and Jews were less common, because of the larger size of the respective communities and the tendency to retire in ethnic neighbourhoods. It is precisely from these urban centres that much of the public discourse originates on which macro-level studies base their conclusions. This has led to an unjust urban bias in the analysis of Polish-Jewish relations that focuses on competition and anti-Semitism. More attention to rural settings, in which a relatively large proportion of Jews lived in prewar Poland, may force us to reassess that interpretation of the Polish-Jewish past.

While this analysis has very much focused on the specifics of the Polish-Jewish relationship, we can nevertheless draw some implications for the field of interethnic relations. First of all, it was shown that the values and opinions held by informants are far from consistent. It is useful to make an analytical distinction between ideology, stereotypical cultural notions, and actual behaviour. A single focus on what people say may all to easily lead to a lopsided representation of inter-cultural relations. Second, it was shown that values and attitudes are dynamic and differ from one generation to another. Care should thus be taken in generalising observations based on the views expressed by a single generation. Finally, the study has shown that hostility and conflict between groups with a different ethnic background living in close proximity is far from inevitable. At this point, the framework of patron-client ties has proven to be a useful perspective of analysis. Similar patterns of structural interdependence in interethnic relations may therefore be a fruitful subject for further study.

Notes

1. During the Second World War the grave-stones of the Jewish cemetery of Jaśliska were used by the Ukrainian village head (*sołtys*) of Jaśliska to build an embankment in the nearby river.

APPENDIX
Cadastral Registers

The cadastral or real estate registers (*księgi wieczyste*) were a product of the land reforms in 1848, when land ownership became an important indicator for land redistribution policies. In the research area a first cadastral survey was conducted in 1851. The later real estate registers and cadastral maps were based on these data.[1] The real estate registers are now located in the court of law in Krosno (for the period 1874-1940) and the municipal council in Dukla (for the period 1945-1965).[2] With the help of the real estate registers and the cadastral maps, all transactions in the town real estate among the Jews and between the Jews and Poles were recorded for the period between 1874 and 1939; transactions of agricultural plots were considered to fall outside the scope of the present work. Table 1 reflects the balance between Polish and Jewish holdings for the period 1874 to 1947 in terms of numbers and percentages of Jewish-owned building lots. Maps 3, 4 and 5 give a picture of the distribution of Polish and Jewish building lots in Jaśliska for the period between 1874 and 1947.

It should be noted that some of the mortgage records have been lost and that it has therefore become impossible to determine the absolute number of Jewish and Polish lots. In this respect the year of 1947 forms an exception. Data for this year are based on the mortgage index of 1947, which gives a complete picture of the postwar status quo.[3] Because the Jews of Jaśliska had been deported and murdered in the summer of 1942, the proportion of the Jewish real estate in 1947 reflects the situation as it was left by the Jews in 1942. Due to this different and more complete source for 1947, the absolute number of Jewish lots in this year is higher than in 1939, as the data for the latter year are based on the older and incomplete real estate records. Still, the percentage of Jewish lots in 1947 equals that of 1939 (see Table 1). All in all, it is safe to assume that the real estate registers give

---

Notes for this section begin on page 196.

an accurate picture of the proportion of Jewish-owned holdings to that of the Polish townsmen.

Table 1   Proportion of Building Lots Completely and Partially Owned by Jews in Numbers and Percentages (1874-1947)

Year	All lots*	Jewish lots		Partially owned	Total
		Completely owned			
	number	number	*% of all lots*	number	% of all lots
1874	178	29	*16.2*	4	18.5
1880	168	28	*16.6*	3	18.5
1885	167	28	*16.6*	3	18.6
1890	168	29	*17.2*	3	19.0
1895	172	34	*19.7*	4	22.1
1900	173	38	*21.9*	7	26.0
1905	171	41	*23.9*	4	26.3
1910	172	41	*23.8*	2	25.0
1915	172	39	*22.6*	2	23.8
1920	172	36	*20.9*	2	22.1
1925	172	37	*21.5*	1	22.1
1930	172	37	*21.5*	1	22.1
1935	174	36	*20.6*	3	22.4
1939	174	34	*19.5*	4	21.8
1947**	208	41	*19.7*	1	20.2

Notes: *All lots of which records were found; **according to *Wypisy Hipoteczne Gromady Jaśliskiej*, Dukla (1947)
Sources: Księgi Wieczyste, Krosno (1874).

Notes

1. For information concerning the Austrian cadastral survey in 1851, see also Hann (1985) and Bednarska (1982).
2. The registers belong to the cadastral maps of 1896 and 1962/1975.
3. Like the cadastral survey a hundred years earlier, the land registration (Jewish and non-Jewish) in 1947 served the purpose of land reform, this time according to socialist principles.

Map 3 Distribution of Polish and Jewish building lots in 1874

0 20 40 60 80 100 m

Polish lots

shared lots

Jewish lots

no information

North

Based on the cadastral map of 1896 and the
real estate registers for the period 1874-1965

Map 4   Distribution of Polish and Jewish building lots in 1905

0   20   40   60   80   100 m

Polish lots   North ➤

shared lots

Jewish lots

no information

Based on the cadastral map of 1896 and the
real estate registers for the period 1874-1965

Map 5 Distribution of Polish and Jewish building lots in 1947

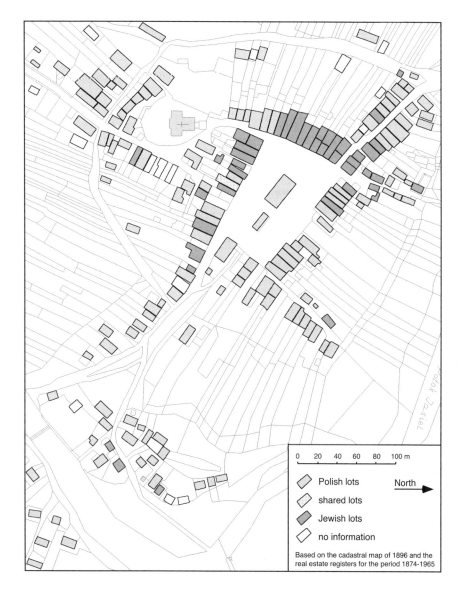

0 20 40 60 80 100 m		

⬦ Polish lots   North ▶

⬦ shared lots

◆ Jewish lots

⬦ no information

Based on the cadastral map of 1896 and the
real estate registers for the period 1874-1965

GLOSSARY

arenda	a lease of monopoly rights
arendarz	a lessee of an *arenda*
czopowe	excise on liquor
czynsz	real estate tax
dzierżawa	a leasehold, usually of real estate
dzierżawca	a lessee of a *dzierżawa*
goy	non-Jew, Gentile (pl. *goyim*)
grosz	a monetary unit
grzywna	a monetary unit, usually used to express the amounts of monetary fines (pl. *grzywny*)
Hasid	member of a religious movement, begun by Israel Ba'al Shem Tov, which emphasised piety and joyous communion with God (pl. *Hasidim*)
Haskalah	Jewish enlightenment movement
kahal	the governing council of a *kehilla*
kehilla	an organised Jewish community
klucz	the basic unit of latifundium consisting of a town or towns, villages, and several manors
Maskil	adherent of the Jewish enlightenment (pl. *Maskilim*)
Pan	nobleman
propinacja	lease on production and sale of alcohol
propinator	lessee of the right to propination
rebbe	a leader of a group of Hasidim, not necessarily a rabbi, whose authority was charismatic
shabbes goy	a Christian who on Sabbath does work which is prohibited to Jews (also: a Jew who scorns the Sabbath)

zaddik	lit. righteous, a Hassidic leader, often raised by their followers to the status of direct intermediaries with God or super human miracle workers (pl. *zaddikim*)
złoty	basic Polish monetary unit

Note: this list is largely based on the glossary by Rosman (1990: 216-220) and Zborowski and Herzog (1962).

BIBLIOGRAPHY

Consulted Archival Sources and Documents

Archiwum Państwowe, Rzeszów
Akta Gminy Jaślisk, 1939-1945.

Archiwum Państwowe, Sanok
Akta Gminy Jaślisk, 1944-1956.
Państwowe Urząd Repatriacyjny: Referat Osadnictwa, 1947-1948.
Państwowe Urząd Repatriacyjny: Referat Przesiedleńczy, 1949.

Archiwum Parafii Jaśliska, Jaśliska
Garbaszewski K. 'Kronika Księdza Karola Garbaszewskiego', 1872-1895.
Moszkowicz J. 'Kronika Księdza Jana Moszkowicza', n.d.
Bogdański Z. 'Kronika Miasteczko Jaślisk', n.d.

Archiwum Szkoły Powszechnej w Jaśliskach, Jaśliska
Stączek K. 'Kronika szkoła', 1944-1951.
'Oceny Sprawowania się i Postępów w Nauce', 1933-1939.

Główny Urząd Statystyczny, Warsaw
Skorowidz Miejscowości Rzeczypospolitej Polskiej, 1924.
Spis Powszechny, 1988.

Muzeum Budownictwa Ludowego, Sanok
Olszański H. 'Stosunki Mieszkańców Jaślisk ze Słowacją', 1985.
'Zgadnienie: Małe Miasteczko Jaśliska', 1978-1985 (collection of
   interviews by Polish students).

Muzeum Historyczne, Sanok
'Księga Zawiadomień Przełożonego Miejscowego w Miasteczkim Jaślisku',
   1958-1880.

Sąd Rejonowy, Krosno
Księgi Wieczyste dla nieruchomości w Jaśliskach, 1874-1958.

Urząd Miejski, Dukla
Wypisy Hipoteczne Gromady Jaśliskiej: 'Rejestr Gruntów wsi Jaśliska',
1947.

Wojewódzkie Archiwum Państwowe, Cracow
Teka 'Schneidera', 678.

Yad Vashem, Jerusalem
'Oral testimony', March 1970, 03/3350 (oral testimony of Israel B.
relating to the murder of the Jewish community of Jaśliska recorded by
Josef Litwak).

Żydowski Instytut Historyzcny, Warsaw
'Domaradz-Obóz w Jaśliskach', n.d., Lb 1076 (oral testimony of
Mordechai D. relating to the Nazi persecutions during the Second
World War recorded by Róża Bauminger).

References

Abercrombie, N., S. Hill and B.S. Turner. *The Penguin Dictionary of
Sociology*, Penguin Books, London, 1984.
Ain, A. 'Swisłocz: Portrait of a Jewish Community in Eastern Europe',
Annual of Jewish Social Sciences 4 (1949): 94-114.
Barth, F. 'Introduction'. In *Ethnic Groups and Boundaries: The Social
Organization of Culture Difference*, edited by F. Barth, 9-38. George
Allen & Unwin, London, 1969.
Bartoszewski, W. 'Jews as a Polish Problem', *Polin: A Journal of Polish-
Jewish Studies* 2 (1987a): 391-403.
Bartoszewski, W. *Uns eint Vergossenes Blut: Juden und Polen in der Zeit der
Endlösung*, S. Fischer Verlag, Frankfurt am Main, 1987b.
Bartoszewski, W., ed. *Under One Heaven: "Więź" Special Issue*, Towarzystwo
"Więź", Warsaw, 1998.
Bauman, Z. 'The Literary Afterlife of Polish Jewry', *POLIN: Studies in
Polish Jewry* 7 (1992): 273-299.
Bauminger, R. 'Domaradz-Obóz w Jaśliskach', Żydowski Instytut
Historyczny (File: Lb/1076), Warsaw, n.d.

Bednarska, A. and Z. Kamieńska, eds. *Lokacja i Zagospodarowanie Miast Królewskich w Malopolsce za Kazimierza Wielkiego (1333-1370)*, Wrocław, 1982.

Bogdański, Z. 'Kronika Miasteczka Jaślisk', Archiwum Parafii Jaśliska, n.d.

Boissevain, J. *Friends of Friends: Networks, Manipulators and Coalitions*, Basil Blackwell, Oxford, 1974.

Bonacich, E. 'A Theory of Middleman Minorities', *American Sociological Review* 38, October (1973): 583-594.

Bostel, F. 'Przyczynek do Dziejów Jaślisk', *Przewodnik Naukowy Literacki* 18, no. 7 (1890): 801-819.

Bryk, A. 'The Hidden Complex of the Polish Mind: Polish-Jewish Relations during the Holocaust'. In *My brother's Keeper? Recent Polish Debates on the Holocaust*, edited by A. Polonsky, 161-183. Routledge, London, 1990.

Budzyński, Z. 'Ludność Żydowska Zachodniej Części Rusi Czerwonej w Drugiej Połowie XVIII Wieku'. In *Żydzi w Małopolsce: Studia z Dziejów Osadnictwa i Życia Społecznego*, edited by F. Kiryk, 137-147. Południowo-Wschodni Instytut Naukowe, Przemyśl, 1991.

Burkolter, V. *The Patronage System: Theoretical Remarks*, Social Strategies Publishers Co-operative Society, Basel, 1976.

Błonski, J. 'The Poor Poles Look at the Ghetto'. In *My brother's Keeper? Recent Polish Debates on the Holocaust*, edited by A. Polonsky, 34-52. Routledge, London, 1990.

Cała, A. 'The Question of Assimilation of Jews in the Polish Kingdom (1864-1897): An Interpretative Essay', *Polin: A Journal of Polish-Jewish Studies* 1 (1986): 130-149.

Cała, A. *Wizerunek Żyda w Polskiej Kulturze Ludowej*, Wydawnictwo Uniwersytetu Warszawskiego, Warszawa, 1992.

Curtin, P.D. *Cross-Cultural Trade in World History*, Cambridge University Press, London, 1984.

Czajkowski, J., ed. *Lemkowie w Historii i Kulturze Karpat* 2, Muzeum Budownictwa Ludowego w Sanoku, Sanok, 1994.

Czajkowski, J., ed. *Lemkowie w Historii i Kulturze Karpat* 1, Muzeum Budownictwa Ludowego w Sanoku, Sanok, 1995.

Davies, N. *Heart of Europe: A Short History of Poland*, Oxford University Press, Oxford, New York, 1986.

Ellenson, D. 'The Orthodox Rabbinate and Apostasy in Nineteenth Century Germany and Hungary'. In *Jewish Apostasy in the Modern World*, edited by T.M. Endelman, 165-188. Holmes & Meier, New York, 1987.

Endelman, T.M. 'Introduction'. In *Jewish Apostasy in the Modern World*, edited by T.M. Endelman, 1-19. Holmes & Meier, New York, 1987.

Fastnacht, A. *Osadnictwo Ziemi Sanockiej w Latach 1340-1650*, Wrocław, 1962.

Foster, B.L. 'Ethnicity and Commerce', *American Ethnologist* 1 (1974): 437-48.

Friedman, P. *Roads to Extinction: Essays on the Holocaust*, The Jewish Publication Society of America and the Conference on Jewish Social Studies, Inc., New York, 1980.

Gajewski, B. *Jaśliska 1366-1996: Zarys Monograficzny*, PUW "ROKSANA", Krosno, 1996.

Garbaszewski, K. 'Kronika Księdza Karola Garbaszewskiego', Archiwum Parafii Jaśliska, 1872-1895.

Glassman, B. *Anti-Semitic Stereotypes without Jews: Images of the Jews in England 1290-1700*, Wayne State University Press, Detroit, 1975.

Gmina. 'Księga Zawiadomień Przełożonego Miejscowego w Miasteczkim Jaślisku', Muzeum Historyczne, Sanok, 1858-1880.

Golczewski, F. 'Rural Anti-Semitism in Galicia before World War I'. In *The Jews in Poland*, edited by C. Abramsky, M. Jachimczyk and A. Polonsky, 97-105. Basil Blackwell, Oxford, 1986.

Goldberg, J. 'The Changes in the Attitude of Polish Society toward the Jews in the 18th Century', *Polin: A Journal of Polish-Jewish Studies* 1 (1986): 35-48.

Gross, J.T. *Polish Society under German Occupation: The General Government, 1939-1944*, Princeton University Press, New Jersey, 1979.

Gross, N. 'Requiem for the Jewish People: Polish Literary Judaica in the years 1987-1989', *POLIN: Studies in Polish Jewry* 6 (1991): 295-308.

Grynberg, H. 'Is Polish Anti-Semitism Special?', *Midstream*, August/September (1983): 19-23.

Grzesik, W. and T. Traczyk. *Od Komańcza do Bartnego*, Wydawnictwo Stanisław Kryciński, Warszawa, 1992.

GUS. *Skorowidz Miejscowości Rzeczypospolitej Polskiej*, Nakład Głównego Urzędu Statystycznego, Warszawa, 1924.

GUS. 'Spis Powszechny', Główny Urząd Statystyczny, Warszawa, 1988.

Gutman, Y. 'Polish and Jewish Historiography on the Question of Polish-Jewish Relations during World War II'. In *The Jews in Poland*, edited by C. Abramsky, M. Jachimczyk and A. Polonsky, 177-189. Basil Blackwell, Oxford, 1986.

Hann, C. 'Christianity's Internal Frontier: The Case of Uniates in South-East Poland', *Anthropology Today* 4, no. 3 (1988): 9-14.

Hann, C.M. *A Village without Solidarity: Polish Peasants in Years of Crisis*, Yale University Press, London, 1985.

Heller, C.S. *On the Edge of Destruction: Jews of Poland between the Two World Wars*, Colombia University Press, New York, 1977.

Hertz, A. *The Jews in Polish Culture*, Northwestern University Press, Evanston, 1988.

Hirszowicz, L. 'The Jewish Issue in Post-War Communist Politics'. In *The Jews in Poland*, edited by C. Abramsky, M. Jachimczyk and A. Polonsky, 199-208. Basil Blackwell, Oxford, 1986.

Hoetink, H.R., E. De Bruyne, J.F. Koksma, R.F. Lissens and J. Presser, eds. *Algemene Winkler Prins Encyclopedie*, Elsevier, Amsterdam & Brussel, 1956.

Hoffman, E. *Shtetl: The Life and Death of a Small Town and the World of Polish Jews*, Secker & Warburg, London, 1998.

Horn, M. 'Żydzi Ziemi Sanockiej do 1650 Roku', *Biuletyn Żydowskiego Instytutu Historycznego*, no. 71 (1970): 3-30.

Hundert, G. 'The implications of Jewish Economic Activities for Christian-Jewish Relations in the Polish Commonwealth'. In *The Jews in Poland*, edited by C. Abramsky, M. Jachimczyk and A. Polonsky, 55-63. Basil Blackwell, Oxford, 1986.

Hundert, G.D. *The Jews in a Polish Private Town: The case of Opatów in the Eighteenth Century*, John Hopkins University Press, Baltimore, 1992.

Informator. *Wyzwolenie Miast i Gmin przez Armię Radziecką i Ludowe WP 1944-1945*, Wojskowy Przegląd Historyczny, Warszawa, 1977.

Irwin-Zarecka, I. *Neutralizing Memory: The Jew in Contemporary Poland*, Transaction Publishers, New Brunswick, 1989a.

Irwin-Zarecka, I. 'Problematizing the 'Jewish Problem'', *POLIN: Studies in Polish Jewry* 4 (1989b): 281-295.

Kamińska, M. 'References to Polish-Jewish Coexistence in the Memoirs of Łódź Workers: A Linguistic Analysis', *POLIN: Studies in Polish Jewry* 6 (1991): 207-222.

Kaufman, J. *A Hole in the Heart of the World: Being Jewish in Eastern Europe*, Viking Penguin, New York, 1997.

Kieniewicz, S. 'Polish Society and the Jewish Problem in the Nineteenth Century'. In *The Jews in Poland*, edited by C. Abramsky, M. Jachimczyk and A. Polonsky, 70-77. Basil Blackwell, Oxford, 1986.

Kozakiewicz, L. 'Jaśliska: Zarys Dziejów Miasta Prywatnego', *Wierchy* (1966): 180-188.

Krajewski, S. "The Jewish Problem' as a Polish Problem'. In *Under One Heaven: "Więź" Special Issue*, edited by W. Bartoszewski, 60-81. Towarzystwo "Więź", Warsaw, 1998.

Krakowski, S. 'Relations between Jews and Poles during the Holocaust: New and Old Approaches in Polish Historiography', *Yad Vashem Studies* 19 (1988): 317-340.

Landman, I., ed. *Universal Jewish Encyclopedia*, New York, 1941.

Lanzmann. *Shoah: An Oral History of the Holocaust. The Complete Text of the Film*, Pantheon Books, New York, 1985.

Lehmann, R. 'Symbiosis and Ambivalence: Poles and Jews in a Small Galician Town' (Master's Thesis, University of Amsterdam, 1995).

Lehmann, R. 'Conflict or Harmony? Poles and Jews in a Small Galician Town', *International Journal on Minority and Group Rights* 4, no. 3/4 (1997): 323-339.

Levine, H. 'Gentry, Jews and Serfs: The Rise of Polish Vodka', *Review* 4, no. 2 (1980): 223-250.

Levine, H. *Economic Origins of Antisemitism: Poland and its Jews in the Early Modern Period*, Yale University Press, New Haven, 1991.

Lichten, J. 'Notes on the Assimilation and Acculturation of Jews in Poland'. In *The Jews in Poland*, edited by C. Abramsky, M. Jachimczyk and A. Polonsky, 106-129. Basil Blackwell, Oxford, 1986.

Litwak, J. 'Oral Testimony', Yad Vashem (File: 03/3350), Jerusalem, 1969.

Macartney, C.A., ed. *The Habsburg and Hohenzollern Dynasties in the Seventeenth and Eighteenth Centuries*, Macmillan, London, 1970.

Mach, Z. *Symbols, Conflict and Identity*, SUNNY Press, Albany, NY, 1993.

Magocsi, P.R. *The Shaping of a National Identity: Subcarpathian Rus', 1848-1948*, Harvard University Press, London, 1978.

Mahler, R. *Hasidism and the Jewish Enlightenment: Their Confrontation in Galicia and Poland in the First Half of the Nineteenth Century*, The Jewish Publication Society of America, Philadelphia, 1985.

Mahler, R. 'Jewish Emigration from Galicia'. In *East European Jews in Two Worlds: Studies from the YIVO Annual*, edited by D.D. Moore, 125-137. Northwestern University Press and the Yivo institute for Jewish research, Evanston (Illinois), 1990.

Meijers, D. *De Revolutie der Vromen: Onstaan en Ontwikkeling van het Chassidisme. Waarin is Opgenomen het Verslag van Reb Dan Isj-Toms Reis door de Eeuwigheid*, Gooi en Sticht, Hilversum, 1989.

Meijers, D. 'The Sociogenesis of the Hasidic Movement: An Orthodox-Jewish Regime and State-Formation in eighteenth-Century Poland'. In *Religious Regimes and State-Formation: Perspectives from European*

Ethnology, edited by E.R. Wolf, 133-153. State University of New York Press, New York, 1991.

Mendelsohn, E. 'Interwar Poland: Good for the Jews or Bad for the Jews?'. In *The Jews in Poland*, edited by C. Abramsky, M. Jachimczyk and A. Polonsky, 130-139. Basil Blackwell, Oxford, 1986.

Moszkowicz, J. 'Kronika Księdza Jana Moszkowicza', Archiwum Parafii Jaśliska, n.d.

Niezabitowska, M. and T. Tomaszewski. *Ostatni: Współcześni Żydzi Polscy*, Wydawnictwa Artystyczne i Filmowe, Warszawa, 1993.

Oldson, W.O. *A Providential Anti-Semitism: Nationalism and Polity in Nineteenth-Century Romania*, The American Philosophical Society, Philadelphia, 1991.

Olszański, H. 'Stosunki Mieszkańców Jaślisk ze Słowacją', Muzeum Budownictwa Ludowego, Sanok, 1985.

Olszański, T.A., ed. *Żydzi w karpatach: Beskid Niski - Bieszczady - Pogorze.*, Towarzystwo Karpackie & Oficyna Wydawnicza "Rewasz", Warszawa, 1991.

Opatoshu, J. *The Jew Legend and Other Stories (Yidn-Legende un Andere Dertsailungen)*, "CYCO"-FARLAG, New York, 1951.

Orla-Bukowska, A. 'Shtetl Communities: Another Image', *POLIN: Studies in Polish Jewry* 8 (1994): 89-113.

Orlik, Z. 'Dzieje Jaślisk' (Praca Magisterska, Wyższa Szkoła Pedagogiczna w Rzeszowie, 1979).

Pismo Diecezjalne. *Rocznik Diecezji Przemyskich*, Przemyśl, 1938.

Polonsky, A., ed. *My Brothers's Keeper? Recent Polish Debates on the Holocaust*, Routledge, London, 1990.

Prochaska, A. 'Jaśliska: Miasteczko i Klucz Biskupów Przemyskich Obrządku Lacińskiego (ciąg dalszy)', *Przewodnik Naukowy i Literacki* 17, no. 3 (1889): 263-270.

Radziwiłł, A. 'The Teaching of the History of the Jews in Secondary Schools in the Polish People's Republic, 1949-88', *POLIN: Studies in Polish Jewry* 4 (1989): 402-424.

Reinfuss, R. *Śladami Lemków*, Wydawnictwo PTTK "Kraj", Warszawa, 1990.

Rosenthal, C.S. 'Deviation and Social Change in the Jewish Community of a Small Polish Town', *The American Journal of Sociology* 60, no. 2 (1954): 177-181.

Rosman, M.J. *The Lords' Jews: Magnate-Jewish Relations in the Polish-Lithuanian Commonwealth during the 18th Century*, Harvard University Press, Cambridge (Massachusetts), 1990.

Roth, C., ed. *Encyclopaedia Judaica*, Jerusalem, 1971.

Runes, D.D., ed. *Dictionary of Judaism: the Tenets, Rites, Customs and Concepts of Judaism*, Carol Publishing Group, New York, 1991.

Scharf, R.F. 'In Anger and in Sorrow: Towards a Polish-Jewish Dialogue', *Polin: A Journal of Polish-Jewish Studies* 1 (1986): 270-277.

Segev, T. *The Seventh Million: the Israelis and the Holocaust*, Hill and Wang, New York, 1993.

Stàczek, K. 'Kronika Szkoła', Archiwum Szkoły Powszechnej w Jaśliskach, 1944-1951.

Sulimierski, F., B. Chłembowski and W. Walewski. *Słownik Geograficzny Królestwa Polskiego*, Warszawa, 1882.

Tomaszewski, J. 'Wstęp'. In *Najnowsze Dzieje Żydów w Polsce*, edited by J. Tomaszewksi, 5-9. Wydawnictwo Naukowe PWN, Warszawa, 1993.

Turowicz, J. 'Polish Reasons and Jewish Reasons', *Yad Vashem Studies* 19 (1988): 379-388.

Van Arkel, D. 'De groei van het Anti-Joodse Stereotype: Een Poging tot een Hypothetisch-Deductieve Werkwijze in Historisch Onderzoek', *Tijdschrift voor Sociale Geschiedenis* 10, no. 33 (1984): 34-69.

Van Arkel, D. 'Genealogisch Verband van Antisemitische Vooroordelen'. In *Wat is Antisemitisme? Een Benadering vanuit Vier Disciplines*, edited by R.W. Munk, 48-74. Uitgeversmaatschappij J.H. Kok B.V., Kampen, 1991.

Van Hulten, M.H.M. 'De Collectivisatie van de Landbouw in de Volksrepubliek Polen, 1944-1960' (Ph.D. Diss., University of Amsterdam, 1962).

Vansina, J. *Oral Tradition as History*, Heinemann Kenya, Nairobi, 1985.

Vermeulen, H. *Etnische Groepen en Grenzen: Surinamers, Chinezen, Turken*, Het Wereldvenster, Weesp, 1984.

Vermeulen, H. 'Handelsminderheden: Een Inleiding', *Focaal*, no. 15 (1991): 7-18.

Walicki, A. 'The three traditions of Polish patriotism'. In *Polish Paradoxes*, edited by A. Polonsky and S. Gomulka, 22-39, London & New York, 1990.

WAPK. 'Verzeichniß der Wahlberechtigten Gemeindebürger und Angehörigen', Wojewódzkie Archiwum Państwowe w Krakowie (File: Teka Schneidera/678), 1867a.

WAPK. 'Wählerliste für die Landtagswahlen', Wojewódzkie Archiwum Państwowe w Krakowie (File: Teka Schneidera/678), 1867b.

WAPK. 'Lista Wyborców dla Wyborów Sejmowych', Wojewódzkie Archiwum Państwowe w Krakowie (File: Teka Schneidera/678), 1870a.

WAPK. 'Spis Członków Gminy i Przynależnych do niej, którzy są
   Uprawnieni do Wyboru', Wojewódzkie Archiwum Państwowe w
   Krakowie (File: Teka Schneidera/678), 1870b.
Weinryb, B.D. *The Jews of Poland: A Social and Economic History of the
   Jewish Community in Poland from 1100-1800*, The Jewish Publication
   Society of America, Philadelphia, 1972.
Weisser, M.R. *A Brotherhood of Memory: Jewish Landsmanshaftn in the New
   World*, Cornell University Press, Ithaca, London, 1989.
Wisse, R.R. 'Poland's Jewish Ghosts', *Commentary* 83, no. 1 (1987): 25-33.
Wolf, E.R. 'Kinship, Friendship, and Patron-Client Relations in Complex
   Societies'. In *The Social Anthropology of Complex Societies*, edited by M.
   Banton, 1-22. Tavistock Publications, London, 1966.
Wróbel, J. 'Between Co-existence and Hostility: A Contribution to the
   Problem of National Antagonism in Łódź in the Inter-War Period',
   POLIN: Studies in Polish Jewry 6 (1991): 201-206.
Yad Vashem. *Pinkas Hakehillot Encyclopaedia of Jewish Communities*,
   Cooperative Press, Jerusalem, 1984.
Zborowski, M. and E. Herzog. *Life is with the People: The Culture of the
   Shtetl*, Shocken Books, New York, 1962.
Zenner, W.P. *Minorities in the Middle: A Cross-Cultural Analysis*, State
   University of New York Press, New York, 1991.
Zimand, R. 'Wormwood and Ashes (Do Poles and Jews Hate Each
   Other?)', *POLIN: Studies in Polish Jewry* 4 (1989): 313-353.

INDEX